Palgrave Studies in Sustainable Business In Association with Future Earth

Series Editors
Paul Shrivastava
Pennsylvania State University
University Park, PA, USA

László Zsolnai
Corvinus University Budapest
Budapest, Hungary

"This is a very practical framework that executives will find quite useful in guiding their thinking to develop a truly sustainable business model. It should be read by all who are deeply concerned with sustainable business."
—R. Edward Freeman, University Professor,
The Darden School, University of Virginia

"The sustainable business agenda is mainstreaming at last, a process that coincides with the evolution and deployment of radically different mindsets, technologies and business models. Entire industries and economies will be disrupted. In *RESTART*, Sveinung Jørgensen and Lars Jacob Tynes Pedersen indicate where this grand convergence is now headed—and explain how business leaders and their organisations can help drive the necessary system change. Recommended reading."
—John Elkington, Chairman & Chief Pollinator, *Volans*

"RESTART represents a thoughtful, well-researched and extremely practical approach to making business models sustainable for the future. The field of sustainability has lacked a comprehensive and practical approach for sustainable

Sustainability in Business is increasingly becoming the forefront issue for researchers, practitioners and companies the world over. Engaging with this immense challenge, Future Earth is a major international research platform from a range of disciplines, with a common goal to support and achieve global sustainability. This series will define a clear space for the work of Future Earth Finance and Economics Knowledge-Action Network. Publishing key research with a holistic and trans-disciplinary approach, it intends to help reinvent business and economic models for the Anthropocene, geared towards engendering sustainability and creating ecologically conscious organizations.

More information about this series at
http://www.palgrave.com/gp/series/15667

business model innovation, and RESTART fills this vital need. The case studies illustrate the framework in illuminating ways that senior executives can readily understand and use."

—Ram Nidumolu, CEO, *Academy for Innovation & Management*, award-winning *HBR* author

"In the effort to solve the big sustainability challenges of our time, innovative business models are essential. In this book, Jørgensen and Pedersen show how companies can turn problems into solutions by giving their business models a RESTART. This book gives managers the tools for contributing to build a sustainable future."

—David Katz, Founder and CEO, *The Plastic Bank*

"In *RESTART Sustainable Business Model Innovation*, Jørgensen and Pedersen offer a practical and inspiring framework for designing more sustainable business models. The book offers rich material on companies that aim to align sustainability and profitability, both in the Nordic setting and beyond. *RESTART* is a valuable read for practitioners and scholars alike."

—Robert Strand, Executive Director & Lecturer, *Center for Responsible Business, Haas School of Business, University of California, Berkeley* and Associate Professor of Leadership & Sustainability, *Copenhagen Business School*

Sveinung Jørgensen
Lars Jacob Tynes Pedersen

RESTART Sustainable Business Model Innovation

Sveinung Jørgensen
Inland Norway University of Applied Sciences
Lillehammer, Norway

Lars Jacob Tynes Pedersen
NHH Norwegian School of Economics
Bergen, Norway

Palgrave Studies in Sustainable Business In Association with Future Earth
ISBN 978-3-030-06338-2   ISBN 978-3-319-91971-3 (eBook)
https://doi.org/10.1007/978-3-319-91971-3

© The Editor(s) (if applicable) and The Author(s) 2018 This book is an open access publication.
Softcover re-print of the Hardcover 1st edition 2018
Open Access This book is licensed under the terms of the Creative Commons Attribution-NonCommercial-NoDerivatives 4.0 International License (http://creativecommons.org/licenses/by-nc-nd/4.0/), which permits any noncommercial use, sharing, distribution and reproduction in any medium or format, as long as you give appropriate credit to the original author(s) and the source, provide a link to the Creative Commons license and indicate if you modified the licensed material. You do not have permission under this license to share adapted material derived from this book or parts of it.
The images or other third party material in this book are included in the book's Creative Commons license, unless indicated otherwise in a credit line to the material. If material is not included in the book's Creative Commons license and your intended use is not permitted by statutory regulation or exceeds the permitted use, you will need to obtain permission directly from the copyright holder.
This work is subject to copyright. All commercial rights are reserved by the author(s), whether the whole or part of the material is concerned, specifically the rights of translation, reprinting, reuse of illustrations, recitation, broadcasting, reproduction on microfilms or in any other physical way, and transmission or information storage and retrieval, electronic adaptation, computer software, or by similar or dissimilar methodology now known or hereafter developed. Regarding these commercial rights a non-exclusive license has been granted to the publisher.
The use of general descriptive names, registered names, trademarks, service marks, etc. in this publication does not imply, even in the absence of a specific statement, that such names are exempt from the relevant protective laws and regulations and therefore free for general use.
The publisher, the authors and the editors are safe to assume that the advice and information in this book are believed to be true and accurate at the date of publication. Neither the publisher nor the authors or the editors give a warranty, express or implied, with respect to the material contained herein or for any errors or omissions that may have been made. The publisher remains neutral with regard to jurisdictional claims in published maps and institutional affiliations.

Cover illustration: © MB Photography/Moment/Getty; all rights reserved, used with permission

Printed on acid-free paper

This Palgrave Macmillan imprint is published by the registered company Springer Nature Switzerland AG
The registered company address is: Gewerbestrasse 11, 6330 Cham, Switzerland

*To Endre and Rannei Johanne,
Marie and Ada*

Foreword

Our world now appears to be gripped once more by zero-sum thinking and an intensifying "winner-takes-all" approach in a range of sectors. For companies choosing between sustainability and profitability, or economic growth and social equity, are artificially limiting the choices at our disposal. This is the case that Jorgensen and Pedersen make in this book—for companies to see that their viability and profitability are not threatened, but rather can be enhanced, by embracing sustainable practices.

The World Economic Forum recognizes the importance of changing this mind-set. This is why it has been working since its founding in 1971 to convene diverse stakeholders from government, business and civil society around a common agenda, to create win-win solutions and to transform false dichotomies into real synergies. It means being able to consider, as the authors do, the short- and long-term challenges and opportunities facing companies as they navigate conflicting interests and constituencies to balance growth, prosperity, sustainability and profitability.

For this reason, and in a world that is to an increasing extent divided and dominated by echo-chambers, this book could not be more timely.

By showing how to reconcile the bottom line and environmental sustainability, it points the way forward for any entrepreneur that has the best interest of its shareholders—as well as the planet—in mind.

Geneva, Switzerland   Børge Brende

Preface

"Dear passengers. We remind those of you who will be leaving the plane at Kigali International Airport that all plastic bags must be left on board. It is not allowed to bring bags into Rwanda."

We looked at each other, and then we looked around. Quite right: the passengers took items out of their plastic bags and carried the contents out in their hands. We were not disembarking the plane in Rwanda—it was a stopover on the way to Kampala in Uganda. We went there to advise a delegation of the Ugandan authorities, led by the Minister of Water and Environment, Ephraim Kamuntu, as well as companies from the Eastern African countries, in their preparation for the United Nations Climate Change Conference in Paris in 2015, also known as COP21. The plastic problem that was the reason for the surprising message on the plane was a hot topic in Uganda and the other East African countries too. In the Indian Ocean off the coast of East Africa, there is an area full of plastic garbage—the Indian Ocean Garbage Patch, which is larger than South Africa and Ethiopia added together. There are five such patches in the world oceans—they have become symbols of pollution and ecosystem destruction, and they are increasing in size.

Therefore, Sveinung was not surprised when only six months later he stood on the grounds of The Plastic Bank in Port-Au-Prince, Haiti, along with one of the managers in the company. Sveinung was there doing research for this book, and together, they looked at the huge amounts of plastic garbage the company had collected by creating jobs for the poor people on the island. The Plastic Bank had simply realized that it could do two things at once: it could do business in a way that prevented plastic from reaching the sea. At the same time, it could become profitable and create jobs exactly by "turning trash into cash" and by collaborating with companies that use recycled plastic in their products. The Plastic Bank realized that plastic is not just waste, and it is not just a problem: it also represents a misuse of resources that have great economic value if brought back to productive use.

Today, we have all started getting used to companies, customers and authorities putting sustainability on the agenda—whether this relates to plastic or water, CO_2 emissions or additives in food production, human rights or gender equality, corruption or poverty. It has even come to the point where more and more companies are realizing that it is possible to be both sustainable and profitable. In our work, we meet small and large companies that find new and innovative ways of doing business that are less harmful to society and the environment. Not only that—many of the companies even aim to have a net positive footprint, for instance, by integrating United Nations' Sustainable Development Goals (SDGs) into their strategies.

It has not always been like this. Quite a few years ago, we found ourselves in the Baltics, where we were working with a financial institution. The company was aiming to ensure that it conducted its banking practices in the region responsibly, even in a difficult market with corruption, money laundering and environmental criminality. At lunch with the company, one of the older managers in the company leaned over to Lars Jacob and said with a sly smile, *We try to make this work—we really do. But remember: Until recently, the business model of our industry was "steal-and-run"*. Since then, we have discussed sustainable business model innovation with everything from private equity firms in Oslo to investment banks in London, and there are indications that sustainability has become mainstream even in the financial industry (e.g., Jeucken 2010; Eurosif 2014; Eccles et al. 2011).

In our work as researchers and advisors for companies, we see how this happens across all industries—to an increasing extent and with increasing pace. In the years of research involved in writing this book, we have discussed alternative business models with the oil industry; had workshops with social entrepreneurs; brainstormed with fish-farming companies about the possibilities of green growth at sea; sparred with the automotive industry about the implications of the electric car revolution for its service market; discussed with logistics companies what the green transport system of the future could look like and worked with Norwegian entrepreneurs from various industries on the opportunities and challenges of bringing a sustainable business model to the global market. We work with an increasingly varied set of companies all over the world that have similar challenges: they all influence society and the environment, for better or worse, but how can they succeed in doing business in a way that allows them to align sustainability and profitability—both in the short and long term?

Questions like this are also at the core of our discussions with current and future managers at the master's and executive courses in sustainable business model innovation that we teach in Norway and abroad: why has Apple taken the trouble to develop a robot that can dismantle old cell phones? What lies behind Renault's decision to enter into a long-term relationship with a company that recycles steel? Why does Refettorio Gastromotiva in Rio de Janeiro collect soon-to-be-discarded food from grocery stores and have top Brazilian chefs cook three-course dinners for the homeless, while simultaneously offering cooking education to the poor? Why is it that LEGO will use one billion Danish kroner to find an alternative to the plastic used in the LEGO blocks? Why does Equinor (formerly Statoil) capture large amounts of CO_2 and give it to scientists at the company CO2BIO, which cultivates algae for making nutritious fish feed? What makes companies such as Bright Products develop solar energy solutions for impoverished people in the African market? Why does the Norwegian consumer products company Orkla develop an organic and vegan alternative to its personal hygiene and laundry detergents and deliver these products in recycled plastic bottles? And what makes the aquaculture industry move its fish farms on land and collaborate with partners who can collect, rinse and dry the wastewater from the farms and turn it into fertilizer and energy?

We argue that these companies are doing what they are designed to do: they find problems that can be solved in profitable ways, and the natural thing is to start with the problems that matter. But which problems are important enough so that customers are willing to pay to get them fixed? Many of the biggest problems we face as a society today relate to social and environmental sustainability. Contemporary business leaders face a sustainability problem of enormous dimensions. Research indicates that we already have to prepare for significant climate change, while overconsumption and population growth leads to depletion of key resources for both business and society. Simultaneously, the problem of poverty persists and causes distress, social unrest, corruption and an unstable society. These developments cause the ground to tremble under businesses that are now beginning to realize that "business as usual" may be going "out of business". This is precisely why there are so many indications that in the coming decades, sustainability problems may be among the biggest sources of profitable business opportunities for the companies that embrace them (cf. Nidumolu et al. 2009; Porter and Kramer 2011). At the same time, of course, sustainability may be a source of major problems for companies that are not able to deal with these developments (e.g., Hofmann et al. 2014; Weber et al. 2010; Richardson et al. 2009).

Companies have played a big role in creating the problems we currently face around the world. This has severe consequences for the future of our planet and our societies. Moreover, it affects companies' legitimacy in society and it matters for how regulators will choose to act in the face of growing social and environmental problems. This situation will greatly affect the conditions of doing business. There are expectations that states as well as international agreements will use both carrots and sticks in the wake of the COP21 climate summit in Paris and the development of the SDGs. In addition, not at least, the depletion of important natural resources that companies depend on will determine what production, logistics and consumption will look like in the future.

In this book, we argue that companies can be, and are becoming, an important part of the solution and that the problems we are talking about here are and will likely remain a source of business opportunities and competitive advantage. There are already plentiful examples of companies that change their business models in ways that allow them to contribute to a more sustainable world—either by improving their own footprint or by helping others to improve theirs (see, e.g., Jørgensen and

Pedersen 2017a). Importantly, however, they try to do so in a manner that is compatible with, and can even promote, profitable operations.

This movement in a more sustainable direction is, however, probably just beginning. In order to get the necessary momentum and actually solve the sustainability problems we face today, there is a pressing need for fundamental business model innovations. Thus, the point of departure of this book is simple: In order for companies to be part of the solution rather than part of the problem, we need comprehensive changes to business models. And in order to achieve this, there is a need for knowledge to support such changes. In this book, we aim to contribute to these changes by developing a research-based framework for sustainable business model innovation. Our conceptual framework for what this entails is coined RESTART—an acronym of seven letters reflecting seven key characteristics related to business models. Such a RESTART of business is likely to require large-scale sustainable business model innovation, in which companies add more value than they take. More sustainable business models will need to address the social and environmental problems we face, be informed by the technological opportunity space of digitalization and the fourth industrial revolution and be adapted to the changing mindsets of consumers, employees and other stakeholders. This book provides a conceptual and empirical investigation of seven business model characteristics that are central to such a RESTART. It shows how business leaders can use it in practice and how it can spark new and important avenues of research on sustainable business model innovation.

The book comprises three parts. In part I, "What is the problem?", we outline the purpose of the book. We discuss the need for sustainable business model innovation, explore three key trends and developments that are pushing us in that direction and briefly introduce the seven components of the RESTART framework. In part II, "The RESTART framework", we develop the RESTART framework and discuss each of the seven components of the framework in depth. Finally, in part III, "Implications and future research", we outline practical implications, including a process model for sustainable business model innovation, as well as avenues for future research, including two case studies based on the RESTART framework.

For videos and materials based on this book and more information about us and our work, please visit our website www.JorgensenPedersen. no. We would love to hear from you, whether you are a manager, researcher, politician, student or simply a fellow citizen of this planet who also wants to engage in a *RESTART*. On our website, you can share your stories, insights and examples with us, and you can find out how to join the discussion on social media.

Lillehammer, Norway Sveinung Jørgensen
Bergen, Norway Lars Jacob Tynes Pedersen

References

Eccles, R. G., Feiner, A., & Verheyden, T. (2016). *Sustainability and financial performance of Scandinavian companies*. Unpublished manuscript, Harvard Business School.
Eurosif. (2014). *European SRI study 2014*. Paris: Eurosif.
Hofmann, H., Busse, C., Bode, C., & Henke, M. (2014). Sustainability-related supply chain risks: Conceptualization and management. *Business Strategy and the Environment, 23*(3), 160–172.
Jeucken, M. (2010). *Sustainable finance and banking: The financial sector and the future of the planet*. London: Routledge.
Jørgensen, S., & Pedersen, L. J. T. (2017a). Designing sustainable business models. In T. W. Andreassen, S. Clatworthy, M. Lüders, & T. Hillestad (Eds.), *Innovating for trust*. Cheltenham, UK: Edward Elgar Publishing.
Nidumolu, R., Prahalad, C. K., & Rangaswami, M. R. (2009). Why sustainability is now the key driver of innovation. *Harvard Business Review, 87*(9), 56–64.
Porter, M. E., & Kramer, M. R. (2011). Creating shared value: How to reinvent capitalism—And unleash a wave of innovation and growth. *Harvard Business Review, 89*(1–2), 62–77.
Richardson, K., Steffen, W., Schellnhuber, H. J., Alcamo, J., Barker, T., Kammen, D. M., & Stern, N. (2009). *Climate change-global risks, challenges & decisions: Synthesis report*. Copenhagen: Museum Tusculanum.
Weber, O., Scholz, R. W., & Michalik, G. (2010). Incorporating sustainability criteria into credit risk management. *Business Strategy and the Environment, 19*(1), 39–50.

Acknowledgments

Any book is the product of the sum of efforts, contributions and support of many different people, and this manuscript is no exception. The present work is the outcome of our joint research efforts since 2006, and we are grateful to all our collaborators who have inspired and informed us during this time and who have contributed directly and indirectly to this work.

We are grateful to our editor, Madeleine Holder at Palgrave Macmillan, who expertly and efficiently led us through the process toward publication. We also thank Gabriel Everington for his work in helping us prepare the manuscript for publication. We are highly grateful to the blind reviewers whose valuable comments allowed us to improve the manuscript substantially. We owe considerable gratitude to Professors László Zsolnai and Paul Shrivastava, who are editors of the *Palgrave Studies in Sustainable Business In Association with Future Earth* series, in which this book is included. We consider it a privilege that our book is published as part of this important and inspiring series.

We are grateful to our Norwegian editor Cappelen Damm Akademisk (CDA), which published an earlier and shorter version of the present work as *RESTART: 7 veier til bærekraftig business [RESTART: 7 Steps to Sustainable Business]* in Norwegian in 2017. Thank you Dorte Østreng, Lisbeth Opøien, Åsne Lund Godbolt and Wegard Kyoo Bergli and the rest of the editorial team at CDA. We are also immensely grateful to our former editors at CDA, Tor Paulson and Erlend Aas Gulbrandsen, who have since joined us in academia. Tor and Erlend were "midwives" for the present work when stimulating us to write the book *Ansvarlig og lønnsom [Responsible and Profitable]* almost a decade ago, thus sending us on a journey that has culminated in this book.

We are very thankful for the support—financial and otherwise—from our respective institutions *Inland Norway University of Applied Sciences* and *NHH Norwegian School of Economics*. They have given us freedom to pursue the exciting adventures that have led to this book, and more generally allowed us to play entrepreneurial—or, rather, intrapreneurial—roles in our work with research, teaching and communication. In particular, we thank the Center for Service Innovation, the Centre for Ethics and Economics and NHH Executive at NHH. We moreover thank the research boards at both institutions for providing financial support that allowed us to publish the book as open access.

We are grateful to friends, colleagues, executive and master students and collaborators at academic institutions, companies and other organizations at home and abroad who have given us ideas, input, feedback and energy. In particular, we are grateful to the managers of companies with whom we conduct research, many of whom are covered in this book, for their willingness and enthusiasm to share knowledge and insights from their companies' operations. We appreciate the efforts of students of all ages who have read, participated in the testing of the material and provided feedback. A big thank you to our eminent designer Ingrid Bygjordet Vaterland, who designed logos, figures and illustrations inside the book. Finally, we are grateful to the *Norwegian Non-Fiction Writers and Translators Organization* for a project grant in the early stage of writing this book.

Above all, we are grateful to family and friends for the many ways they contribute to everything we do. A special thank you to Ingrid and Kjersti.

Contents

Part I What is the Problem? ... 1

1 Why Sustainable Business Model Innovation? ... 3
 1.1 A RESTART of Business Models for a Brighter Future Earth ... 5
 1.2 The Methodological Approach of This Book ... 7
 1.3 Let Us RESTART Sustainable Business Model Innovation ... 10
 References ... 10

2 The Seven Steps of the RESTART Framework ... 13
 2.1 A RESTART for Business Models of the Future ... 14
 2.2 A Brief Introduction to the RESTART Framework for Sustainable Business Model Innovation ... 18
 References ... 19

3 RESTART: What, Why, How and So What? ... 23
 3.1 Responsibility and Opportunity ... 23
 3.2 Sustainable and Profitable ... 29

xvii

	3.3 The Next Step: Aligning Financial, Social and Environmental Bottom Lines	34
	References	43

Part II The RESTART Framework — 47

4 Roadmap to a RESTART — 49
References — 52

5 Redesign Rather than Standstill — 55
5.1 The Business Model as the Story of How the Company Works — 56
5.2 Redesigning Business Models — 66
References — 72

6 Experimentation Rather than Turnaround — 75
6.1 The Science of Profitability — 76
6.2 Asking the Right Questions — 82
References — 87

7 Service-Logic Rather than Product-Logic — 89
7.1 At Your Service — 90
7.2 Access to Everything — 95
References — 100

8 The Circular Rather than the Linear Economy — 103
8.1 The Future Goes in Circles — 104
8.2 Resources Astray — 110
References — 119

9 Alliances Rather than Solo-runs — 121
9.1 Unite and Collaborate! — 122
9.2 Creating and Sharing Value — 126
References — 132

10	**Results Rather than Indulgences**	135
	10.1 With an Eye on the Ball	136
	10.2 Prioritize What Matters	141
	References	149

11	**Three-Dimensionality Rather than One-Dimensionality**	153
	11.1 Take the Lead	154
	11.2 Building a Better World	159
	References	166

12	**RESTART Before It is Too Late**	169
	12.1 It is Not Going to Be Easy	172
	12.2 Ready, Set, RESTART!	173
	Reference	175

Part III Implications and Future Research 177

13	**A Recap of the RESTART Framework**	179

14	**A Process Model for Sustainable Business Model Innovation**	183
	14.1 A Closer Look at the Four Phases of the Sustainable Business Model Innovation Process	187
	14.2 Why the Business Model RESTARTer?	190
	14.3 Starting the RESTART	190
	References	192

15	**Avenues for Future Research**	193
	15.1 Mind the Gap!	194
	15.2 Research Designs and Methodologies	196
	15.3 A RESTART Research Agenda	198
	15.4 An Ocean of Opportunities	203
	References	204

16	**Case Study: A RESTART for Scanship**		209
	16.1 Business Opportunities on the Floating City		211
	16.2 Solutions for Cleaner Oceans		213
	16.3 Toward Uncharted Waters		215
	16.4 Restarting Scanship: Practical Challenges and Research Opportunities		216
	References		219
17	**Case Study: A Circular Business Model for Orkla and BIR?**		221
	17.1 Orkla and Its Ecosystem		222
	17.2 BIR: From Waste Manager to Circular Business Partner?		224
	17.3 Recognize—Rethink—Reinvent—Reorganize		225
	17.4 Restarting Together: More Cake for All?		228
	Reference		228

References 231

Index 249

List of Figures

Fig. 1.1	Three trends driving the development of new business models	5
Fig. 3.1	Sustainability as responsibility and as opportunity (Jørgensen and Pedersen 2017)	27
Fig. 3.2	The net effect of sustainability efforts (based on McDonough and Braungart 2010)	32
Fig. 3.3	A sustainable interaction between economy, society and environment	35
Fig. 4.1	A roadmap to RESTART	52
Fig. 5.1	Redesign Rather than Standstill	55
Fig. 5.2	The business model: creating, delivering and capturing value from business opportunities	59
Fig. 5.3	The value proposition	61
Fig. 6.1	Experimentation Rather than Turnaround	75
Fig. 6.2	Questions underlying business model experimentation in practice	86
Fig. 7.1	Service-logic Rather than Product-logic	89
Fig. 8.1	The Circular Rather than the Linear Economy	103
Fig. 8.2	A traditional linear value chain	106
Fig. 8.3	Different types of upcycling in circular business models	108
Fig. 8.4	The two basic cycles (based on McDonough and Braungart 2013)	110
Fig. 9.1	Alliances Rather than Solo-runs	121

Fig. 9.2	A smaller part of a larger cake	126
Fig. 9.3	The organization and its stakeholders	130
Fig. 10.1	Results Rather than Indulgences	135
Fig. 10.2	How sustainability influences the company's performance (based on Esty and Winston 2009)	139
Fig. 10.3	Which issues are material—for the company and for its stakeholders?	142
Fig. 11.1	Three-dimensionality Rather than One-dimensionality	153
Fig. 11.2	Four elements of organizing for sustainability	161
Fig. 13.1	A roadmap to RESTART	181
Fig. 14.1	Three trends driving the development of new business models	184
Fig. 14.2	The business model RESTARTer for sustainable business model innovation	185

List of Tables

Table 5.1	The business models of various music services	65
Table 10.1	"Push" and "pull" factors in sustainable business model innovations	148
Table 14.1	Questions to guide the four phases of the sustainable business model innovation process	186

Part I

What is the Problem?

In this part of the book, we outline the purpose and scope of the book. We begin by discussing the urgent need for sustainable business model innovations, which are necessary in order for more business models to become both sustainable and profitable. In doing so, we explore three key trends and developments that are pushing us in that direction, namely (1) the sustainability problem, (2) digitalization and the technological opportunity space and (3) changing consumer preferences and lifestyles. We also briefly introduce the seven components of the RESTART framework that we develop and discuss in the remainder of the book.

1

Why Sustainable Business Model Innovation?

> *"Just a few years ago, nobody questioned the footprint of our products. The fact that our house insulation products decreased customers' energy consumption was more than good enough. Today, however, we must redesign our business model completely, for instance by no longer using coal as the main energy source in our many factories. We are expected to make our products recyclable and reusable, and we are even faced by a need to make them smarter, by using sensors that connect them to the Internet. Not at least, we need to find new ways of interacting with our customers and other players in collaboration with competitors and different platform-based networks. In order to do that, we need to rethink the whole idea of who we are, what we deliver to whom and how, and how we are going to make a profit."*

The CEO of the big, international corporation was excited and uncomfortable at the same time. He had been in the insulation business his whole career. We met him at a roundtable discussion that we facilitated with executives from key companies in the construction industry. During the conversation, he told us that his company was searching for innovative and more sustainable solutions along its entire value chain, including designing new products and services, developing new ways of sourcing, manufacturing and prolonging the life of its products and finding new ways of distributing and monitoring them by means of new technology and new alliances.

This is not the only CEO or top-level manager currently experiencing such challenges. During the 15 years we have studied corporate sustainability, we have experienced firsthand that the business landscape has changed tremendously. When we started researching corporate sustainability, the people in charge of corporate social responsibility (CSR) and sustainability issues were typically powerless communication managers with low budgets, who were unwillingly tasked with managing such issues as a small part of their job description. Neither corporate responsibility nor sustainability issues were anchored at the top of the organization. Furthermore, the relatively few stakeholders within the companies who cared about these issues were mostly activists pushing this agenda. Today, however, we get to discuss sustainable business model innovation in boardrooms and executive offices, and sustainability and its implications for business models have become a strategic priority across all industries—sometimes as a threat, but more and more often as an opportunity.

This does not mean that designing innovative and sustainable business models is a walk in the park. We propose that it is possible, and as we will show you throughout this book, there is a growing body of research within the field of corporate sustainability indicating that companies can be both sustainable and profitable at the same time. There is, however, still a long way to go, and the path toward sustainable business is a rocky and risky one. We argue that sustainable business model innovation requires hard work and even a solid dose of bravery. We also argue that we still lack research-based insights that can guide practitioners who want to embark on the sustainability journey, such as the CEO described above. Our purpose with this book is thus to develop a research-based framework or a map that can empower leaders in their quest for sustainable and profitable business models and that can pave the way for more research on such business model innovation in the near future.

1.1 A RESTART of Business Models for a Brighter Future Earth

We have coined our framework for sustainable business model innovation *RESTART*. We introduce this framework briefly in the next chapter, and we develop and discuss it in detail in the second part of the book. Before we introduce the framework, we will shortly discuss three interwoven trends that we argue drive the development of new business models and that drive the need for *sustainable business model innovations*: (1) the sustainability problem, (2) digitalization and the technological opportunity space and (3) changing consumer preferences and lifestyles (Fig. 1.1).

The comprehensive sustainability problem with which we are faced comprises numerous social and environmental challenges that need to be solved. In this age of digitalization, however, companies at the same time find themselves in the midst of an ocean of technological opportunities that allow for new and smarter business models, and societal trends enable companies to deliver their products and services in new ways that are attractive to a new generation of consumers. Taken together, this is fertile ground for business model innovation. Taken together, however, these ongoing trends and drivers also represent many unknown factors that managers need to take into consideration when developing and implementing their strategies.

Managers often ask us how they are supposed to achieve sustainable and profitable business models in practice in this new business landscape. In our talks and strategy seminars, we often use "the dark room" as a

Fig. 1.1 Three trends driving the development of new business models

metaphorical starting point for sustainable business model innovation. In any innovation process, the light switch is hidden somewhere inside the dark room. Outside of the room—in the light—lies the known territory for the managers and their companies, often illuminated by practices that are woven deep into the culture or the DNA of the company. The sustainability problem, the technological changes we are witnessing and the changes in customers' expectations are all beyond the known part of this territory. It often feels safer for managers and other stakeholders out there in the light, where they can maneuver in safe environments without having to take unnecessary risks. However, as the CEO above describes, contemporary business managers operate in a competitive landscape that requires them to redesign their business models and break loose from business as usual. Often, this involves entering dark rooms in search of the light switch that "turns on" innovative ideas and business models. This also means that they need to start looking at the sustainability problem, the new technologies and the changes in customers' expectations as opportunities, rather than as threats.

In order to find the light switch, the first thing managers need to do is to enter the dark room, which can be challenging in its own right. When entering the dark room, they meet many challenges: the light switch seems to move from time to time and the furniture seems to move around as well. This implies that once they think they have found an innovative solution to a sustainability problem, other factors interfere and complicate the situation—conditions may have changed, competitors may have acted or other players may have entered the industry and changed the rules of the game. True innovators thus need to work together to understand the problem better and to find new solutions that can push them forward toward their goals and objectives—that is, to find the switch that turns on the light.

In the following chapters, we invite you to join us in the hunt for the light switch to sustainable business model innovations. To create a brighter future, everyone needs to contribute to this search—whether you are a researcher, a student, a manager in the middle of an innovation process or a concerned citizen who believes we are in need of a shift toward more sustainable business models. Our experience is that entering such dark rooms may not seem very tempting at first, but it helps to be prepared when entering the darkness. This involves conducting the search for new business models based on knowledge and insights that can lead to asking better questions and being more precise in the search for the answers to those questions. The research-based framework RESTART that we develop in this book can support managers in their attempt to *rethink, reinvent* and *reorganize* the ways in which they create, deliver and capture value through their business models.

Such innovative efforts are necessary for companies that want to take part in the ongoing movement from a brown to a green economy, from an analog to a digital economy and from an old-fashioned to a modern economy. This book addresses this transition. It discusses why such a transition is needed, how new and smarter business models can be designed and how researchers can study such innovation processes. We argue that there are massive changes going on that require new lenses through which we can understand business. The business landscape has changed comprehensively, and new maps are needed to maneuver in this rapidly changing territory.

The managers of contemporary companies need to identify and step into their dark rooms, and not only that: they also need to inspire their coworkers to join them in the search for the light switch. We propose that many companies have failed to design sustainable business models because they have not yet asked the right questions. This book thus attempts to provide knowledge and insight that can be helpful for asking the questions that can spark the necessary transition toward business models that are fit for the future—whether you are a researcher, a manager, a student, a regulator or a legislator, or just a citizen interested in business, society and the environment.

1.2 The Methodological Approach of This Book

This book outlines the RESTART framework, which is a conceptual framework that is intended to capture the characteristics of new business models that can be sustainable and profitable at the same time. We moreover consider the framework as a research agenda, as each of the seven components of the framework will require comprehensive research, and toward the end of the book, we point out fruitful avenues for research related to several of these components.

We have developed the framework over a period of many years, through a combination of quantitative, qualitative and action-based research in close collaboration with companies in several sectors. Across several different research projects, we have collected data through structured and unstructured interviews with executives, managers and sustainability officers, which have formed the basis for a deeper understanding of the kinds of changes companies are attempting to make to their business models. We use many of these companies as cases and examples throughout this book, and their business models are used as examples to shed light on various characteristics of more sustainable business models. Among those companies are Norwegian companies, such as Bright Products, Orkla and Norsk Gjenvinning, and international companies, such as The Plastic Bank and Scanship. Structured and unstructured interviews with managers and executives in these companies and others have been central to the empirical inquiry on which the book builds.

In addition, we have conducted surveys and field experiments with companies that also inform our account of the changes taking place and further business model innovations that might become widespread. For instance, our inquiry is informed by our field experiments on sustainability investing in Skandiabanken (Døskeland and Pedersen 2015, 2017), our survey of sustainability practices and performance in Norwegian service firms (Gulbrandsen et al. 2017) and the management control and governance practices in the same firms (Gulbrandsen et al. 2015), as well as our empirical investigations of the relationship between sustainability efforts and consumer trust (Jørgensen et al. 2018).

Finally, we build on secondary data and information from a vast and manifold set of reports, documents and scientific studies that have informed our understanding of the business modeling trends that are ongoing, and that are likely to shape the business models of the future. In our research projects in collaboration with the companies outlined above and many others, we have been granted access to numerous documents that have allowed us to dig deeper into how these companies are working in order to adapt their business models to the sustainability problem, technological changes that are underway and changing consumer preferences and lifestyles.

When considering the methodological approach of our book, however, we should also note that we have gradually tested the framework on a variety of managers and executives. We have done so in Executive MBA programs, in company-internal workshops with managers of companies trying to design new and more sustainable business models and in other events with a corporate audience, over a period of several years. This has given us valuable feedback on how concepts are understood and the relative importance of various aspects of the framework and characteristics of business models. We believe that one of the strengths of the framework outlined in this book is that we have continuously tested the ideas upon which the framework rests on both the companies with which we have conducted empirical studies and managers from other companies that are struggling with the same kinds of challenges that this book addresses.

From a scientific point of view, we consider the framework better suited as a point of departure for asking better questions, rather than a framework that gives answers. At the time of writing, we are designing empirical studies—including field experiments, surveys and other research designs—aimed at investigating the seven components of the RESTART framework. This includes studies of sharing-economic business models, alliances for business models at the bottom of the pyramid and circular-economic business models. For this reason, we encourage academic readers of this book to read it as a contribution not just to conceptualizing sustainable business models, but also to the research agenda in which we need plentiful of studies investigating the attempt to align sustainability and profitability when designing and innovating new business models.

1.3 Let Us RESTART Sustainable Business Model Innovation

In 2028, ten years from now, the CEO of the insulation company outlined above will probably have retired, but it will be interesting to see what company he leaves behind. Will he have been successful at innovating its business model to become more sustainable, leveraging new technologies and fit for the future expectations of its customers? In 2028, we will probably look back at 2018 and say, "Why didn't we grab the opportunities then?" We are going to look back and think that at the time it should have been easy to exploit the new technological opportunities to develop new, smarter and more sustainable business models. We will look back at 2018 as the time when one could exploit all the novel technologies comprised in the fourth industrial revolution to make new products and services that have a smaller footprint while delivering high-quality and convenient solutions in line with customer expectations. We argue that achieving this requires a RESTART. In the following chapters, we discuss what such a RESTART might entail, how it can be studied empirically and how managers can utilize such a framework in an attempt to design and implement the business models of the future.

References

Døskeland, T., & Pedersen, L. J. T. (2015). Investing with brain or heart? A field experiment on responsible investment. *Management Science, 62*(6), 1632–1644.

Døskeland, T., & Pedersen, L. J. T. (2017). Does the wealth of investors matter? Evidence from a field experiment on responsible investment. *Working paper*, NHH Norwegian School of Economics.

Gulbrandsen, E. A., Jørgensen, S., Kaarbøe, K., & Pedersen, L. J. T. (2015). Developing management control systems for sustainable business models. *Beta: Scandinavian Journal of Business Research, 29*(1), 10–25.

Gulbrandsen, E. A., Jørgensen, S., & Pedersen, L. J. T. (2017). Sustainability practices and performance in Norwegian knowledge-intensive service companies. *Working paper*, NHH Norwegian School of Economics.

Jørgensen, S., Pedersen, L. J. T., & Skard, S. (2018). Does going green build trust? The relationship between sustainability efforts, perceived innovativeness and trust. *Working paper*, NHH Norwegian School of Economics.

Open Access This chapter is licensed under the terms of the Creative Commons Attribution-NonCommercial-NoDerivatives 4.0 International License (http://creativecommons.org/licenses/by-nc-nd/4.0/), which permits any noncommercial use, sharing, distribution and reproduction in any medium or format, as long as you give appropriate credit to the original author(s) and the source, provide a link to the Creative Commons license and indicate if you modified the licensed material. You do not have permission under this license to share adapted material derived from this book or parts of it.

The images or other third party material in this chapter are included in the chapter's Creative Commons license, unless indicated otherwise in a credit line to the material. If material is not included in the chapter's Creative Commons license and your intended use is not permitted by statutory regulation or exceeds the permitted use, you will need to obtain permission directly from the copyright holder.

2

The Seven Steps of the RESTART Framework

If you ask the executives of the shipping company Wilhelmsen Ship Services (WSS), the fourth industrial revolution has already begun, and it is allowing the company to reduce its footprint significantly. This is evident when looking at the innovations put in place by WSS in 2017 alone. Several such innovations have been developed in collaboration with the company Pracademy. For example, WSS has introduced a drone service that delivers documents, money, medicines and other small packages from ports to WSS's ships. Historically, the ships have had to enter the ports for such purposes, which increases emissions close to land and which is also more costly for the company. WSS has furthermore developed "intelligent ropes"—that is, ropes with sensors that let operators know when they are about to be destroyed or worn out, thus avoiding risky and damaging situations caused by ropes breaking. Moreover, WSS has started three-dimensional (3D) printing of spare parts in strategically positioned ports around the world, rather than having to stock parts and to travel back and forth to get them. Thus, the footprint of providing these parts is reduced while provision is more efficient. And finally, by using the so-called Internet of Things (IoT) sensors in the kettles aboard its ships, operators at WSS's headquarters can monitor

© The Author(s) 2018
S. Jørgensen, L. J. T. Pedersen, *RESTART Sustainable Business Model Innovation*, Palgrave Studies in Sustainable Business In Association with Future Earth, https://doi.org/10.1007/978-3-319-91971-3_2

and manage pH levels and temperature in the kettles. This makes it unnecessary for staff on the ship to carry out this risky job that—when managed insufficiently—can lead to dangerous situations that can ultimately result in injury or casualties. By introducing innovative new technologies in their operations, then, WSS also changes the work-life for its workers on ships, in ports and elsewhere in its global supply chain.

As discussed in the previous chapter, our book's point of departure is that three concurrent major trends indicate the need for a RESTART—that is, for sustainable business model innovations. These three are all reflected in the innovations by WSS outlined above. First, we are facing a massive sustainability problem (e.g., Rockström et al. 2009), which we will illuminate throughout this book. The comprehensive social and environmental issues comprised in the sustainability problem are simultaneously a threat and a source of opportunities for companies. In both ways, sustainability issues are drivers of innovation (cf. Nidumolu et al. 2009). Second, the technological revolution we are facing has a double effect: it renders old business models obsolete and it creates huge possibilities for creating value in new ways. Increasingly, the technological opportunities comprised in the digital and physical technologies, often referred to as the fourth industrial revolution (Schwab 2016), have enabled the development of smarter and leaner business models that can have a lesser footprint while remaining equally good customer experiences. Finally, changes in consumer preferences, lifestyles and consumption patterns help make new types of value creation possible—for example, through sharing-economic business models, access-based services and so on.

2.1 A RESTART for Business Models of the Future

In the expectations of future business models articulated by managers, academics and other pundits, we are already seeing the contours of how these three trends may shape the ways value will be created, delivered and captured in the future. How many years will it, for instance, take before we no longer own our own car, but rather subscribe to a shuttle service based on a fleet of driverless cars? How long will it take until we rent a drill whenever we need one and get it delivered at home within minutes by the same driverless cars? And how should the car industry prepare itself for this transition, or any other industry for that matter?

At which point will we be sitting at home browsing Facebook with our Virtual Reality (VR) goggles, looking at clothes that are digitally generated, customized to us, and we will simply say: "Order the shirt. Charge my Bitcoin account". Will the shirt be 3D printed and flown to our homes by a drone that picks up the shirt from a warehouse with no people involved, while payment is executed automatically? When will we put our laundry in the washing machine and the clothes will have sensors that tell the machine the garments' washing instructions? And how long will it be until we get smart light bulbs, clothes, carpets and other products for "free" because they are linked to the Internet and are financed by generating valuable data about us for energy companies and others who benefit from this information?

When will we scan products in the grocery store with our smartphones or augmented reality devices, upon which we are instantly told in detail how the products were made, from where their components originate, how far the products have traveled, what impacts they will have on our bodies and the environment, and so on? This extreme traceability and transparency are expected to become a reality in the not very distant future, due to the combination of increased consumer expectations, technological opportunities related to IoT sensors, blockchain-based and other information systems and digital interfaces that allow consumers access to the right information at the right time. Again, we see how such a future is simultaneously driven by the sustainability problem, the technological opportunity space and changing consumer preferences.

In recent years, we have seen that what a few years ago almost appeared as science fiction is becoming more science and less fiction. Just look at how quickly companies like Alibaba and Amazon have built their gigantic ecosystems online, through which they offer more products and services than what we thought possible only a short time ago. For instance, Amazon and Fiat Chrysler recently began working together to sell cars online at heavily discounted prices, and Amazon has purchased Whole Foods, thus making a move to enter the food industry. Another example is Apple's new wireless headphones, which according to the World

Economic Forum constitute the first step toward integrating our mobile phones in our bodies. When you speak, the wireless earpiece can "hear" you, and it has software that removes noise and makes your voice clear. This makes it possible for you to ask Siri to send a message to a colleague or to order goods for you on Amazon, or you can ask your thermostat from Nest to turn down the heat in the room or turn on the alarm system in selected parts of your house. That is, of course, if you need it, with the recent developments in artificial intelligence and machine learning, the different bots in our surroundings will know who you are, if you want the alarm off or on and what temperature you like in which parts of the house at different times of the day.

The same kinds of developments are taking place with production processes that allow companies to reduce their footprints. Think about how 3D printing has quickly enabled companies to produce in ways that significantly reduce excess materials from manufacturing, since more and more products are 3D printed "from scratch", rather than carved out of a piece of metal, wood or other materials. In addition, this allows for printing on demand, which makes it unnecessary to keep large inventories of products that can be printed when needed. Similarly, virtual reality and augmented reality technologies are allowing health care providers to treat stroke patients in rehabilitation through Virtual Reality (VR) where they reside, thus eliminating the need for comprehensive transportation services of those patients to and from health care facilities. The list of such solutions that allow for product and service delivery of high quality, but with very significant reduction of footprints, is growing steadily.

These technological changes are occurring at record speed, and consequently current business models must change rapidly (Teece 2010). Had we written this book a few years ago, for instance, we had not been familiar with Tesla's new strategy. The company's new cars will have an app that allows car rental by neighbors or others without the car owner being involved. Allegedly, the new Tesla cars already have hardware to enable self-driving functionality when legislation allows the implementation thereof. Both Google and Apple are expected to produce such cars in the not too distant future. These cars are almost like rolling smartphones, and given that we will continue to buy our own cars, we will likely not pay much in advance. Instead, we will pay per kilometer and perhaps for different services we access while being driven around by our cars. In this way, we can reduce the "structural waste" that surrounds us everywhere; that is, the overcapacity in all the things we already possess (e.g., Morlet et al. 2016). Why build new cars, when most existing cars stand idle most of the day (and have available seating most of the time while they are in motion)? By simple app-based sharing models, we can instead exploit the capacity of the cars we already have. The same is true for office space, agricultural equipment like tractors, slalom skis and drills in our houses and so on.

These radical technological changes, which can help mitigate the sustainability problem, imply that the fourth industrial revolution is already ongoing (Schwab 2016). This concept refers to the almost all-encompassing transformation characterized by new technologies like artificial intelligence, robotics, the IoT, 3D printing and advanced materials. It further comprises the emergence of autonomous vehicles, new forms of energy, genetic engineering, nanotechnology and drones (see, e.g., Kelly 2016). In parallel with these technological developments, online solutions and platforms that bring together suppliers and demanders of goods, services and social capital also challenge traditional business model (Choudary et al. 2016). Moreover, new sharing-economic and circular-economic business models are deviating from conventional business thinking (see, e.g., Botsman and Rogers 2010; McDonough and Braungart 2010). Overall, these trends point toward a comprehensive transformation of current business models that imply new ways of producing, transporting, consuming and reusing materials, components and products (e.g., Bocken et al. 2014; Boons and Lüdeke-Freund 2013; Jørgensen and Pedersen 2015). These smarter business models will enable more efficient resource use and customization of products and services in a way that can improve the offering to customers while reducing the footprint thereof.

In this book, we investigate such developments in business models. We shed light on changes that have already taken place, we illuminate business model innovations that are ongoing at the time of writing and we even attempt to "look into the crystal ball". Thereby, we offer some indications of what the business models of the future might look like if we take the three developments outlined above and their implications into account.

2.2 A Brief Introduction to the RESTART Framework for Sustainable Business Model Innovation

In Part II of the book, we will dig deeper into the RESTART framework. Briefly put, RESTART is an acronym of seven letters that correspond with seven features of more sustainable business models. They can meaningfully be categorized into three groups of features ("RE", "STA" and "RT", respectively), and the framework was designed with these three in mind.

The first category, "RE"—*redesign* and *experimentation*—relates to the development that companies are increasingly faced with the need to redesign their business models (see, e.g., Johnson et al. 2008), which in turn necessitates controlled experimentation (Andries et al. 2013; McGrath 2010). The second category, "STA"—*service-logic, the circular economy* and *alliances*—reflects three central developments in contemporary business modeling for sustainability: the emphasis on services rather than products (or functionality rather than ownership; cf. Bocken et al. 2014), on circular business models rather than linear ones (see, e.g., Bocken et al. 2016; Linder and Williander 2017) and on alliances and collaboration rather than single companies competing in isolation (e.g., Kiron et al. 2015). The third category, "RT"—results and three-dimensionality—relates to the governance and control challenges associated with implementing a sustainable business model, which are crucial for its success (e.g., Eccles et al. 2014; Perrini and Tencati 2006).

We contrast each of the seven features with their opposites, all of which are arguably characteristics of business-as-usual. In this way, the framework highlights seven main changes that can make business models smarter and more sustainable:

REDESIGN rather than standstill
EXPERIMENTATION rather than turnaround
SERVICE-LOGIC rather than product-logic
THE CIRCULAR rather than the linear economy
ALLIANCES rather than solo-runs
RESULTS rather than indulgences
THREE-DIMENSIONALITY rather than one-dimensionality

Based on these seven characteristics, we will argue throughout the book that the business models of the future are likely, in systematic ways, to look very different from the business models of the past. Specifically, we suggest the following propositions about the business models of the future:

>…they will require frequent REDESIGN,
>…which necessitates controlled EXPERIMENTATION.
>…and be characterized by SERVICE-LOGIC
>…based on ideas from THE CIRCULAR economy.
>…which will make ALLIANCES even more important,
>…in order to achieve the right RESULTS
>…in a world where the scorecard is THREE-DIMENSIONAL.

More and more companies are trying to make the world more sustainable. But not only that: they are trying to make money while doing so. If companies embrace these opportunities and take on this responsibility, we might be able to achieve the so-called green growth: economic growth while reducing the use of resources and thus the emissions that contribute to a worsening climate (e.g., Ekins 2002; Popp 2012). There will arguably still be a need for solutions that go beyond what companies can achieve on their own since not all problems can be solved in a manner that is consistent with profitability and some problems arguably need regulation and other solutions. The opportunity space for solutions by companies is still immense, but it is not going to be a walk in the park. It will require major transformation of corporate activities, and hence our way of life—as customers, employees and contributors to the economic engine. We need smarter manufacturing, logistics and transport, packaging, consumption and reuse. We argue that this requires a RESTART.

References

Andries, P., Debackere, K., & Looy, B. (2013). Simultaneous experimentation as a learning strategy: Business model development under uncertainty. *Strategic Entrepreneurship Journal, 7*(4), 288–310.

Bocken, N. M., de Pauw, I., Bakker, C., & van der Grinten, B. (2016). Product design and business model strategies for a circular economy. *Journal of Industrial and Production Engineering, 33*(5), 308–320.

Bocken, N. M. P., Short, S. W., Rana, P., & Evans, S. (2014). A literature and practice review to develop sustainable business model archetypes. *Journal of Cleaner Production, 65*, 42–56.

Boons, F., & Lüdeke-Freund, F. (2013). Business models for sustainable innovation: State-of-the-art and steps towards a research agenda. *Journal of Cleaner Production, 45*, 9–19.

Botsman, R., & Rogers, R. (2010). *What's mine is yours. The rise of collaborative consumption*. New York, NY: HarperCollins.

Choudary, S. P., Van Alstyne, M. W., & Parker, G. G. (2016). *Platform revolution: How networked markets are transforming the economy—And how to make them work for you*. New York, NY: WW Norton & Company.

Eccles, R. G., Ioannou, I., & Serafeim, G. (2014). The impact of corporate sustainability on organizational processes and performance. *Management Science, 60*(11), 2835–2857.

Ekins, P. (2002). *Economic growth and environmental sustainability: The prospects for green growth*. London: Routledge.

Johnson, M. W., Christensen, C. M., & Kagermann, H. (2008). Reinventing your business model. *Harvard Business Review, 86*(12), 57–68.

Jørgensen, S., & Pedersen, L. J. T. (2015). *Responsible and profitable: Strategies for sustainable business models*. Oslo: Cappelen Damm Akademisk.

Kelly, K. (2016). *The inevitable: Understanding the 12 technological forces that will shape our future*. Penguin.

Kiron, D., Kruschwitz, N., Haanaes, K., Reeves, M., Fuisz-Kehrbach, S. K., & Kell, G. (2015). Joining forces: Collaboration and leadership for sustainability. *MIT Sloan Management Review, 56*(3), 1–31.

Linder, M., & Williander, M. (2017). Circular business model innovation: Inherent uncertainties. *Business Strategy and the Environment, 26*(2), 182–196.

McDonough, W., & Braungart, M. (2010). *Cradle to cradle: Remaking the way we make things*. London: Macmillan.

McGrath, R. G. (2010). Business models: A discovery driven approach. *Long Range Planning, 43*(2), 247–261.

Morlet, A., Blériot, J., Opsomer, R., Linder, M., Henggeler, A., Bluhm, A., & Carrera, A. (2016). *Intelligent assets: Unlocking the circular economy potential*. London: Ellen MacArthur Foundation.

Nidumolu, R., Prahalad, C. K., & Rangaswami, M. R. (2009). Why sustainability is now the key driver of innovation. *Harvard Business Review, 87*(9), 56–64.

Perrini, F., & Tencati, A. (2006). Sustainability and stakeholder management: The need for new corporate performance evaluation and reporting systems. *Business Strategy and the Environment, 15*(5), 296–308.

Popp, D. (2012). The role of technological change in green growth (No. w18506). National Bureau of Economic Research.

Rockström, J., Steffen, W., Noone, K., Persson, Å., Chapin, F. S., Lambin, E. F., & Nykvist, B. (2009). A safe operating space for humanity. *Nature, 461*(7263), 472–475.

Schwab, K. (2016). *The fourth industrial revolution*. Geneva: World Economic Forum.

Teece, D. J. (2010). Business models, business strategy and innovation. *Long Range Planning, 43*(2), 172–194.

Open Access This chapter is licensed under the terms of the Creative Commons Attribution-NonCommercial-NoDerivatives 4.0 International License (http://creativecommons.org/licenses/by-nc-nd/4.0/), which permits any noncommercial use, sharing, distribution and reproduction in any medium or format, as long as you give appropriate credit to the original author(s) and the source, provide a link to the Creative Commons license and indicate if you modified the licensed material. You do not have permission under this license to share adapted material derived from this book or parts of it.

The images or other third party material in this chapter are included in the chapter's Creative Commons license, unless indicated otherwise in a credit line to the material. If material is not included in the chapter's Creative Commons license and your intended use is not permitted by statutory regulation or exceeds the permitted use, you will need to obtain permission directly from the copyright holder.

3

RESTART: What, Why, How and So What?

3.1 Responsibility and Opportunity

In 2014, the technology company Dell entered into an agreement with the supplier Newlight Technologies—an innovative plastics manufacturer from California. The thing to note about Dell's new supplier was that the plastic it delivered to Dell was certified carbon-negative.

In order to produce the plastic, Newlight captures CO_2 from the chimneys of other companies and uses it as the most important input in its plastic production. In other words, the more plastic Newlight produces, the larger the reduction of CO_2 in the atmosphere. In addition, the plastic produced by Newlight is biodegradable. Newlight can deliver this product because it has developed technology that makes it possible to capture greenhouse gases in the air and turn them into biodegradable plastic.

Newlight plastic is competitive in quality and price, and it is used for everything from plastic chairs to the bags in which Dell packages its laptops. This implies that Newlight not only contributes to solve the climate problem, it has also established a business model that could potentially provide it with clients both upstream and downstream in its value chain.

Upstream, it could be paid by companies that have a surplus of CO_2 and a need to get rid of it. Downstream, it is already paid by customers of its plastic. In this way, the company could eventually get a double revenue model. Dell, like many other comparable companies, wants greener products as part of an attempt to reduce the environmental footprint of its value chain. Therefore, Newlight already has a long list of clients on the Fortune 500 list aiming to reduce the negative impact of their plastic use. And in 2016, Newlight entered into a comprehensive partnership with IKEA, through which Newlight will supply IKEA with carbon-negative plastic for use in its products.

Some 20 years earlier, in 1994, Ray Anderson, the founder and CEO of Interface, was asked to comment on the company's environmental vision at an internal work meeting. Interface was a large player in the international carpet market, and the reason for the meeting was that the company's customers and collaborative partners had begun to question how its carpets were manufactured and what influence Interface had on society and the environment (Anderson 2002). Ray drew inspiration for his speech from reading Paul Hawken's *The Ecology of Commerce* (Hawken 1993). It suddenly occurred to him that the company he had been running for 21 years not only lacked an environmental vision but rather the company was an environmental culprit. This was a revelation to Anderson, and it led to his vision of reducing Interface's ecological footprint to zero by 2020 ("Mission Zero"). This required an entirely new way of thinking and a completely new business model to turn the company around from being an environmental villain to becoming a leader in sustainability (Anderson 2010).

To achieve this ambitious objective, the company needed to develop new products and had to turn its processes upside down to find new ways of designing, manufacturing and distributing its carpets. In addition, it aimed to find alternative sources of energy. Perhaps most fundamentally, Interface changed its business model from one based on selling carpets to end users to a business model based on a so-called product-service system. This implied that it leased carpets to its customers, in a way that the company had the responsibility for maintenance, cleaning and so on. When carpet tiles were destroyed or worn down, Interface replaced them and collected the old tiles for reuse in the production of new carpets. In this way, Interface could sell more services to its customers, while at the same time driving down the cost of input factors for its carpets (see, e.g., Botsman and Rogers 2010; Jørgensen and Pedersen 2017). Interface is still working toward these goals today—even after Anderson's death—and the company has made good progress toward realizing its environmental vision, while at the same time remaining a market leader in its industrial segment.

These two companies, Newlight and Interface, both actively address the environmental and social issues facing the world, and they have developed business models that strive to be both sustainable and profitable. While Ray Anderson experienced an epiphany that led him to take responsibility for the sustainability issues of his company, we can say that Newlight has based its business model on the opportunity the sustainability issue provides for businesses to find profitable solutions to these pressing problems. This book revolves around both of these approaches: responsibilities and opportunities for creating more sustainable economies. Most importantly, however, it addresses how these companies aim to align sustainability and profitability.

Companies are Problem Solvers

Increasing attention is being paid to sustainability issues in companies across all industries (e.g., Kiron et al. 2012). This is not only because the severity of the problem has begun to dawn on our societies, but also because companies are realizing that in order to remain profitable over time, they will have to take sustainability into account and, ideally, deal with the problems we face (e.g., Eccles et al. 2015; Khan et al. 2016). This may involve changing their business models to adapt to the sustainability issue or it could involve designing business models that actively contribute to solving the problem (e.g., Wells 2013; Boons and Lüdeke-Freund 2013). Therefore, insurance companies are working to ensure that customers can adapt to the new climate reality, fish farming companies are changing their production methods to become more sustainable and an increasing part of assets under management in financial markets take the so-called ESG (environmental, social, governance) factors into account.

On the one hand, the sustainability issue is important to business because it affects the conditions for economic activities (Pachauri and Meyer 2014; Rockström et al. 2009). When resources become scarcer because of overuse or climate change, the costs and risks associated with resources increase and the rewards of adapting increase (e.g., Evans 2011; Krautkraemer 1998). When markets become unstable due to geopolitical and environmental risks, the stability of the economy is also disturbed (e.g., Fitzpatrick 1983; Miller 1992; Søreide 2016). And not least: when customers, employees, investors and other stakeholders place greater demands on social and environmental performance, openness and transparency, and expect that products and services are made more sustainable, it becomes less attractive to be the company that cannot live up to those expectations (e.g., Sen et al. 2016; Skarmeas and Leonidou 2013). Perhaps this is why companies such as Equinor and Shell choose to pull out of oil sands mining, and food producers like Orkla stop using palm oil as an input factor? More and more research shows that sustainability and profitability are possible to align and that improving sustainability performance can even lead to certain types of competitive advantage that are unavailable to businesses that are not sustainable (Eccles et al. 2015, 2016; Khan et al. 2016; Kiron et al., 2012; Jørgensen and Pedersen 2015). This means that the incentives to become greener become stronger.

On the other hand, the sustainability issue is important to business simply because companies are part of the problem. Companies have played a major role in the development of our sustainability problems, and it is difficult to imagine that these problems can be solved without their efforts. To achieve this, there is a need for both companies that take responsibility for reducing their negative influence on society and the environment and companies that manage to find profitable ways to exploit the business opportunities that arise because of those problems. Fortunately, we see that both things are happening—although perhaps not quickly enough.

Responsibility and Opportunity: Two Drivers of Sustainable Business Models

In other words, we outline two different approaches to the sustainability problem. On the one hand, there are companies that take responsibility for their culpability in contributing to the problem and consequently take measures to reduce their negative impact on society and the environment. On the other hand, there are companies that see potential for solving the problem and consequently build business models that enable them to offer profitable products and services that address the footprint made by others. In addition, of course, there are companies that apply both approaches at the same time. This distinction between sustainability as responsibility and as opportunity can be illustrated as follows (Fig. 3.1).

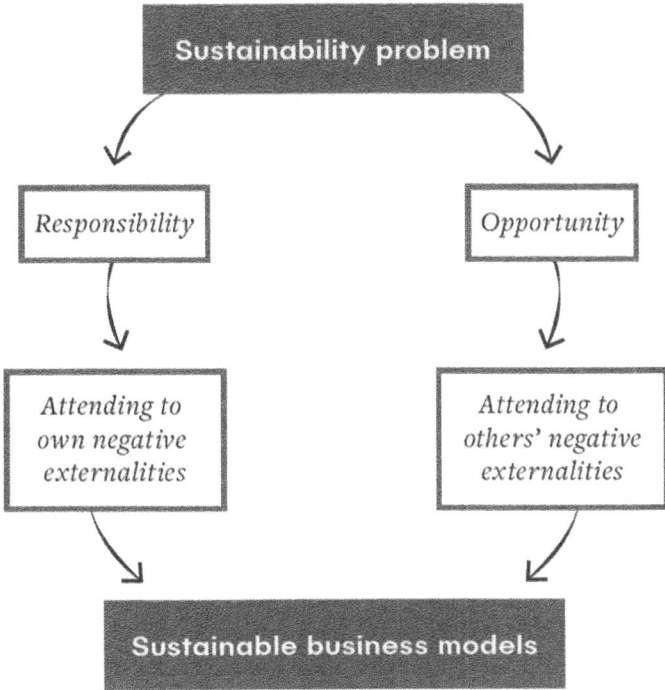

Fig. 3.1 Sustainability as responsibility and as opportunity (Jørgensen and Pedersen 2017)

We use the term sustainability problem to denote the sum of challenges we face with regard to both society and the environment. The part of these problems arising from companies' operations are due to what we call negative externalities (Cornes and Sandler 1996). This refers to the negative effects of a company's activities on society and the environment, and it thus reflects an impact that would not have been there if the company did not exist. Depending on how the company sees its relationship to any given sustainability problem, it may experience a responsibility for the problem (e.g., Carroll 1999) or it may see an opportunity in resolving it (e.g., Jenkins 2009; Grayson and Hodges 2017). The former typically involves dealing with one's own negative externalities, whereas the latter typically involves helping to cope with the negative externalities of others. When we are talking about sustainable business models, such characteristics of the company are an integral part of the way it operates.

For some sustainability problems, it is common to think that individual companies are responsible (e.g., Freeman 2010). Seemingly, this was the experience of Ray Anderson when he initiated the turnaround at Interface. Similarly, such thinking might underlie Dell's desire to reduce the footprint of its operations by switching from oil-based to carbon-negative plastic. Thus, the company can tell its customers and other stakeholders that it is greening its operations. Other problems are clearly caused by others than the company itself, and there is little reason to argue that the company is responsible for such problems. For instance, Newlight is not responsible for the CO_2 emissions of others. However, the company still sees a significant business opportunity in those problems, and consequently develops a business model by which it can contribute to solving the sustainability problem while making money thereof.

There are more and more examples that businesses find innovative solutions to solve sustainability problems profitably (Nidumolu et al. 2009; Porter and Kramer 2011). Companies are uniquely fitted to do this because they are basically problem solvers—they are designed to identify business opportunities in the problems faced by existing or potential customers and to find profitable ways to solve them.

Toward Sustainable Business Models

When Mark Herrema and Kenton Kimmel founded Newlight in 2003, they were two young men who experimented with technology in their garage. The idea emerged from what was barely a start-up company. When Ray Anderson had his ecological epiphany, however, he had already been the CEO of the market-leading company Interface for 21 years, and he transformed the business model of the company completely. Such innovations are possible in small companies as well as large, in goods-producing companies as well as in the service sector, in Norway as well as in California, and in modern knowledge-intensive companies as well as in organizations that are more traditional.

We will now take you on a journey from supermarkets in Paris to football pitches in Rio de Janeiro; from financial institutions in Bergen, Norway to technology companies in Silicon Valley; from clothing manufacturers in Madrid to industrial parks in Denmark. In all of these places, there are companies that have taken appropriate steps to become more sustainable, and that have succeeded in maintaining or increasing profitability at the same time. These firms have come a long way toward succeeding in implementing sustainable business model innovations. Many other companies could do so too.

3.2 Sustainable and Profitable

Does a recycling company need a sustainable business model innovation? In 2011, the private equity firm Altor bought the largest recycling company in Norway, Norsk Gjenvinning (NG), for about 250 million USD. The new owners quickly realized that the company was in need of a major cleanup.

In 2014, the company publicly disclosed details of the dirty practices hidden in the company's operations and in the waste industry in general. This was not popular in the industry. NG argued that in 2013 alone, it spent close to 15 million USD on a "moral cleanup" of the company, which has 1500 employees, 40,000 customers and approximately

400 million USD in annual revenue. NG handles about 25 percent of all waste in Norway and operates in Sweden, Denmark and Great Britain as well. Among the issues that Altor discovered when taking over NG in 2011 was that a lot of money was being made by illegal means of getting rid of waste. Moreover, parts of the recycling industry were characterized by corruption, partly because of a cash economy and lax controls. Hazardous waste was not being handled in compliance with relevant laws, waste was exported illegally and there was considerable collusion between players in the industry.

The management team of NG, with CEO Erik Osmundsen in the lead, set a goal to achieve what they refer to as "real sustainability". They started in their own ranks, with a new vision and new corporate values. At the same time, they worked to get the rest of the industry, as well as the government and customers to understand the urgency of the situation. About half of the managers of the company were replaced, one of its former managers was jailed for 13 months and whistleblowing systems were designed to unveil all problems. NG's efforts to move in the direction of real sustainability continues unabated, and even in this supposedly "green" industry, improvement has required major corporate restructuring (Serafeim and Gombos 2015). At the end of 2017, the company's movement in this direction gained further momentum when Altor's stake was purchased by the private equity firm Summa Equity—led by Reynir Indahl, one of the partners who had previously acquired NG when working at Altor. At the time of the acquisition, Indahl stated that "*[t]he company is proof of the financial attractiveness of providing solutions that improve environmental sustainability.*" The firm further added its intention to make NG a leader in the transition to a circular economy—thus improving the footprint of its business model in new ways.

More of Everything That is Good

The story of NG is largely a story about externalities—the positive and negative side effects of corporate activities on society and the environment. We call this the sunny side and the shadowy side of companies, respectively (Jørgensen and Pedersen 2015; Eells and Walton 1969).

Through their operations, companies shed light and cast shadow. Put simply, companies shed light when they solve problems that are caused by others, and they cast shadows when they cause problems for others through their operations. NG strives to minimize the shadowy side of their operations, which includes corruption, pollution and much more. Moreover, the company aims to shed light by helping other businesses to become more sustainable. This is really the essence of the company's business model—it deals with excess resources and waste and brings them back into productive purposes, and at the same time, the company advises other companies on how to reduce their footprints (Serafeim and Gombos 2015). Among other things, NG collaborates with Norsk Hydro and Nespresso to create systems for recycling aluminum containers used for Nespresso coffee machines. Aluminum containers represent a big shadow of Nespresso's products and Norsk Hydro uses large amounts of energy to produce new aluminum but only five percent of its energy usage to recycle aluminum. Working together, all three players have found a market-based solution that improves the total footprint of the companies' operations.

All organizations cast shadows and all businesses can shed more light. This applies not only to oil companies or to industry giants. Even a charity like the Red Cross has negative externalities, while it of course could have done even more to solve the world's problems. All organizations will necessarily to a greater or lesser extent cast shadows that would not have been there if they did not exist. Yet how extensive the shadows of the individual organization are will depend on the design of its business model—hence, it has an opportunity to design more sustainable business models. In the same way, all organizations also create some positive externalities that would not have been there if they did not exist, and we can therefore think in terms of "net impact" on society and the environment from any organization's operations.

NG want to contribute to what its managers call "real sustainability"—that is, not only implement measures to become *more* sustainable but also to attain the state of actually *being* in harmony with society and the environment. Therefore, the company aims to develop a business model that operates within planetary and societal boundaries. Interface has a stated goal of attaining a zero footprint by 2020, and Newlight has developed a production method that makes its plastic carbon negative. In different ways, then, these three actors expressed the same kind of objective: They do not want their companies cast unnecessary shadow—they even want to shed light, so that any positive consequences outweigh the negatives. They aim to achieve what is often called green growth—increased economic growth with reduced impact on society and the environment (Stoknes 2015). If so, they can provide a net positive contribution to our sustainability problems.

Figure 3.2 depicts the positive and negative externalities of a company—the total amount of light and shadow that follows from its operations (McDonough and Braungart 2010). On the vertical axis, we distinguish between what is 100 percent positive and what is 100 percent negative (both of which are of course theoretical—no company will end up in either of those extremes). The bars in the graph depict the company's sunny and shadowy sides. Companies with a large shadow side and a small sunny side would be placed in the far left of the diagram, while the far right would reflect the opposite. The dotted lines illustrate two desir-

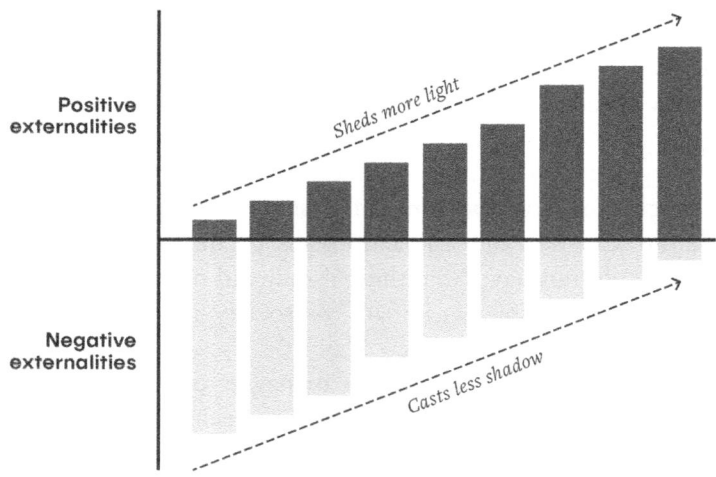

Fig. 3.2 The net effect of sustainability efforts (based on McDonough and Braungart 2010)

able movements or trajectories, respectively, to shed more light and to cast less shadow. Both of these trajectories reflect contributions to more sustainable business, but it should be noted that reducing shadows is a linear movement toward zero footprint—it is about doing as little bad as possible. The other trajectory, however, is in some sense endless—there is no limit to how comprehensive a company's positive externalities might become, and in this sense, doing more good carries in it the potential for exponential positive impact.

An organization like the Red Cross would typically be placed at the right of the diagram, as one would see it as shedding much more light than shadow, from the societal and environmental points of view. Through ensuring children education, food and health care, it helps to reduce social inequalities and to ensure that children become environmentally aware. Meanwhile, of course, the Red Cross also has a shadowy side related to the negative effects of its operations, including travel, logistics and so on. Manufacturers of cluster bombs and gambling companies, however, would typically represent the far left in the diagram. This is because of their substantial shadows stemming from their core offerings, despite the fact that they obviously create jobs, pay taxes and that their operations have other positive effects.

What, then, is most important? Is it primarily desirable that companies shed light and thus contribute to positive consequences for society and the environment? Or is it more important that they "clean up their own nests" by taking steps to cast less shadow? The answer to this question perhaps depends on both the objectives of the company and the urgency of the sustainability issue in question. Any company that operates in an unsustainable manner is in a sense sawing of the branch on which it is sitting. The question is whether it is sufficient to saw more slowly or whether it needs to stop sawing altogether, that is, instead finding new and more sustainable ways of operating. Short-term profitability can in many cases be achieved without thinking about light and shadow at all, but as we will see, the long-term profitability of companies is closely tied to their social and environmental performance.

3.3 The Next Step: Aligning Financial, Social and Environmental Bottom Lines

In 2011, the sports equipment manufacturer PUMA, under the leadership of CEO Jochen Zeitz, published the company's first sustainability report. In this report, PUMA disclosed that the cost of its negative impact on the environment was 145 million euros, while its profits in the same year were 202 million euros.

If the company should have paid the cost of these negative externalities, its profits would thus have been reduced by 72 percent. In reality, PUMA's profits were largely borrowed from the resources of future generations. When presenting the sustainability report, Zeitz stated that we are overexploiting the resources and services that the environment provides and added, "The world has changed, and sustainable business cannot be expected or achieved without radical changes in our economic models. It's as simple as that."

When PUMA published its report, it also implemented a number of measures to reduce its shadow. However, the environmental data shows that PUMA is still in "debt" to Earth, although it is trying to become more sustainable. With few exceptions—such as CO_2 emissions within the EU—a price has still not been put on the use of resources such as clean air, fresh water and topsoil. This means that the environmental costs PUMA refers to are not actual costs for companies—they do not have to be paid. In contrast, the consumption of these resources is a very real cost to the Earth, not at least for those who will live here after us (cf. Zeitz 2011).

What, then, is sustainable business? Simply put, it is about creating a harmonious and sustainable interaction between economy, society and the environment in which economic activity strengthens the social and environmental systems they exist within, rather than breaking them down (Lozano 2008; O'Higgins and Zsolnai 2017). Our perspective is a business-economic one, which implies that we look at the world from the point of view of companies. We are particularly concerned with the characteristics of companies that aim to attain both financial and non-financial objectives, both in the short and long term. However, as the example of PUMA illustrates, companies can shoot themselves in the foot if they do not take into account the social and environmental dimensions of their performance. Companies are directly dependent on society and the environment in the sense that their operations rely on both the human and natural resources extracted from these sources. Companies are also indirectly dependent on how their activities affect society and the environment since customers, employees, investors and other stakeholders can be more or less willing to support the company, depending on how they perceive its footprint.

A Sustainable Interplay

A sustainable future depends on a more harmonious interplay between business, society and the environment. Today, we are experiencing a comprehensive sustainability problem, partly because of the activities of business generating large negative externalities for society and the environment, while the positive externalities thereof are not extensive enough to compensate for companies' shadows. This is based on a simple, but important, premise for understanding how the economy, society and environment are interrelated, as illustrated in Fig. 3.3.

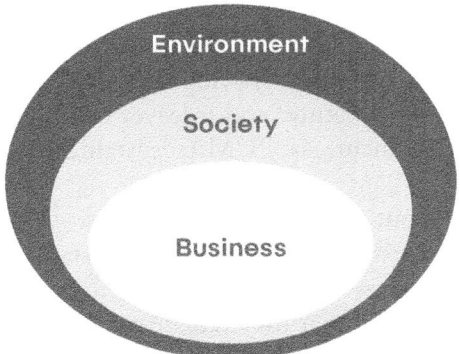

Fig. 3.3 A sustainable interaction between economy, society and environment

The economic system exists within societal boundaries (e.g., Thompson and Macmillan 2010; Dyllick and Hockerts 2002). Companies supply resources of great value to society, such as salaries and important goods and services, and they also make use of societal resources, such as labor, and infrastructure, such as education, roads and so on. When we say that companies shed light and cast shadow on society, the sunny side relates to such issues as paying taxes, creating jobs and delivering products and services, while the shadowy side, for instance, relates to exploitation of workers, corruption, tax evasion, food products that lead to obesity and so on.

There is as such an intimate interplay between business and society, and over time, companies depend on a sustainable society in which there is trust, educational institutions that can provide workers with needed skills and well-functioning democratic systems as well as political and legal institutions that make business operations possible. When these assumptions fail, it harms companies that depend on these conditions (cf. Carroll and Shabana 2010).

Moreover, both business and society exist within environmental boundaries (Ingebrigtsen and Jakobsen 2007). This does not only relate to the physical environment on land. The environment extends deep into the oceans and far into space (Rockström et al. 2009). As shown in Fig. 3.3, society and the environment are both embedded in the ecological system. As described above, business and society are interdependent, and both of these two systems are reliant on nature. Earth can exist just fine without humans (cf. Holmes 2006), but humans are completely dependent on a viable ecological system. Of course, business activity also depends on inputs from nature, and it leaves behind a significant footprint on the environment, as PUMA's sustainability report aims to highlight.

When we talk about sustainability problems, we refer to a discord between these three systems, which cannot be sustainable over time. The challenge thus consists in finding business models that are in harmony with the three systems, so that they remain profitable while being more sustainable. Thankfully, we see that more and more companies are achieving this. It should, however, be noted that in the pursuit of more sustainable business, many companies will not survive. Perhaps many companies are simply not fit for the future. Perhaps there are products, services—even entire industries that we will get rid of in a more sustainable future. Another related, and important, point is that there are probably also limits to the problems that can be solved on the part of companies themselves. Regulations are clearly needed and perhaps other means of facilitating greener lifestyles, consumption patterns and solutions will also be necessary. The point of departure of this book is to investigate the solutions that can be offered by companies. And while they may lead to considerable business opportunities, attaining them will not be a simple feat.

Sustainability Can Pay—But It is No Walk in the Park

It is of course still possible to make money while completely ignoring any impact on society and the environment, and this will probably be the case for the foreseeable future (e.g., Hong and Kacperczyk 2009; Salaber 2007). Companies that are willing to compromise on social and environmental standards, for example, by producing goods in countries with no restrictions on either pollution or worker rights, will at least reap short-term benefits thereof. It is entirely possible for companies to be irresponsible without going bankrupt. However, a number of developments—for example, related to sustainability reporting, regulation, changing customer preferences and increased attention from investors about environmental risks—suggest that it is becoming increasingly difficult to hide and to get away with irresponsible practices (see, e.g., Fernandez-Feijoo et al. 2014; Mol 2015; Unruh et al. 2016). Consequently, the best path to profitability is perhaps no longer leniency when it comes to social and environmental impact.

Recent research in fact suggests that companies that succeed in integrating sustainability into their overall strategies and business models are more profitable in the long term. This is the key finding in a study conducted by a group of researchers led by Robert G. Eccles at Harvard Business School (Eccles et al. 2015). They studied the effect of sustainability efforts on companies' financial performance and compared 180 US companies over a 20-year period. They divided the firms into two groups: the so-called high and low sustainability companies, respectively. The companies are matched so that they are comparable in important characteristics that could explain differences in performance, so that any remaining differences in profitability can most likely be attributed to differences in the companies' approach to sustainability.

The conclusion of the study is that high sustainability firms over time outperform low sustainability firms, both when measured with stock market data and accounting data. The difference is greater for companies that are relatively more exposed to end consumers Business to customer (B2C) than for those who mostly sell to other companies Business to business (B2B). The difference is also greater for companies that compete on brand and reputation, and for companies that are more dependent on using large amounts of natural resources.

What, then, characterizes the sustainable companies? In these companies, the board of directors are more often responsible for corporate sustainability strategy and results, and they are more likely to have implemented financial incentives for senior executives that are linked to sustainability performance. Moreover, these companies have more comprehensive procedures and systems for stakeholder engagement, they have longer-term horizons, they are generally more open and transparent, and their control systems and reporting include both financial and non-financial measures. A number of these characteristics are also emphasized in other studies wherein companies self-report the characteristics of their sustainability efforts and the financial performance implications thereof.

We should note that although this study includes companies from a variety of industries, the sample is limited to US companies. It is in other words unclear if one would find similar results in markets in other parts of the world, although recent studies suggest that some of the same relationships exist, for example, in Scandinavian companies (Eccles et al. 2016; Gulbrandsen et al. 2015). Nevertheless, the trends we have described above suggest that the competitive advantages related to being sustainable will be stronger in the years to come. They are not easy to achieve, however, and although it is possible to align sustainability and profitability, it requires extensive changes in companies and their business models because the problems that need to be solved are comprehensive.

Our Collective Luxury Trap

Every year, the Global Footprint Network (GFN) announces Earth Overshoot Day (see, e.g., Global Footprint Network 2011). It is the day of the year when we have used all the resources we have available that year if we were to manage our resources sustainably. In 2017, the day fell on 2 August—six days earlier than in 2016, when it was 8 August. Hence, we are moving in the wrong direction with quite some speed. We use a full year's worth of the earth's resources during the first eight months of the year, and for the remainder of the year, we borrow all the resources we consume from future generations. GFN has calculated that we need 1.6 planets to support our current consumption, while we of course only have access to one. By comparison, in 1960, we only needed three-quarters of our planet to support our consumption. Currently, the Earth's population is annually using more than 50 percent of its resources and producing more waste, including CO_2, than the planet can handle.

One example is that every year, we emit twice as much CO_2 that the forests and the sea manage to capture and turn into oxygen. With regard to greenhouse gas emissions alone, we need the equivalent of two planets. There are of course huge differences between countries: while it takes just less than four "Italies" to meet Italy's needs, we need more than 12 "Saudi Arabias" to support Saudi Arabia. Earth Overshoot Day is also referred to as Earth Debt Day, and our collective overconsumption can be seen as an ecological luxury trap, in which we borrow increasingly from the earth. Moreover, we transfer ecological debt to future generations, who will therefore have fewer resources to live from and will have to deal with a more unstable climate. They will thus incur great costs—both financial and non-financial—in order to deal with the situation that our current lifestyle imposes on them.

Such a debt-ridden development is clearly not sustainable since sustainable development is defined as development that meets present needs without compromising the ability of future generations to satisfy their needs. The term sustainable development was popularized through the UN report, Our Common Future, which was published by the World Commission on Environment and Development in 1987 (also known as the Brundtland Commission after its leader Gro Harlem Brundtland). Sustainable development is an overarching political understanding of the concept. Sustainability essentially refers to the survival of an ecological system, like a forest or an ocean. More recently, the concept has been used to refer to the broader survivability of both business and society (see also Dixon and Fallon 1989).

It is obvious that we are challenging the earth's carrying capacity. But how much can it endure? What kind of action space do we have? And how is the threat changing from year to year? The Stockholm Resilience Center (SRC) has developed a framework that covers nine planetary boundaries that are under pressure (e.g., Rockström et al. 2009). Each year, the center publishes reports in which they attempt to measure the progress in these nine areas. The nine areas together capture the planet's carrying capacity:

- Stratospheric ozone depletion
- Loss of biosphere integrity
- Chemical pollution and the release of novel entities
- Climate change
- Ocean acidification
- Freshwater consumption and the global hydrological cycle
- Land system change
- Nitrogen and phosphorus flows to the biosphere and oceans
- Atmospheric aerosol loading

According to the SRC, several of these areas are already under considerable pressure. The degree of pressure on each area varies, but the center also points out that due to unsafe methods of measurement, we do not yet have sufficient knowledge of the magnitude of the negative impact for many of these areas (cf. Steffen et al. 2015).

Societal Boundaries

In the same way that the planet has limits to what it can withstand, the societal fabric can also be stretched too far. However, we can obviously not see society and the environment as completely disconnected from each other (cf. Margolis and Walsh 2003; Smith et al. 2013). For example, we know that the environmental consequences of climate change are disproportionately borne by the poorest people in the world (see, e.g., Duraiappah 1998; Intergovernmental Panel on Climate Change 2014). Another example is the relationship between slave labor and greenhouse gas emissions. Recent research shows that the economic activity performed by slaves has a disproportionately high carbon footprint. Calculations conducted by the researcher Kevin Bales suggests that if slavery were a country, it would have had Canada's population and Angola's gross domestic product, but it would have been the third largest emitter of CO_2 globally, surpassed only by China and the United States (Bales 2016). These examples show that there is a correlation between social and environmental problems and that they may therefore be mutually self-reinforcing. The upside of this is that one may in fact solve environmental problems by solving social problems and vice versa.

The social dimension of sustainability includes a variety of characteristics of the endurance of communities, which are not necessarily as easy to capture and measure as are the abovementioned environmental attributes (cf. Hutchins and Sutherland 2008). For instance, the UN Sustainable Development Goals (SDGs), which were published in 2015, include social phenomena such as poverty, health, gender equality, diversity, social justice and social inclusion. We know that poverty is gigantic—almost half the world's population lives on less than 2.5 dollars a day, while economic inequality is increasing (cf. Banerjee and Duflo 2011; Atkinson 2015).

The social footprint of business affects all of these outcomes. When economic entities are corrupt, social justice is undermined and corruption maintained, and the differences between rich and poor may be worsened (Søreide 2016). When companies develop unhealthy or harmful products, this has consequences for both human health and quality of life (e.g., Collins and Fairchild 2007). And when companies enter markets with weak background institutions and carry out exploitative business practices in order to get cheap labor working under hazardous or high-risk conditions, several social values are under pressure (e.g., Simas et al. 2014).

The business models of the future must be adapted to this resource situation. Companies rely on employees wanting to work for them. They also depend on societal legitimacy in order to maintain operations without being subject to activism, stricter regulations and negative reputational effects. And they rely on the social environment within which they operate being sufficiently safe and predictable so that they get the human and social resources they need.

The social boundaries are perhaps less tangible than are the planetary boundaries. We can identify when we are running out of precious metals and clean water, and we can observe the rising sea levels. We note rising average temperatures and the effects thereof. However, how do we know when the social fabric is about to break? Perhaps, then, is this challenge even more difficult to manage for companies than are the environmental ones, and in many instances such social issues will also be significantly more local in nature. Therefore, there might be reason to believe that companies are more likely to address problems related to environmental sustainability than those relating to social sustainability. That does not mean, however, that the latter category is not as important.

Next Stop: RESTART

PUMA realized that it really owed three-quarters of its profits to the planet because it was extracting more resources than it provided and because it polluted the planet and the atmosphere. In recent years, PUMA and many other companies have taken steps to contribute to more sustainable development. They are becoming "more sustainable" and over time, they will perhaps become "truly sustainable", which is the stated objective of Norsk Gjenvinning. Given the overall sustainability problems we have outlined above, however, it is easy to become both pessimistic and paralyzed. The warning lights are flashing in the measurements of the Stockholm Resilience Center. Even for the indicators where we are currently within the limits of the Earth's carrying capacity, such as the use of fresh water, the analysis shows that these resources are also under pressure. And there are problems seemingly not addressed by any companies because they do not perceive them as being important for their business performance.

The response from the global community is strikingly passive in the face of such dramatic developments. Moreover, while there are plenty of examples of companies that make large and small steps to become more sustainable—or at least appear to be—there are still relatively few of the kinds of business models of which we have sketched the contours above. The treasure chest of business models that make the world greener rather than browner therefore needs replenishing. We need more truly sustainable business models that can give us a RESTART.

References

Anderson, R. (2002). Mid-course correction: Toward a sustainable enterprise. *Journal of Business Administration and Policy Analysis, 30*, 415.

Atkinson, A. B. (2015). *Inequality*. Cambridge, MA: Harvard University Press.

Bales, K. (2016). *Blood and earth: Modern slavery, ecocide, and the secret to saving the world*. Spiegel & Grau.

Banerjee, A. V., & Duflo, E. (2011). *Poor economics: A radical rethinking of the way to fight global poverty*. New York, NY: Public Affairs.

Boons, F., & Lüdeke-Freund, F. (2013). Business models for sustainable innovation: State-of-the-art and steps towards a research agenda. *Journal of Cleaner Production, 45*, 9–19.

Botsman, R., & Rogers, R. (2010). *What's mine is yours. The rise of collaborative consumption*. New York, NY: HarperCollins.

Carroll, A. B. (1999). Corporate social responsibility: Evolution of a definitional construct. *Business & Society, 38*(3), 268–295.

Carroll, A. B., & Shabana, K. M. (2010). The business case for corporate social responsibility: A review of concepts, research and practice. *International Journal of Management Reviews, 12*(1), 85–105.

Collins, A., & Fairchild, R. (2007). Sustainable food consumption at a subnational level: An ecological footprint, nutritional and economic analysis. *Journal of Environmental Policy & Planning, 9*(1), 5–30.

Cornes, R., & Sandler, T. (1996). *The theory of externalities, public goods, and club goods*. Cambridge: Cambridge University Press.

Dixon, J. A., & Fallon, L. A. (1989). The concept of sustainability: Origins, extensions, and usefulness for policy. *Society & Natural Resources, 2*(1), 73–84.

Duraiappah, A. K. (1998). Poverty and environmental degradation: A review and analysis of the nexus. *World Development, 26*(12), 2169–2179.

Dyllick, T., & Hockerts, K. (2002). Beyond the business case for corporate sustainability. *Business Strategy and the Environment, 11*(2), 130–141.

Eccles, R. G., Feiner, A., & Verheyden, T. (2016). *Sustainability and financial performance of Scandinavian companies*. Unpublished manuscript, Harvard Business School.

Eccles, R. G., Ioannou, I., & Serafeim, G. (2015). The impact of corporate sustainability on organizational processes and performance. *Management Science, 60*(11), 2835–2857.

Eells, R. S. F., & Walton, C. C. (1969). *Conceptual foundations of business*. Homewood, IL: R.D. Irwin.

Evans, A. (2011). *Resource scarcity, climate change and the risk of violent conflict*. Washington, DC: The World Bank.

Fernandez-Feijoo, B., Romero, S., & Ruiz, S. (2014). Effect of stakeholders' pressure on transparency of sustainability reports within the GRI framework. *Journal of Business Ethics, 122*(1), 53–63.

Freeman, R. E. (2010). *Strategic management: A stakeholder approach*. Cambridge: Cambridge University Press.

Global Footprint Network. (2011). What happens when infinite-growth economy runs into a finite planet. *Global Footprint Network 2011 Annual Report*. Oakland, CA: Global Footprint Network.

Grayson, D., & Hodges, A. (2017). *Corporate social opportunity! Seven steps to make corporate social responsibility work for your business*. Sheffield, UK: Greenleaf.

Gulbrandsen, E. A., Jørgensen, S., Kaarbøe, K., & Pedersen, L. J. T. (2015). Developing management control systems for sustainable business models. *Beta: Scandinavian Journal of Business Research, 29*(1), 10–25.

Hawken, P. (1993). *The ecology of commerce: How business can save the planet*. London: Weidenfeld & Nicolson.

Holmes, B. (2006). Earth without humans. *New Scientist, 192*(2573), 36–41.

Hong, H., & Kacperczyk, M. (2009). The price of sin: The effects of social norms on markets. *Journal of Financial Economics, 93*(1), 15–36.

Hutchins, M. J., & Sutherland, J. W. (2008). An exploration of measures of social sustainability and their application to supply chain decisions. *Journal of Cleaner Production, 16*(15), 1688–1698.

Ingebrigtsen, S., & Jakobsen, O. D. (2007). *Circulation economics: Theory and practice* (Vol. 3). Oxford: Peter Lang.

Intergovernmental Panel on Climate Change. (2014). *Climate change 2014— Impacts, adaptation and vulnerability: Regional aspects*. Cambridge: Cambridge University Press.

Jenkins, H. (2009). A 'business opportunity' model of corporate social responsibility for small-and medium-sized enterprises. *Business Ethics: A European Review, 18*(1), 21–36.

Jørgensen, S., & Pedersen, L. J. T. (2015). *Responsible and profitable: Strategies for sustainable business models*. Oslo: Cappelen Damm Akademisk.

Jørgensen, S., & Pedersen, L. J. T. (2017). Designing sustainable business models. In T. W. Andreassen, S. Clatworthy, M. Lüders, & T. Hillestad (Eds.), *Innovating for trust*. Cheltenham, UK: Edward Elgar Publishing.

Khan, M., Serafeim, G., & Yoon, A. (2016). Corporate sustainability: First evidence on materiality. *Accounting Review, 91*(6), 1697–1724.

Kiron, D., Kruschwitz, N., Haanaes, K., & von Streng Velken, I. (2012). Sustainability nears a tipping point. *MIT Sloan Management Review, 53*(2), 69–74.

Krautkraemer, J. A. (1998). Nonrenewable resource scarcity. *Journal of Economic Literature, 36*(4), 2065–2107.

Lozano, R. (2008). Envisioning sustainability three-dimensionally. *Journal of Cleaner Production, 16*(17), 1838–1846.

Margolis, J. D., & Walsh, J. P. (2003). Misery loves companies: Rethinking social initiatives by business. *Administrative Science Quarterly, 48*(2), 268–305.

McDonough, W., & Braungart, M. (2010). *Cradle to cradle: Remaking the way we make things*. London: Macmillan.

Miller, K. D. (1992). A framework for integrated risk management in international business. *Journal of International Business Studies, 23*(2), 311–331.

Mol, A. P. (2015). Transparency and value chain sustainability. *Journal of Cleaner Production, 107*, 154–161.

Nidumolu, R., Prahalad, C. K., & Rangaswami, M. R. (2009). Why sustainability is now the key driver of innovation. *Harvard Business Review, 87*(9), 56–64.

O'Higgins, E., & Zsolnai, L. (Eds.). (2017). *Progressive business models: Creating sustainable and pro-social enterprise*. Springer.

Pachauri, R. K., & Meyer, L. (red.) (2014). *Climate change 2014: Synthesis report*. Geneva, Switzerland: IPCC.

Rockström, J., Steffen, W., Noone, K., Persson, Å., Chapin, F. S., Lambin, E. F., & Nykvist, B. (2009). A safe operating space for humanity. *Nature, 461*(7263), 472–475.

Salaber, J. M. (2007). The determinants of sin stock returns: Evidence on the European market. *Working paper*, Université Paris-Dauphine.

Sen, S., Du, S., & Bhattacharya, C. B. (2016). Corporate social responsibility: A consumer psychology perspective. *Current Opinion in Psychology, 10*, 70–75.

Serafeim, G., & Gombos, S. (2015). Turnaround at Norsk Gjenvinning. Harvard Business School Case, 1.

Simas, M. S., Golsteijn, L., Huijbregts, M. A., Wood, R., & Hertwich, E. G. (2014). The "Bad Labor" footprint: Quantifying the social impacts of globalization. *Sustainability, 6*(11), 7514–7540.

Skarmeas, D., & Leonidou, C. N. (2013). When consumers doubt, watch out! The role of CSR skepticism. *Journal of Business Research, 66*(10), 1831–1838.

Smith, W. K., Gonin, M., & Besharov, M. L. (2013). Managing social-business tensions: A review and research agenda for social enterprise. *Business Ethics Quarterly, 23*(3), 407–442.

Søreide, T. (2016). *Corruption and criminal justice: Bridging economic and legal perspectives*. Edward Elgar Publishing.

Steffen, W., Richardson, K., Rockström, J., Cornell, S. E., Fetzer, I., Bennett, E. M., & Folke, C. (2015). Planetary boundaries: Guiding human development on a changing planet. *Science, 347*(6223), 1259855.

Stoknes, P. E. (2015). *What we think about when we try not to think about global warming: Toward a new psychology of climate action*. Chelsea Green Publishing.

Thompson, J. D., & MacMillan, I. C. (2010). Business models: Creating new markets and societal wealth. *Long Range Planning, 43*(2), 291–307.

Unruh, G., Kiron, D., Kruschwitz, N., Reeves, M., Rubel, H., & Zum Felde, A. M. (2016). Investing for a sustainable future: Investors care more about sustainability than many executives believe. *MIT Sloan Management Review, 57*(4), 3–25.

Wells, P. E. (2013). *Business models for sustainability*. Cheltenham, UK: Edward Elgar Publishing.

Zeitz, J. (2011). Puma completes first environmental profit and loss account. *The Guardian*, November 16.

Open Access This chapter is licensed under the terms of the Creative Commons Attribution-NonCommercial-NoDerivatives 4.0 International License (http://creativecommons.org/licenses/by-nc-nd/4.0/), which permits any noncommercial use, sharing, distribution and reproduction in any medium or format, as long as you give appropriate credit to the original author(s) and the source, provide a link to the Creative Commons license and indicate if you modified the licensed material. You do not have permission under this license to share adapted material derived from this book or parts of it.

The images or other third party material in this chapter are included in the chapter's Creative Commons license, unless indicated otherwise in a credit line to the material. If material is not included in the chapter's Creative Commons license and your intended use is not permitted by statutory regulation or exceeds the permitted use, you will need to obtain permission directly from the copyright holder.

Part II

The RESTART Framework

In the second part of the book, we develop the RESTART framework. We outline each of the seven components of the framework—R, E, S, T, A, R, T—and explore how they relate to the attempt to align sustainability performance and financial performance in business model design and innovation. In doing so, we outline a conceptual framework that can be the basis for further empirical investigation, practical application and teaching, which we discuss further in the third and final part of the book.

4

Roadmap to a RESTART

In the next seven chapters, we introduce the RESTART framework and its seven components. The letters in the acronym RESTART each represent one characteristic of more sustainable business models. In the seven chapters associated with each letter of the acronym, we will argue that the following seven characteristics are central to sustainable business model innovation that can lead to a RESTART. In the following, we briefly introduce each of the seven components of the framework and their corresponding chapters.

The necessary changes will not take place unless companies make them happen, and they will hardly be possible to achieve without substantial **redesign** of current business models. Standstill is not an option when the world is moving, and redesign of business models is therefore essential. Moreover, business model innovation appears to become both more frequent and more important in order to keep up with competitive pressures (Johnson et al. 2008; Mitchell and Coles 2003). In Chap. 5, *Redesign rather than standstill*, we discuss what a business model is and how business models can be redesigned to ensure innovation with regard to how the company creates value for customers and thereby achieves profitability.

Although significant changes are necessary, they will not be done overnight and companies cannot risk everything on one endeavor. Instead, they should move forward in a controlled manner and with an experimental mindset in order to find out what works and how new business models can function over time. Rather than doing a sudden turnaround, **experimentation** is therefore necessary (e.g., List and Gneezy 2014; Andries et al. 2013). In Chap. 6, *Experimentation rather than turnaround*, we show the importance of experimentation for the success of business model innovations in general and for sustainable business model innovations in particular.

An important step toward more efficient use of resources is to move beyond the notion that the customer needs ownership of products. Such a product-logic has dominated companies' offerings to customers, but companies are instead increasingly embracing a **service-logic** to promote sustainable business. This involves thinking in terms of access and functionality rather than ownership and designing services that are equally attractive to the customer as a product that can be bought and owned (e.g., Bocken et al. 2014; Baines et al. 2009). In Chap. 7, *Service-logic rather than product-logic*, we show how applying service-logic can contribute to smarter and more resource-efficient consumption that can reduce waste and pollution.

One of the most important changes needed to achieve a sustainable future is the smarter use of the scarce resources we have available. This means that we have to move away from the linear "take, make and dispose" approach upon which traditional business economics is based. Instead, companies should build circular business models based on reuse, resource efficiency and closed loops (e.g., Bocken et al. 2016; McDonough and Braungart 2009; Webster 2015). **The circular economy** is thus a key for greener and more efficient business. In Chap. 8, *The circular rather than the linear economy*, we look at how circular business models are central to the transition to a greener, smarter economy.

Being successful with changes of this magnitude requires collaboration. When considering the sustainability of companies' business models, it is too limiting to look solely at what goes on within the walls of the individual company. Achievements of this kind are difficult to reach through solo-runs, but rather requires appropriate **alliances** between companies, which together can solve problems they would not be successful in resolving alone (e.g., Kiron et al. 2015; Tencati and Zsolnai 2009; Chesbrough 2006). In Chap. 9, *Alliances rather than solo-runs*, we discuss the role alliances play in enabling sustainable innovations that span across organizations.

Implementing the comprehensive changes that lead to sustainable business requires prioritization. This implies that one cannot do everything and that it is more important to do the right thing than to do what looks good. For a sustainable future to be possible, it is not sufficient that companies conduct indulgences. Instead, companies should deliver **results**, that is, succeeding in making sustainability improvements that actually make a difference and that solve the important problems (e.g., Khan et al. 2016; Eccles and Serafeim 2013). In Chap. 10, *Results rather than indulgences*, we look at how sustainability performance can be achieved and how it can be aligned with financial performance.

To succeed with a transition of this caliber, the entire organization must be designed in a way that makes all organizational members pull in the right direction. Sustainable business models involve an intimate interplay between social, environmental and financial performance, and this must be reflected in goal structures, measurements and indicators, incentives, rewards and organization design in general (e.g., Jørgensen and Pedersen 2015; Schaltegger 2011; Gond et al. 2012; Figge et al. 2002). It involves moving from a one-dimensional emphasis on financial performance toward designing the entire organization for **three-dimensionality**. In Chap. 11, *Three-dimensionality rather than one-dimensionality*, we show how objectives, priorities, measurement and reporting are key elements to achieve sustainability and profitability.

We have now drawn up the roadmap for a RESTART. In the next seven chapters, we discuss each of the seven components of the RESTART framework in order to shed light on the types of business model innovation it proposes (Fig. 4.1).

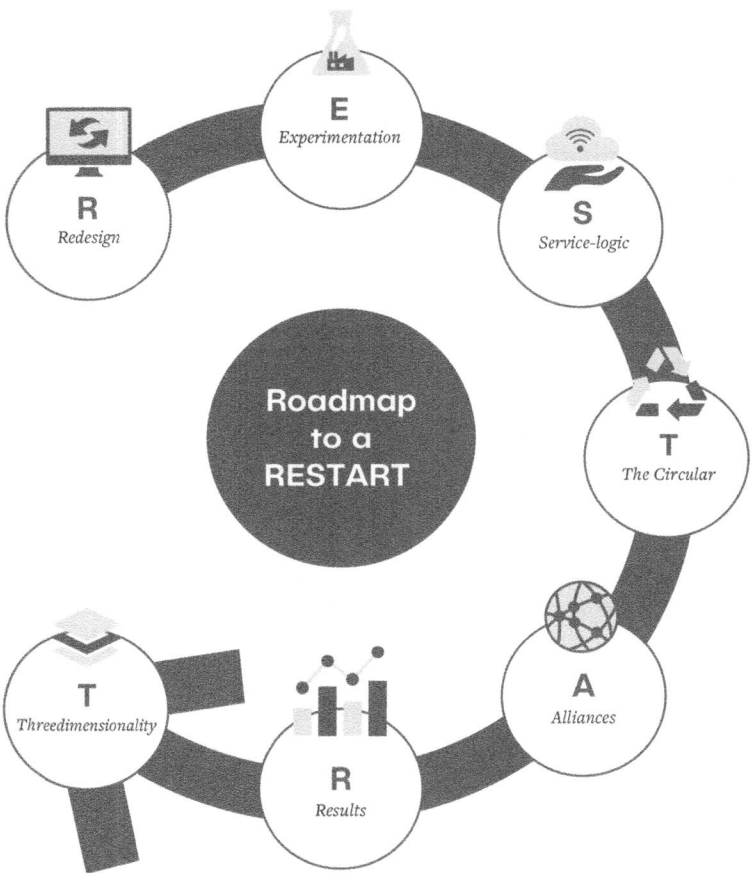

Fig. 4.1 A roadmap to RESTART

References

Andries, P., Debackere, K., & Looy, B. (2013). Simultaneous experimentation as a learning strategy: Business model development under uncertainty. *Strategic Entrepreneurship Journal, 7*(4), 288–310.

Baines, T. S., Lightfoot, H. W., Benedettini, O., & Kay, J. M. (2009). The servitization of manufacturing: A review of literature and reflection on future challenges. *Journal of Manufacturing Technology Management, 20*(5), 547–567.

Bocken, N. M., de Pauw, I., Bakker, C., & van der Grinten, B. (2016). Product design and business model strategies for a circular economy. *Journal of Industrial and Production Engineering, 33*(5), 308–320.

Bocken, N. M. P., Short, S. W., Rana, P., & Evans, S. (2014). A literature and practice review to develop sustainable business model archetypes. *Journal of Cleaner Production, 65*, 42–56.

Chesbrough, H. W. (2006). *Open innovation: The new imperative for creating and profiting from technology*. Cambridge, MA: Harvard Business Press.

Eccles, R. G., & Serafeim, G. (2013). The performance frontier. *Harvard Business Review, 91*(5), 50–60.

Figge, F., Hahn, T., Schaltegger, S., & Wagner, M. (2002). The sustainability balanced scorecard–linking sustainability management to business strategy. *Business Strategy and the Environment, 11*(5), 269–284.

Gond, J. P., Grubnic, S., Herzig, C., & Moon, J. (2012). Configuring management control systems: Theorizing the integration of strategy and sustainability. *Management Accounting Research, 23*(3), 205–223.

Johnson, M. W., Christensen, C. M., & Kagermann, H. (2008). Reinventing your business model. *Harvard Business Review, 86*(12), 57–68.

Jørgensen, S., & Pedersen, L. J. T. (2015). *Responsible and profitable: Strategies for sustainable business models*. Oslo: Cappelen Damm Akademisk.

Khan, M., Serafeim, G., & Yoon, A. (2016). Corporate sustainability: First evidence on materiality. *Accounting Review, 91*(6), 1697–1724.

Kiron, D., Kruschwitz, N., Haanaes, K., Reeves, M., Fuisz-Kehrbach, S. K., & Kell, G. (2015). Joining forces: Collaboration and leadership for sustainability. *MIT Sloan Management Review, 56*(3), 1–31.

List, J., & Gneezy, U. (2014). *The why axis: Hidden motives and the undiscovered economics of everyday life*. New York, NY: Random House.

McDonough, W., & Braungart, M. (2009). *Cradle to cradle: Remaking the way we make things*. North Point Press.

Mitchell, D., & Coles, C. (2003). The ultimate competitive advantage of continuing business model innovation. *Journal of Business Strategy, 24*(5), 15–21.

Schaltegger, S. (2011). Sustainability as a driver for corporate economic success: Consequences for the development of sustainability management control. *Society and Economy, 33*(1), 15–28.

Tencati, A., & Zsolnai, L. (2009). The collaborative enterprise. *Journal of Business Ethics, 85*(3), 367–376.

Webster, K. (2015). *The circular economy: A wealth of flows*. Coew, UK: Ellen MacArthur Foundation Publishing.

Open Access This chapter is licensed under the terms of the Creative Commons Attribution-NonCommercial-NoDerivatives 4.0 International License (http://creativecommons.org/licenses/by-nc-nd/4.0/), which permits any noncommercial use, sharing, distribution and reproduction in any medium or format, as long as you give appropriate credit to the original author(s) and the source, provide a link to the Creative Commons license and indicate if you modified the licensed material. You do not have permission under this license to share adapted material derived from this book or parts of it.

The images or other third party material in this chapter are included in the chapter's Creative Commons license, unless indicated otherwise in a credit line to the material. If material is not included in the chapter's Creative Commons license and your intended use is not permitted by statutory regulation or exceeds the permitted use, you will need to obtain permission directly from the copyright holder.

5

Redesign Rather than Standstill

Companies that aim to be both sustainable and profitable must redesign their business models. It implies changing how companies create, deliver and capture value in a manner that reduces the shadow they cast on society and the environment, doing it in such a way that the companies shed more light on their surroundings, and doing it in a way that promotes their ability to be competitive in the markets in which they operate.

Fig. 5.1 Redesign Rather than Standstill

5.1 The Business Model as the Story of How the Company Works

"*Those were the days my friend, we thought they'd never end*", Mary Hopkin sang in 1968. It is easy to imagine that the record industry meets annually and sings this refrain because the music industry has been through many and violent upheavals ever since Hopkin's song was released (Fig. 5.1).

For a long time, most of us bought music in physical formats. Even before that, people mostly went to concerts in order to experience music. Not too many years ago, the common consumption of music was buying CDs and other formats in physical stores like Virgin Megastore and HMV. Throughout the 2000s, as more and more people gained access to faster computers and broadband Internet connections, music became digitized and an increasing number of people downloaded music illegally through services like Napster and The Pirate Bay. The music industry stuck its head in the sand and argued that customers would not want files with inferior sound quality, but that they would rather prefer having the CDs on their bookshelves, being able to touch the album covers and to display their great music tastes through a well-stocked record collection. They were wrong.

Digitization of music and the development of business models that capitalized on new forms of music consumption showed that customers did not require owning the physical music product. Admittedly, vinyl records have received a sales boost in recent years, but they still have a market share of less than ten percent. More and more people are instead willing to access and play music digitally, without having the ability to hold the physical album cover in their hands. Indeed, the value of the album in its conventional sense has gradually decreased in the digital age. The music industry's reaction was first an attempt to prevent this development. Through copy protection technology, lawsuits against file-sharers and so on, they tried to stop a development that seemed unstoppable. Many musicians were also skeptical about the development. Of course, illegal file sharing went directly at the expense of record sales, and musicians were forced to think in new ways about where their revenues would come from. The entire industry thus needed to adapt to find new ways to create, deliver and capture value.

In 2001, Apple launched the music service iTunes, through which users could buy digital audio files that could be played on their MP3 players, iPods and computers, and eventually also on iPhones, iPads and other devices. This business model was striking, not at least because it managed to challenge the illegal downloading of music, even if it required payment by customers. Its success was perhaps especially due to iTunes making it easy to buy the products, through a simple user interface on an attractive platform. In addition, Apple's comprehensive contracts with suppliers made sure they had a very rich catalog of music. It is important to remember, however, that Apple's business model was still based on the customer owning the product—the music—albeit as a digital file instead of as a physical product (see, e.g., Johnson et al. 2008; Osterwalder and Pigneur 2010).

A strong competitor to the iTunes business model emerged in 2006 when the Swedish company Spotify launched its service. Spotify had a new hypothesis about what the customer wanted and instead offered music through a subscription-based streaming service. Instead of buying individual files or albums, customers were now able to stream all the music in the Spotify catalog whenever they wanted and as much as they wanted. Spotify thus changed the consumption of music from providing customers with ownership of the product to providing them with mere access to the music (see, e.g., Stampfl et al. 2013; Gassmann et al. 2014). The situation today is that the physical format (CDs, vinyl records, etc.), digital audio files for purchase (iTunes, Amazon, etc.) and digital audio files for streaming (Spotify, Tidal, etc.) all coexist, but the digital business models increasingly dominate the landscape.

The golden age of the music industry will perhaps never return, and streaming services like Spotify will likely not be the last revolution in this industry. And to keep track with this development, Spotify has recently started hiring research scientists who can work on leveraging the company's data to deliver better services in an uncertain competitive future. Over time, the story of how music is distributed and consumed has been retold many times. The entire industry can perhaps best be described as waves of subsequent business model innovations—of business models redesigned repeatedly. This is how innovation happens in many industries, although in some more frequently than in others. A natural consequence of this is that many companies and even entire industries perish, precisely because they have not been able to make necessary changes in time. Rather than innovating, they have become victims of the innovative business models of others. But what exactly is a business model, and how can it help us understand how companies work?

Companies as Stories

The business model is sometimes referred to as the story that explains how the company works (Magretta 2002). What, then, does characterize companies that work? At least, they create value for both the customer and for themselves by offering a product or service that the customer wants and for which he or she is willing to pay. The business model captures the essence of how companies succeed with this in practice (Osterwalder et al. 2014).

If we want to become better acquainted with companies like Spotify and find out how such a company works, we can ask questions such as:

- What is Spotify?
- For whom does Spotify exist?
- How does Spotify create value for itself and for others?
- Which markets does Spotify operate in, and how does it differ from its competitors in these markets?
- How do Spotify's customers pay?
- How does Spotify ensure that its revenues are greater than its costs so that it remains profitable?
- What ambitions for growth and scope does Spotify have over time?

A common denominator of business models is that they reflect how companies create, deliver and capture value from business opportunities (Osterwalder and Pigneur 2010; Teece 2010; Johnson et al. 2008). This is illustrated in Fig. 5.2.

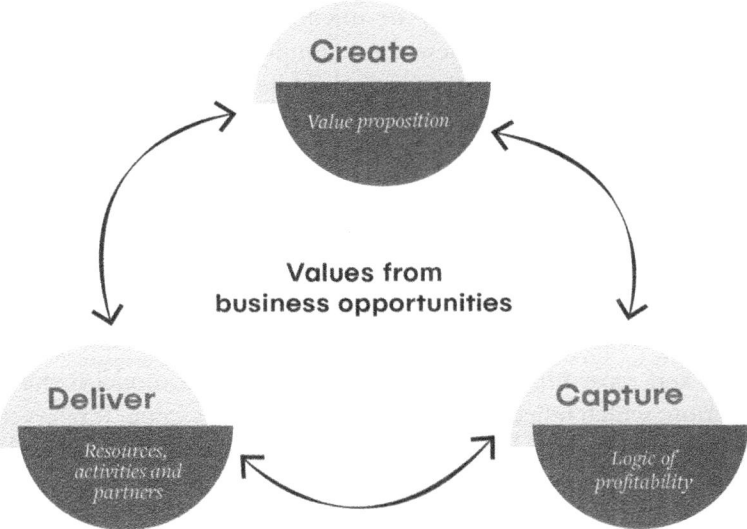

Fig. 5.2 The business model: creating, delivering and capturing value from business opportunities

There are several ways to define the business model, and one can think of business models as consisting of a set of interrelated components that can be conceptualized in various ways. However, as pointed out by Foss and Saebi (2017) in their review of business model innovation, most definitions seem to converge around the notion that business models comprise the "design or architecture of the value creation, delivery, and capture mechanisms" of a company (cf. Teece 2010). In this book, we similarly build on a conceptualization of the business model that consists of three parts (Jørgensen and Pedersen 2015):

1. *Value creation*: How the company helps customers to solve a problem or perform a job-to-be-done at a given price (often referred to as the value proposition).
2. *Value delivery*: The key resources, activities and partners that are needed for the company to carry out what the value proposition requires.
3. *Value capture*: How the company makes money by means of a given revenue model and a given cost structure.

All organizations consciously or unconsciously operate based on a business model that reflects these three components. We have placed values from business opportunities in the middle of the model since that is what the company is trying to achieve—it represents the opportunity around which the business model is built. Overall, these components tell the story of how the company works, and all three parts are vital to business success.

Creating Value Through Successful Value Propositions

The first and most fundamental part of the business model is the value proposition, which reflects how the company creates value. It refers to the company's offering that helps the customer solve a problem or perform a job-to-be-done at a given price (Osterwalder et al. 2014). The "job" metaphor introduced by Christensen et al. (2007) conceives of transactions as customers "hiring" products to do a "job". Then, it is crucial to understand what type of job the customers need done. And by extension, what does the company offer, and how does it offer it, so that customers are willing to "hire" them again and again?

You use Spotify to solve the problem of how to listen to music in one way, while a physical CD or vinyl record purchased in a record store solves the problem in a different way. Common to both the value proposition of Spotify and of the record store is that they allow you to listen to the music. However, they clearly do it in different ways. Spotify streams the music online and its service gives you access to an endless supply of artists and songs, while you can buy physical records in stores whether they are big or large and whether they are physical stores or online stores. Or you can even stream the music on YouTube and enjoy the music video at the same time—another feature of music services that do different jobs for its users.

Such basic choices are captured in the company's value proposition, and they are indicative of different solutions to the same basic problem. Successful value propositions have a coherence between what the

Fig. 5.3 The value proposition

company offers and what job the customers would like done, as illustrated in Fig. 5.3.

Theodore Levitt once said that managers might think that they are selling a drill to the customer. However, it is not a drill the customers want to buy, argues Levitt: It is the hole in the wall customers want (Levitt 1972). The hole in the wall is an example of a job the customer wants done. This reflects the company's business opportunity: It is an opportunity to create value for the customer at a given price by offering a solution in the form of a product (such as a drill) or a service (such as carpentry). Different customers have different needs. Therefore, they really have different jobs they want done (Christensen 2012). If they feel that other products or services can do the same job, customers will rather choose those products or services. This is particularly true if the substitutes can do an equally good or better job at the same price or at a lower price than what is already offered (Johnson et al. 2008).

It is important to remember that the costs of the customer are not just a matter of money. It is also about time and effort costs (e.g., Christensen 2012). Therein lies another possibility of a business model innovation: new or existing companies can identify problems that are not at present resolved in a satisfactory manner. For example, mobile phones have largely taken over the job done by digital cameras when it comes to photography in everyday life, and a major reason is that they give the user a simple and accessible solution. Even if your company has a value proposition that solves the customer's problem, there is still a long way to go before both the customer and the company are happy. The next question is how to deliver that value to the customer reliably and over time, and there can be considerable differences between the ways in which companies do so.

To Deliver What You Promise

Value delivery refers to the configuration of the most important resources, activities and partners that are needed in order to deliver and be paid for the value proposition (e.g., Morris et al. 2005). Simply put, resources are anything the company *has*, while activities comprise everything the company *does*. The company owns some resources itself, while it relies on partners to access other resources. For instance, many companies collaborate with research institutions in order to develop new technologies or other inputs. Likewise, companies perform some activities on their own, while other activities are outsourced or carried out in collaborative projects. For example, most banks purchase the IT services upon which their online solutions are built, and some wholesalers collaborate with other players in the industry on joint logistics. Not all resources, activities and partners are equally important, and when telling the story of how the company delivers value, we should therefore concentrate on the most important ones.

Key resources—whether they are physical, human, financial or intellectual—are the inputs required to deliver on what the value proposition promises the customer. It is, however, not enough to possess such resources—the company must use them to perform activities that enable them to deliver value over time (see, e.g., Barney 2001). The company must therefore organize itself in a manner that ensures that it does not need to reinvent the wheel each time the customer knocks on the door. To function properly, companies need to conduct several recurring activities that include everything from budgeting, customer service, manufacturing, training, market research and so on. Without these activities, which comprise both the production of the goods or services the company offers and the support functions needed to do this effectively, companies will neither succeed in delivering on the value proposition nor monetize it (cf. Johnson et al. 2003).

Value delivery thus reflects the strategic and organizational conditions that must be in place for the company being able to create, deliver and capture value over time (Morris et al. 2005; Teece 2010). However, companies cannot do all this just with their own resources. In order to deliver value, they need suppliers and partners, whether to provide resources the company itself does not possess or to perform activities it cannot carry out on its own (e.g., Dyer and Singh 1998). In this way, partners can unlock new modes of value delivery for the company. In other words, there are costs to delivering value to the customer. Therefore, in order to be profitable, the solution offered to customers must cost less to produce than the customer is willing to pay for it. This necessitates, however, that the company manages to capture value through an effective logic of profitability.

Getting a Bigger Share of the Pie

We have seen above that the value proposition is the offering that helps the customer to solve a problem at a given price. It does not take much imagination to understand that it is costly for companies to obtain the necessary resources and to use them to perform value-adding activities. The story of how the company works must therefore also include a logic of profitability (Johnson et al. 2008). How does the company generate profitability by means of a given revenue model and a given cost structure? What is the relationship between the price of the offering and the volume sold to customers? The logic of profitability will also include more specific measures, such as how much the company must make on each transaction and how quickly resources and inventory must be turned over to achieve the desired level of profitability.

How companies capture value has become such a central topic that the various payment models have gotten their own names. Spotify's main payment model is a subscription service, while the model advertising-funded version Spotify uses is often called the "free model" (or just "free"). The media companies have offered online newspapers for a long time, but we now see that several online newspapers are beginning to charge in different ways. These models are given names like "total payment", in which customers have to pay for everything; the "metered model", in which customers receive a number of free articles in a given period; and "freemium", in which customers are offered a combination of free and paid content.

Note that these names reveal only a little about how the company actually creates value and how it is delivered to its users. Two newspapers that use the total payment model can address very different segments with very different content, and they can deliver their value propositions in a variety of ways, based on dissimilar resources and activities. It is therefore important to be aware that value capture is an important part of the story of how the company works, even though it may not always be the most telling part of the business model.

Many companies, such as Würth, Volvo and Rolls Royce, have traditionally generated revenues by producing and selling products. In recent years, however, it has become more common that they also offer services by leasing their products to customers. Consequently, they have developed a business model using the so-called servitization, product service systems or product-as-service, by which companies lease products rather than selling them (see, e.g., Jørgensen and Pedersen 2017; Scholl 2006). This implies that the customer is still paying for the physical product, but as a service (i.e., functionality) rather than as a product of which the customer takes ownership (cf. Bocken et al. 2016). Moreover, the customer therefore also pays in other ways than when purchasing the product in a conventional way, which implies that the profitability logic is changed because of the change in the value proposition.

The Hypothesis of What the Customer Wants

It is obvious that the arrival of iTunes and Spotify turned the music industry upside-down. Any business model is based on a value proposition, which in turn reflects a hypothesis about what the customer wants. This hypothesis can of course be right or wrong. A successful business model is able to offer what the customer actually wants at a price the customer can accept, and successful business models both create and deliver value in a way that enables the company to capture value for itself and its owners (Kaplan 2012).

The business models of the music industry, which we have used as examples, have reflected three somewhat different hypotheses about what kind of problem customers want to have solved (Table 5.1). In addition,

Table 5.1 The business models of various music services

	Record store	iTunes	Spotify
Creating value	Ownership of the physical record in exchange for payment per unit	Ownership of the digital music file in exchange for payment per file	Access to stream as many digital music files as you like in exchange for a monthly subscription fee, or funded by advertising embedded in the service
Delivering value	Stores, employees with competence, supplier contracts, sales, marketing and so on	Digital platform, contracts with record companies, software developers, online store and so on	Digital platform, contracts with record companies and advertisers, software developers, online journalists and so on
Capturing value	The customer pays per record, the store has costs associated with purchasing, inventory and staff and so on	The customer pays per downloaded music file, the company has costs related to operations, contracts and so on	The customer pays a monthly fee, or the service is financed by advertising. The company has costs associated with the payment of music rights and operation of the platform and so on

through their intense growth, the new digital music services have made life difficult for the more traditional players in completely different industries since they actually also solve some of the problems of customers who have previously used the products or services of firms in those industries. For instance, when more and more people use Spotify's services on their office laptops or through their mobile phones connected to the car stereo, it means that they are also making life more difficult for radio stations competing for the same customer attention. Similarly, social media like Facebook and Twitter are trying to outcompete the traditional hypothesis that "the customer wants a newspaper that presents the most important news from the past day", or for that matter the more recent hypothesis that "the customer wants the website of a newspaper to update with news in real time".

From time to time, new business models emerge based on new hypotheses about what the customer really wants (Christensen 2012). In such situations, established players quickly lose their customer base. It is enough to recall what happened to the market for relatively inexpensive digital cameras: after Apple, other producers began to integrate good camera features in the iPhone and other smartphones. Companies like Canon and Kodak became "victims" of such business model innovation. This involves a new hypothesis about what the customer wants, a new way to deliver value or new ways to charge the customer for the value, for instance, via a new payment model. In such a situation, standing still might be a recipe for disaster for many companies. In other words, it might be necessary to redesign the company's business model in order to meet the competition. Here, the case of Fujifilm—as a contrast to the plight of Canon—can be instructive. When realizing that digitalization would transform the photography (camera and film) industry, Fujifilm redefined its business as being related to imaging more broadly and successfully entered new markets in medical imaging, information technology and so on (see, e.g., Inagaki and Osawa 2012). In this way, the company steered clear of the downfall that some of its competitors faced.

We have not yet heard the swan song of the music industry. However, the many innovations in the industry imply that old giants might be about to fall and that new players will enter the stage and outperform existing solutions with new products and services, new technologies and new payment models. The challenge for companies in the music industry and in many other industries is to reinvent themselves before someone else makes them redundant.

5.2 Redesigning Business Models

Stanford University is widely known as the hotbed of many of the most successful technology companies in Silicon Valley. But did you know that successful companies have also emerged from the relatively less glamorous study halls of the University of Bergen, Norway?

In 1997, Siri M. Kalvig was already widely known as Norway's first female weather presenter. As a young meteorology student, however, she went on to establish Storm Weather Center with the equivalent of a few thousand dollars in initial capital. In 2014, the Swedish private equity company EQT bought her weather forecasting company, which by then had been renamed StormGeo, for approximately 200 million USD.

What happened on the way in order to enable this massive growth? A possible answer to the question is the way in which Kalvig and her colleagues reformulated the story of the company when they went from being a company that reported the weather to become a company that also reported the consequences of the weather. StormGeo had long delivered weather services for television, newspapers and digital platforms. However, after the reformulation of what it was supposed to be, and for whom, a door was opened to an ocean of new and exciting business opportunities (Jørgensen and Pedersen 2015).

The ocean was also the arena for which the company specialized: StormGeo has developed a range of services that it sells to companies in the shipping, offshore and oil and gas industries. These companies are highly dependent on the weather and the need for timely and reliable information on how their operations are affected by the weather. StormGeo offers decision support systems to enable the weather-sensitive operations of these companies. An example of this is a service that helps shipping companies choose routes that allow them to use the force of the currents in the ocean, thus reducing both their fuel consumption and their environmental footprint. All of StormGeo's services originate in the same resource that rendered StormGeo able to deliver its original service of weather reports on television and other platforms. When the managers began to think again about other ways that these resources could be used, it led to a green innovation that proved to be very profitable. This resulted in a comprehensive redesign of the company's business model.

StormGeo has offices and customers all over the world, and a common characteristic of its customers is that they need knowledge about the consequences of the weather. From being a company associated with regular weather forecasts, StormGeo has retold the story of what it will deliver to whom, how this should be done and how to charge the customer for its services. StormGeo is thus an example of a company that has discovered the possibilities inherent in the sustainability issue and has adapted its business model accordingly. Kalvig has long been a pioneer in the battle against climate change, and she has said that the business model innovation of StormGeo has been motivated in part by a desire to take responsibility for contributing to climate solutions, while at the same time embracing the opportunities inherent in the climate problem.

Innovation of Business Models

Innovation involves renewal, novelty and change, and we usually think of it as a positive concept. Innovation is not just about new products and services—it also relates to innovation of business models (Chesbrough and Rosenbloom 2002); in other words, changes in the way companies create, deliver and capture value. This means that innovation can occur in connection with all three components of the business model: First, it may be an innovative value proposition offering new types of value. Second, it may be linked to value delivery, for example, with regard to the innovative use of resources or design of value-adding activities alone or in collaboration with others. Third, it can be linked to value capture, for instance, in the form of innovative payment models or novel revenue streams.

As pointed out by Schumpeter (1911), innovations vary in their degree of novelty. Zott and Amit (2007) argue that business model designs differ in the degree to which they are centered on efficiency or novelty. Mirroring this distinction, it is common to distinguish between incremental and radical innovations (Ettlie et al. 1984; Dewar and Dutton 1986). Although the latter type gets most of the attention, research shows that most innovations are in fact incremental. Incremental changes take place gradually, while radical changes entail an abrupt break from existing solutions.

A much-discussed type of radical innovations are the so-called disruptive innovations (Christensen 2012). This refers to new products or services that deviate radically from existing offerings, typically by being simpler and less expensive (Johnson et al. 2008). This implies that they usually make a technology or new solution available to many more people. Such innovations often turn markets upside-down, and a typical example is how mobile cameras disrupted the market for more expensive and more advanced digital cameras. The first mobile cameras had significantly poorer quality, but their quality was sufficient and customers found it easier to use them. Hence, as their quality gradually improved, they completely overtook the mass market for photography.

When talking about business model innovations, one often immediately thinks of such radical changes by which new or established businesses change the rules of the game in an industry by changing the way value is created, delivered and captured. Spotify's entry into the music industry is a good example of this. Spotify's hypothesis about what the customer wanted differed significantly from the existing hypothesis. Importantly, the new hypothesis was based on the assumption that ownership was not important. Customers could access the streaming service either by paying a monthly subscription fee or by choosing an advertisement-funded version. Therefore, Spotify also had to show that it could solve a problem for advertisers: after all, ad revenue was supposed to finance part of its operations.

Spotify's value proposition was a novelty, and it required that the company managed to convince several different stakeholders—customers, record companies and artists—that its solution was attractive and useful. Spotify also needed to acquire completely different types of resources and perform completely different types of value-adding activities compared with what previous distributors of music had done. Not at least, their business model had a new way of capturing value—a payment model that made it likely that customers would use it. Overall, Spotify's business model innovation resulted in an entirely new way of thinking that challenged the rules of the game in the industry.

Disrupt or Die?

Companies that do not innovate and change when needed are in danger of becoming "netflixed", to use Saul Kaplan's (2012) phrase. Similarly, there is often speak of the "uberification" of various markets. The radical shifts that have characterized, for instance, the entertainment industry and the taxi industry seem to have created a concern across all industries that the next radical innovation is waiting around the next corner.

Netflix, which today is best known for its offering of TV and movie streaming, started in the late 1990s as a company that offered customers DVD rentals online. At the time, it was common to go to the rental kiosk and rent movies, and Netflix was established as a response to one of the founders having to pay a late delivery fee. Later, Netflix also introduced the service we know today, which is based on the streaming of movies and TV shows online.

One consequence of the success of Netflix was that the rental giant Blockbuster went bankrupt. Blockbuster was unable to renew itself, and thus became a victim of Netflix's innovative services. For companies to survive and grow, they sometimes need to change the story of how they function, and they do this through changes in how they create, deliver and capture value. Blockbuster was not able to adapt—first from a traditional rental store to a provider of online rentals, and thereafter to online streaming. An interesting part of the story is that Blockbuster was invited to buy Netflix for 50 million USD in the early 2000s. At the time, however, it did not realize the potential of Netflix's new business model and therefore declined the offer. Ten years later, the market value of Netflix was nearly 20 billion dollars.

The innovation researcher Clayton Christensen argues that established companies are best at doing incremental innovations, which often involves making a product as sophisticated and as good as possible (Christensen 2012). The problem is that such products often become so advanced that almost only the most ardent and wealthy clients can afford or need them. That creates an opportunity for newcomers that have the opportunity to enter the market with cheaper and simpler products or services able to reach new customer groups. A classic example is the computer industry, in which clear patterns emerged over time. The big players competed to get better storage, and PCs became bigger, stronger and better. Surprisingly, however, new players emerged in the market with small, laptop computers with less storage capacity. These new products initially addressed very different customer segments, and the established companies had not been able to see these opportunities. Instead, they were very fixated on more incremental innovations through which they were creating improved versions of what already existed.

One of the reasons that incumbents fail to come up with disruptive innovations is perhaps that they are too busy to meet (what they believe) are the needs of existing customers—that is, that they are ridden by "marketing myopia" (Levitt 1960). To innovate successfully, it is necessary to break free from the mindsets that block new ideas and solutions. In other words, successful innovators fail to reinvent when they do not turn their attention from making improved products to try to solve the real job the customer wants done instead. Because what is really the customer's "hole in the wall"? There is no use in creating an even more powerful and better drill if your competitors are simultaneously launching products or services that help customers solve the problem in a cheaper and easier way.

In the music industry, the long-lasting established truth was that the customer wanted to own the product, whether it was a CD or an MP3 file. Spotify, however, proved that it is sufficient for most customers to access music through streaming services, even if that also requires them to have a physical product in the form of a computer, smartphone or the like. In many ways, streaming music is also an inferior product: The sound quality is allegedly slightly worse, artists reportedly receive less pay and customers who use the free version of the service are somewhat bothered by the advertisements. Nevertheless, customers are increasingly migrating toward these services, and Spotify has even largely managed to oust illegal music file sharing online because they offer a set of services that customers find attractive enough to pay the subscription fee. Importantly, however, the company is still struggling to become profitable and therefore needs to continue fine-tuning its business model (e.g., Hufford 2017).

StormGeo's redesign of its business model was slightly different. Kalvig and her colleagues simply discovered that their existing resources could be used to solve much bigger problems than what they were initially doing. Thus, the company was able to offer much more profitable services. StormGeo reformulated its value proposition and redesigned its organization in a manner that rendered it able to deliver these services in a way that was attractive to entirely new customer segments.

The concepts innovation and entrepreneurship are closely related, and it is difficult to imagine innovation without entrepreneurs, whether in the form of the so-called intrapreneurship or outside the company. Entrepreneurs are willing to take risks, and they are often rule-breakers in a positive sense—by questioning and experimenting (cf. Christensen 2012). Some entrepreneurs even manage to develop completely new and often disruptive business models. Even in established companies, there are "intrapreneurs" who find new ways to rearrange the building blocks of which the company consists, in order to rewrite the story of the company.

It is said that organizations are born as movements and die as institutions. Being in motion can therefore be understood as a fundamental prerequisite for companies to survive and grow over time. New ideas and business models challenge the old, in the music industry as in most other industries. Companies that do not want to be "netflixed" should therefore look over their shoulders and ask themselves how they should change in order to prevent others from making them redundant. Standing still is not an option—in the future, companies will have to redesign their business models more and more frequently. In order to be successful, however, such changes will require experimentation, which is the topic of the next chapter.

References

Barney, J. B. (2001). Resource-based theories of competitive advantage: A ten-year retrospective on the resource-based view. *Journal of Management, 27*(6), 643–650.

Bocken, N. M., de Pauw, I., Bakker, C., & van der Grinten, B. (2016). Product design and business model strategies for a circular economy. *Journal of Industrial and Production Engineering, 33*(5), 308–320.

Chesbrough, H., & Rosenbloom, R. S. (2002). The role of the business model in capturing value from innovation: Evidence from Xerox Corporation's technology spin-off companies. *Industrial and Corporate Change, 11*(3), 529–555.

Christensen, C. (2012). *The innovator's dilemma: When new technologies cause great firms to fail*. Cambridge, MA: Harvard Business Review Press.

Christensen, C. M., Anthony, S. D., Berstell, G., & Nitterhouse, D. (2007). Finding the right job for your product. *MIT Sloan Management Review, 48*(3), 38.

Dewar, R. D., & Dutton, J. E. (1986). The adoption of radical and incremental innovations: An empirical analysis. *Management Science, 32*(11), 1422–1433.
Dyer, J. H., & Singh, H. (1998). The relational view: Cooperative strategy and sources of interorganizational competitive advantage. *Academy of Management Review, 23*(4), 660–679.
Ettlie, J. E., Bridges, W. P., & O'Keefe, R. D. (1984). Organization strategy and structural differences for radical versus incremental innovation. *Management Science, 30*(6), 682–695.
Foss, N. J., & Saebi, T. (2017). Fifteen years of research on business model innovation: How far have we come, and where should we go? *Journal of Management, 43*(1), 200–227.
Gassmann, O., Frankenberger, K., & Csik, M. (2014). *The business model navigator: 55 models that will revolutionise your business*. Harlow, UK: Pearson UK.
Hufford, A. (2017, June 15). Spotify's paid users surged last year but loss doubled. *The Wall Street Journal*. Retrieved January 12, 2018, from https://www.wsj.com/articles/spotify-paid-users-surged-last-year-but-loss-doubled-1497539725.
Inagaki, K., & Osawa, J. (2012, January 20). Fujifilm thrived by changing focus. *The Wall Street Journal*. Retrieved January 12, 2018, from https://www.wsj.com/articles/SB10001424052970203750404577170481473958516.
Johnson, G., Melin, L., & Whittington, R. (2003). Micro strategy and strategizing: Towards an activity-based view. *Journal of Management Studies, 40*(1), 3–22.
Johnson, M. W., Christensen, C. M., & Kagermann, H. (2008). Reinventing your business model. *Harvard Business Review, 86*(12), 57–68.
Jørgensen, S., & Pedersen, L. J. T. (2015). *Responsible and profitable: Strategies for sustainable business models*. Oslo: Cappelen Damm Akademisk.
Jørgensen, S., & Pedersen, L. J. T. (2017). Designing sustainable business models. In T. W. Andreassen, S. Clatworthy, M. Lüders, & T. Hillestad (Eds.), *Innovating for trust*. Cheltenham, UK: Edward Elgar Publishing.
Kaplan, S. (2012). *The business model innovation factory: How to stay relevant when the world is changing*. London: John Wiley & Sons.
Levitt, T. (1960). Marketing myopia. *Harvard Business Review, 38*(4), 24–47.
Levitt, T. (1972). Production-line approach to service. *Harvard Business Review, 50*(5), 41–52.
Magretta, J. (2002). Why business models matter. *Harvard Business Review, 80*(5), 86–92.

Morris, M., Schindehutte, M., & Allen, J. (2005). The entrepreneur's business model: Toward a unified perspective. *Journal of Business Research, 58*(6), 726–735.

Osterwalder, A., & Pigneur, Y. (2010). *Business model generation: A handbook for visionaries, game changers, and challengers.* London: John Wiley & Sons.

Osterwalder, A., Pigneur, Y., Bernarda, G., & Smith, A. (2014). *Value proposition design: How to create products and services customers want.* London: John Wiley & Sons.

Scholl, G. (2006). Product service systems. In A. Tukker, M. Charter, C. Vezzoli, E. Sto, & M. Munch Andersen (Eds.), *System innovation for sustainability. Perspectives on radical change to sustainable consumption and production* (pp. 25–43). Sheffield, UK: Greenleaf Publishing Ltd.

Schumpeter, J. (1911). *The theory of economic development (1934 translation).* Piscataway, NJ: Transaction Books.

Stampfl, G., Prügl, R., & Osterloh, V. (2013). An explorative model of business model scalability. *International Journal of Product Development, 18*(3–4), 226–248.

Teece, D. J. (2010). Business models, business strategy and innovation. *Long Range Planning, 43*(2), 172–194.

Zott, C., & Amit, R. (2007). Business model design and the performance of entrepreneurial firms. *Organization Science, 18*(2), 181–199.

Open Access This chapter is licensed under the terms of the Creative Commons Attribution-NonCommercial-NoDerivatives 4.0 International License (http://creativecommons.org/licenses/by-nc-nd/4.0/), which permits any noncommercial use, sharing, distribution and reproduction in any medium or format, as long as you give appropriate credit to the original author(s) and the source, provide a link to the Creative Commons license and indicate if you modified the licensed material. You do not have permission under this license to share adapted material derived from this book or parts of it.

The images or other third party material in this chapter are included in the chapter's Creative Commons license, unless indicated otherwise in a credit line to the material. If material is not included in the chapter's Creative Commons license and your intended use is not permitted by statutory regulation or exceeds the permitted use, you will need to obtain permission directly from the copyright holder.

6

Experimentation Rather than Turnaround

Redesigning a business model is not done overnight, and it is wise not to risk everything on one endeavor. To succeed with business model innovations, companies need to conduct controlled experiments on their business models, in order to uncover what works and why. In that way, they can increase the likelihood that the business model will be successful when it is finally implemented in the entire market.

Fig. 6.1 Experimentation Rather than Turnaround

6.1 The Science of Profitability

Imagine if floodlights powered by kinetic energy illuminated the football pitches in poor districts around the world. It would imply that every time kids ran, jumped, did step-overs and tackles—in short, with every step they took on the pitch, electricity would be generated for lighting the pitch. Would not that be great?

If your answer to this question is affirmative, you can take pleasure in this already becoming a reality. There are currently two such pitches. One is located in the heart of Morro da Mineira, a favela in Rio de Janeiro, and the other in Lagos, Nigeria. The energy company Shell and the technology company Pavegen collaborate on the project. Pavegen's kinetic tiles, which generate electricity when someone steps on them, are located under the Astroturf. Previously, these pitches were largely unusable after dark—the kids had to play in the streets, and it was unsafe for them to be out after dark. This project quite literally sheds light, both in that it provides electricity to the lights on the pitch by means of green energy and in the sense that it illuminates the streets surrounding the pitch as a beneficial side effect. In this way, these companies experimented with a concrete solution for alternative energy production (Fig. 6.1).

Shell is unlikely to make a complete turnaround toward renewable energy any time soon, and football players running around on kinetic tiles will probably not solve our future energy needs. Many similar solutions are emerging simultaneously, however, such as the new solar tile-covered sidewalks along parts of Route 66 in the US, where the surface of the road itself generates electricity. Shell and other energy companies are looking for new and renewable energy sources that can meet the increasing energy demand. Therefore, the big players experiment with such innovative solutions, also in cooperation with small companies like Pavegen. Eventually, they will perhaps find solutions that can be scaled up and constitute sustainable innovations in the energy market.

Do Not Put All the Eggs in the Same Basket

Across industries and countries, companies carry out business model innovations to become more sustainable. This comprises innovation in products, services, processes and entire business models. Design and innovation of business models is challenging, and it is perhaps best described as business model experimentation (Chesbrough 2010; Foss and Saebi 2017). We often compare business model innovation to changing the wheels on the car while driving. If you do an online image search, you can in fact find pictures of people who mastered the art of changing the wheels on moving cars, but it is at least wise to change one wheel at a time. The same is true for business model innovation—complete and sudden turnarounds can go wrong and thus be very destructive.

Netflix is often seen as a role model for companies that want to innovate their business model, but Netflix also learned from experience the hard way why experimentation rather than turnaround is the way to go for succeeding with business model innovation. In 2011, Netflix had parallel offerings—its parallel streaming service, as we know it today, and DVD rentals online. The subscription fee for the combined service was 10 USD, and Netflix had decided to increase it to 16 USD but also to give customers the opportunity to choose only one of the two services for 8 USD. When Netflix announced its price changes, it immediately met a storm of complaints from its customers—the company even had to hire new service workers to handle all the requests. Not only that, Netflix's stock price fell by 51 percent in a short time.

However, the bad news was far from over. In an attempt to deal with the self-inflicted crisis, the company made another big move: Netflix announced that it would split the company into two entities; the streaming service would continue as Netflix, while a spin-off company called Qwikster would manage DVD rentals. Customers became even angrier and responded swiftly, which in turn meant that Netflix dropped the plans to split the company.

As pointed out by the leading experimental economists John List and Uri Gneezy, Netflix's pricing blunder was fundamentally a consequence of putting all its eggs in the same basket when it carried out not one but two turnarounds (List and Gneezy 2014). As it turned out, the changes were based on incorrect hypotheses about what customers wanted, and the whole story essentially reads as a study in self-harm. The important question, of course, is why did not Netflix experiment with its pricing model in a controlled manner? It could have tested the new model in only parts of the market—for instance, Texas or Florida—and study the effects of the change while continuing with the old model in the rest of the market. If analyses showed that the change was successful, Netflix could have implemented the model in the rest of the market.

Netflix survived its pricing problems in 2011, and in the US market, its DVD rental service and its streaming service still coexist. Since the stock price drop of 2011, the Netflix stock has risen and risen. However, in the period in question, the company incurred large, unnecessary losses. Who knows how the stock price and the company's reputation in the US market would have fared if it had experimented with its pricing model in a controlled fashion, rather than conduct turnarounds that did not work?

IBM is often viewed as a pioneer in business model experimentation, and the innovation scholar Clayton Christensen has argued that the company is a role model with regard to allowing for experimentation. IBM has made major changes in its value propositions many times: from its huge mainframe computers to the more compact computers it later produced, and then from laptops to information systems and other data-based services. Every time the company has carried out such an innovation process, it placed the new business unit in a new location: Poughkeepsie, New York; Rochester, Minnesota; Boca Raton, Florida, and finally, New York City. In this way, the company created space and freedom for experimentation in the new business units. Out of range of the protectors of the establishment, while still being sheltered by the safe revenue streams from the existing business areas, the developers of new solutions could experiment undisturbed and develop IBM's new products and services. In this way, the company has succeeded in rewriting its history many times, but in controlled ways that enable radical innovations. And who knows where the company will go next, and what it is going to offer from there?

Control, Experiment and Innovate!

To succeed with business model innovation, companies must therefore think like scientists. Experimentation under controlled conditions can provide insight into what works and what does not, and it can reduce the risk of innovation (cf. McGrath 2010; Thomke 2001). In innovation circles, it has become a mantra that entrepreneurs should "fail fast". The logic goes that this allows them to learn from quick failure, instead of working for a long time on wrongful assumptions, and then fail when finally launching the product or service (Ries 2011). However, we should add an important element: If you fail quickly, be sure to fail in a controlled manner. Failure can be an important part of the innovation process, but one should preferably not fail in the manner and on the scale that Netflix did in the pricing story from 2011. Trial and error, however, is a good strategy for business model experimentation, as long as it is done in a controlled way (Davenport 2009).

There are several different ways to experiment with business models (see, e.g., Anderson 2011; Andries et al. 2013; Simester 2017). Firstly, there are the major experiments of the IBM variety, wherein a company is looking for new or alternative ways to create value. In such cases, the company typically explores the possibility of new business models in parallel with the existing business model (see, e.g., Andries et al. 2013). The oil and energy company Equinor's new business area New Energy Solutions and BMW's car sharing service Drivenow in Germany and the UK are examples of large companies exploring alternative business models within the boundaries of business-as-usual. For companies that expect significant changes in customers' consumption patterns in the future, or other changes that would threaten their existing business models, this is a sensible way to approach the transition toward new ways of creating, delivering and capturing value.

Secondly, business model experimentation deals with the many small and large changes in the ways a company creates, delivers and captures value (Morris et al. 2005). At first glance, the change in the pricing model of Netflix is not a major change, but the consequences for the company were dramatic. Business models are never complete—they are typically redesigned continuously and reiteratively, as big and small changes are made in what is offered to the customer, which inputs are used, how products and services are delivered to the customer, how to reduce costs, and so on. An important type of business model experimentation thus relates to conducting controlled trials that make it possible to assess the impact of planned changes.

Changes Big and Small

Experimentation can lead to both major shifts and minor changes in business models. When we talk about innovation, it is easy to think of the large and comprehensive changes. In recent years, there has been a lot of talk about so-called disruptive innovations, and it is almost as if all companies are supposed to be radically innovative. Given how the earth's population is pushing the boundaries of both society and the environment, it is to be expected that academics and others call for fundamental changes and technologies that can turn business upside-down. Many people argue that we are in need of a new "moon landing"—an ambitious goal toward which business and society can strive. In particular, the call for such ambitious action is widespread in relation to the climate problem.

Such breakthrough innovations are important, and there is reason to expect that in the near future companies will revolutionize the way we travel, that they will find new sources of energy, that they will find more sustainable alternatives to our current meat-based diet and that companies can even help solve the poverty problem (see, e.g., Elkington and Zeitz 2014). However, it is important that ordinary companies do not lose heart just because they are not in the business of conducting such radical innovations. Most innovations are actually incremental, and not all sustainable business models need to be radical deviations from existing business models.

Although radical innovations get the most attention, it is often improvements and diffusion of already implemented innovations that have the greatest effect (Christensen 2013). The first electric cars were such a radical innovation, but the subsequent incremental improvements in battery capacity and production method have been crucial for unlocking the impact of this technology on society and the environment. Of course, radical changes that are implemented on a large scale can also have major impact. Interesting examples in our time include 3D printing, which can reduce the need for transport and associated emissions, and large companies replacing fossil fuels with renewable energy on a grand scale. Both incremental and radical innovations can create considerable value to society and the environment.

If we want to stop sawing off the branch we are sitting on, it will require that many companies change their business models in ways that have a large combined effect. Some companies can make small adjustments that have high scalability, while others need to make major changes to their business models for comparable effect on their footprints. What constitutes big and small effects depends on what you measure. If you want to influence the lives of people at the bottom of the pyramid, or ensure better integration of immigrants, the number of people who receive aid and the extent to which they get help is the measure of success. If the objective is to reduce CO_2 emissions, the use of harmful substances or other externalities is what needs to be measured.

People running around on Pavegen's kinetic tiles may not light the large cities of the future. As such, the project's biggest value for Pavegen and Shell is perhaps that it serves as an example of experimentation with the energy industry's business model. However, the technology that Pavegen and Shell are now testing in the Brazilian favela must be seen in conjunction with other rival and complementary technologies that contribute to changes in how energy is generated, stored and distributed. While the Brazilian kids generate electricity by running around on the football pitch, a multitude of companies simultaneously implement a variety of technologies for energy production, thus contributing to the same shift. Scatec Solar builds solar parks in Africa; Bright Products develops solar panels and house systems for poor parts of the world; Otovo Solar puts solar panels on the rooftops of customers; Langlee Wave Power builds systems for exploiting wave power and Statkraft installs more and more wind turbines. The sum of all of these changes can prove significant for the green transition in energy production and consumption.

In order to succeed in a transition to sustainable business, we need both big radical shifts and many small movements in the right direction. And as in the example of the football pitch, we need various players in the market to experiment together to create this movement—thus creating an ecosystem for innovation. Sustainable business requires innovation on a large scale, but a necessary step is to test ideas in new and existing markets (Bocken et al. 2017). This underscores the need for controlled experimentation.

6.2 Asking the Right Questions

I don't understand why investors would want this information. Why should they care about the environment when they invest their savings?

An Italian finance professor had asked the question, after being told about the large field experiment Lars Jacob and his colleague Trond Døskeland had carried out during the launch of the Norwegian bank Skandiabanken's implementation of an ethical labeling system for mutual funds. Skandiabanken (since renamed Sbanken) had developed the system in an attempt to provide the individual investors for whom the system was designed with actionable non-financial information about their investment opportunities. As part of the implementation, the two researchers conducted a large-scale experiment in collaboration with the bank, in order to examine how the labeling system influenced the investment behavior of individual investors.

The labeling system was launched in 2011 and involved a classification of the bank's mutual funds into four categories: "Red funds" are funds containing investments a significant proportion of customers are expected to find problematic. Examples include weapon-producing companies and companies operating in highly corrupt markets. "Neutral funds" are funds that neither contain investments that are considered ethically problematic nor stand out positively in terms of ethicality. "Green funds" were categorized into two levels and contained funds that actively avoid investing in ethically problematic enterprises and funds that actively seek to invest in responsible companies, respectively. When Skandiabanken's customers look at the overview of available mutual funds distributed by the bank, all funds are marked with symbols reflecting one of the four categories. Thus, it is easy for customers to differentiate between mutual funds of different ethicality.

In this way, Skandiabanken made it possible for customers to assess mutual funds also with regard to ethicality. This was a new service to customers—or at least an extension of its existing services. However, little was known about the degree to which customers were interested in this kind of information, and what would be the most effective way to make the information usable for them in their purchasing decisions. To acquire knowledge about this, Lars Jacob and Trond designed a large field experiment together with the management of the bank. In their experiment, they studied the behavior of 140,000 individual investors. They constructed three comparable customer groups and controlled what information each group received about the system. One group received financially framed information, one group received information that emphasized the ethical characteristics of the funds and one control group received no information about the labeling system. This made it possible to investigate which information made it more likely that investors used the information from the ethical labeling system in their investment decisions (see Døskeland and Pedersen 2015, 2017). Based on this insight, Skandiabanken could adapt the communication about the system to all of its customers.

Skandiabanken could have implemented the new system to all of its customers at once. However, by using one month in which they tested different versions on different customer groups, it acquired valuable knowledge about how investors reacted to and used the system. This knowledge could in turn be used in the implementation of the ethical labeling system—a system that has led to changes in customers' investment behavior, and thus shifted their investments in a greener direction (Døskeland and Pedersen 2016).

Experimentation in Practice

Business model experimentation can take many forms, ranging from the design and testing of new product and service prototypes to experimentation with new business models in new markets (Chesbrough 2007). This implies that experimentation may be linked to each of the three components of the business model that we have previously introduced. As illustrated below, a series of questions can be asked as a point of departure for developing experiments relating to each of them.

Regarding value propositions, there are at least three basic questions that must be answered and that can provide ground for experimentation. Who will our customer be, and what kind of market segments will we aim for? What is our hypothesis about what these customers want? And what does that mean for the design of products and/or services that we will offer in order to create value for these customers (Morris et al. 2005)? When Skandiabanken developed its ethical labeling system, it was still unclear whether this was something the average individual investor would benefit from or if a specific niche of ethically conscious investors were the real target group. The research that was carried out showed that the system did in fact change the investment behavior of its customers, which implies that the service may have been more useful than expected among the customers. However, how a service of this type is designed and communicated to customers is central to how it is used. Therefore, controlled trials of how the service works and is used are necessary.

We can explore value delivery using similar questions: Which resources are needed to deliver in line with the value proposition, and how can those resources alternatively be used to solve other problems? Which activities are key to successful value delivery, and what other kinds of problems can be solved by means of comparable activities? Which partners are central for enabling the value delivery the company must carry out, and what other possibilities are there to create value based on the same alliances (cf. Chesbrough 2010; Adner 2006)? There are several examples of companies that have experimented with developing new services based on existing resources. We have previously shown how StormGeo used existing knowledge and meteorological data to develop new services to other market segments. Amazon is another example of a company that has developed a range of innovative services based on its technological platform, which has enabled it to go from being a pure online store to provide a multitude of services within storage, cloud services, research and much more (see, e.g., Brandt 2011; Osterwalder and Pigneur 2010).

Finally, we can ask questions related to value capture, which can inform experimental thinking about revenue streams, payment models, cost structures and so on. How will customers pay? How much does it cost to deliver on the value proposition? And what are the company's ambitions with regard to growth and scope, with regard to what position it wants to take in the market (cf. Morris et al. 2005)? This is fertile ground for experimentation, not at least with regard to payment models. The past decade has seen the emergence of many new payment models, including various streaming services, sharing-economic business models and pay-as-you-go solutions (PAYG), in which the customer pays in installments during the use of the product (see, e.g., Guajardo 2016). There is large potential in finding payment models that are attractive to customers, and it can be the key to attract customers you otherwise would not have. This is particularly evident at the so-called bottom of the pyramid, that is, in markets (e.g., in parts of Africa and Asia) where the purchasing power is so low that large groups of customers cannot afford essential products and services (Prahalad 2012). In these markets, we have seen the emergence of payment models—not at least pay-as-you-go solutions—that have made it possible to penetrate vast markets with customers who would otherwise not have been able to afford products such as solar panels, stoves and so on.

None of these issues directly relates to sustainability as such, but they are nevertheless crucial for companies that aim to conduct sustainable business. Creating sustainable and profitable business models necessitates experimentation with different customers in different markets and with various ways of delivering and capturing value. In our experience, there is increasing willingness among companies to experiment with completely new business models and to make changes to existing ones. We see this across numerous industries, and in order to be successful, companies go

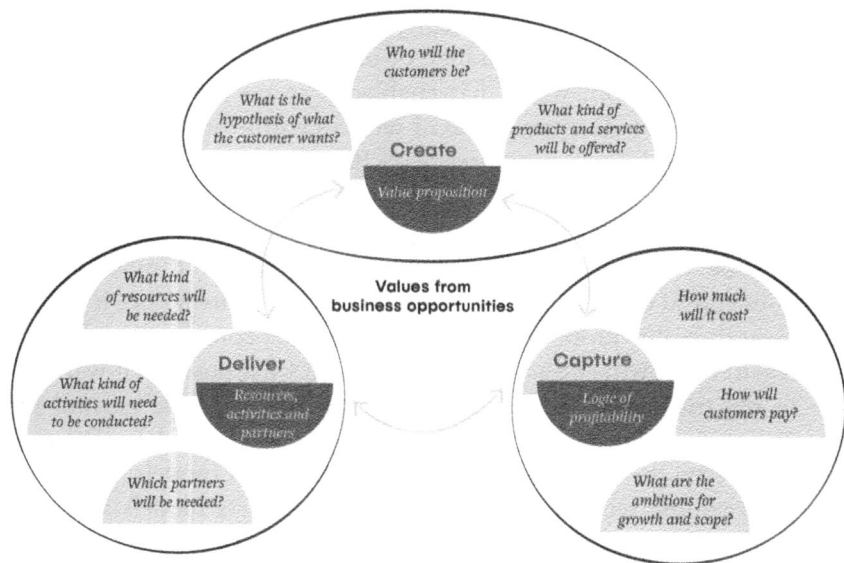

Fig. 6.2 Questions underlying business model experimentation in practice

back to the drawing board and start with questions of the kind we have outlined here (Fig. 6.2).

On the road to sustainable business, many of our current solutions, technologies and production and consumption patterns will likely disappear and be replaced by new ones. It remains to be seen what kind of products and services that will solve our problems, how they will be offered to us from companies and how they will make them, not to mention how we are going to pay for them. However, when all four wheels on the car may need to be replaced while it is still in motion, it means that companies will have to experiment their way forward, systematically. We see this when Levis experiments with the very first 100 percent recycled denim jeans. We see it when aquaculture giants such as Marine Harvest invest in fish farming in closed tanks or in facilities on land. And we see it when companies like Otovo Solar cover the cost of adding solar panels on people's houses, who in turn pay for access to the electricity that is generated, while they can offer excess energy production for sale to their neighbors. Thus, households may get lower costs related to the purchase of electricity. The movement toward sustainable business requires this type of controlled experimentation, so it becomes possible to move in the right direction step by step. In the next chapter, we will show how services can play an important role in this development.

References

Adner, R. (2006). Match your innovation strategy to your innovation ecosystem. *Harvard Business Review, 84*(4), 98.
Anderson, E. T. (2011). A step-by-step guide to smart business experiments. *Development and Learning in Organizations: An International Journal, 25*(6).
Andries, P., Debackere, K., & Looy, B. (2013). Simultaneous experimentation as a learning strategy: Business model development under uncertainty. *Strategic Entrepreneurship Journal, 7*(4), 288–310.
Bocken, N., Miller, K., Weissbrod, I., Holgado, M., & Evans, S. (2017). Business Model Experimentation for Circularity: Driving sustainability in a large international clothing retailer. *Economics and Policy of Energy and the Environment (EPEE)*.
Brandt, R. L. (2011). *One click: Jeff Bezos and the rise of Amazon.com*. London: Penguin.
Chesbrough, H. (2007). Business model innovation: It's not just about technology anymore. *Strategy & Leadership, 35*(6), 12–17.
Chesbrough, H. (2010). Business model innovation: Opportunities and barriers. *Long Range Planning, 43*(2), 354–363.
Christensen, C. (2013). *The innovator's dilemma: When new technologies cause great firms to fail*. Cambridge, MA: Harvard Business Review Press.
Davenport, T. H. (2009). How to design smart business experiments. *Harvard Business Review, 87*(2), 68–76.
Døskeland, T., & Pedersen, L. J. T. (2015). Investing with brain or heart? A field experiment on responsible investment. *Management Science, 62*(6), 1632–1644.
Døskeland, T., & Pedersen, L. J. T. (2016). Does the wealth of investors matter? Evidence from a field experiment on responsible investment. *Working paper*. NHH Norwegian School of Economics.
Døskeland, T., & Pedersen, L. J. T. (2017). Does the wealth of investors matter? Evidence from a field experiment on responsible investment. *Working paper*, NHH Norwegian School of Economics.
Elkington, J., & Zeitz, J. (2014). *The breakthrough challenge: 10 ways to connect today's profits with tomorrow's bottom line*. London: John Wiley & Sons.

Foss, N. J., & Saebi, T. (2017). Fifteen years of research on business model innovation: How far have we come, and where should we go? *Journal of Management, 43*(1), 200–227.

Guajardo, J. A. (2016). Pay-as-you-go business models in developing economies: Consumer behavior and repayment performance. Available at SSRN.

List, J., & Gneezy, U. (2014). *The why axis: Hidden motives and the undiscovered economics of everyday life*. New York, NY: Random House.

McGrath, R. G. (2010). Business models: A discovery driven approach. *Long Range Planning, 43*(2), 247–261.

Morris, M., Schindehutte, M., & Allen, J. (2005). The entrepreneur's business model: Toward a unified perspective. *Journal of Business Research, 58*(6), 726–735.

Osterwalder, A., & Pigneur, Y. (2010). *Business model generation: A handbook for visionaries, game changers, and challengers*. London: John Wiley & Sons.

Prahalad, C. K. (2012). Bottom of the pyramid as a source of breakthrough innovations. *Journal of Product Innovation Management, 29*(1), 6–12.

Ries, E. (2011). *The lean startup: How today's entrepreneurs use continuous innovation to create radically successful businesses*. New York, NY: Crown Books.

Simester, D. (2017). Field experiments in marketing. *Handbook of Economic Field Experiments, 1*, 465–497.

Thomke, S. (2001). Enlightened experimentation: The new imperative for innovation. *Harvard Business Review, 79*(2), 66–75.

Open Access This chapter is licensed under the terms of the Creative Commons Attribution-NonCommercial-NoDerivatives 4.0 International License (http://creativecommons.org/licenses/by-nc-nd/4.0/), which permits any noncommercial use, sharing, distribution and reproduction in any medium or format, as long as you give appropriate credit to the original author(s) and the source, provide a link to the Creative Commons license and indicate if you modified the licensed material. You do not have permission under this license to share adapted material derived from this book or parts of it.

The images or other third party material in this chapter are included in the chapter's Creative Commons license, unless indicated otherwise in a credit line to the material. If material is not included in the chapter's Creative Commons license and your intended use is not permitted by statutory regulation or exceeds the permitted use, you will need to obtain permission directly from the copyright holder.

7

Service-Logic Rather than Product-Logic

Companies conduct services for their customers, whether they do so by means of physical products or not. Sustainable business can be furthered by companies embracing a service-logic across all types of products. This implies thinking in terms of access over ownership, whether we are talking about sharing services, streaming services or leasing-like payment models. By building business models based on service-logic, companies can contribute to improved capacity utilization and less resource waste.

Fig. 7.1 Service-logic Rather than Product-logic

7.1 At Your Service

Every time Apple releases a new iPhone, people tend to drop their old smartphones on the ground or into the sea. The explosion of insurance claims from iPhone owners therefore surge exactly in the days ahead of a new model release (Fig. 7.1).

In this way, of course, people give themselves a reason to buy the latest iPhone model. Apple is obviously pleased at selling new phones. At the same time, however, the company finds it increasingly difficult to obtain raw materials for its new devices, and it has understood that old devices contain a number of resources that can be reused. It is obviously unfortunate for the environment that the resources inside old devices go astray, and we know that, for example, in Norway, only three of ten mobile phones are returned for recycling when the owners replace them.

A few years ago, Apple therefore introduced the "iPhone Upgrade Program"—a service that has since been copied by many other operators. It is a service that gives customers access to a new iPhone whenever they want, and they pay a monthly subscription fee. Apple thus goes from a business model in which the phone is sold to the customer (based on ownership) to a business model that provides customers access to the newest phones at any time (based on access and functionality). In addition, this business model gives the company access to old, used devices (so-called urban mining), which allows them the option of either renting them out again as-is or in refurbished versions or reusing components in the production of new devices. Not at least, the new business model has the advantageous characteristic that it largely provides a "lock-in" of customers to Apple's iPhones, which is also beneficial from a profitability standpoint (see, e.g., Dhebar 2016).

Apple achieves these benefits by introducing a service-logic in its business model, in place of a more traditional product-logic (cf. Lusch and Vargo 2012). Thus, Apple is changing the way it creates, delivers and captures value. The idea is that customer satisfaction will increase because of easy access to the latest models without the need to buy a new device.

In doing so, Apple has turned the product iPhone into a service: paying for access to the latest iPhone model at any time. Apple may in turn capitalize on its "harvested" old devices by leasing them again to new customers, refurbishing them or reusing their components.

The new iPhone models are, unlike previous generations of iPhones, designed in such a way that they can be dismantled for reuse relatively easily. Apple has even developed robots that can dismantle used devices easily and effectively. Such devices contain several valuable resources like gold, lead and platinum. In 2014, Apple harvested a total of 40,000 tons of electronic waste, and the scope of its harvesting is on the increase. Apple's new business model is obviously inspired by the so-called circular economy, which is the topic of the next chapter, and it builds such a circular model in part by moving from a product-logic to a service-logic (see, e.g., Bocken et al. 2014, 2016).

What Do We Mean by Service-Logic?

In recent years, academics and business managers alike have opened their eyes to the service economy. Services largely dominate economic value creation in industrialized countries, to such an extent, in fact, that these countries should perhaps rather be called service economies than industrialized economies (cf. World Bank 2015). In addition, there is an increasing recognition that knowledge is scarce on how to build profitable, service-based business models (e.g., Kastalli and Van Looy 2013; Baines et al. 2009). We use the concept to denote not only services as service providers, in the traditional sense, offer them. It also comprises how products like smartphones, cars and clothes can be understood as services. This implies emphasizing that whatever is delivered to the customer acts as a service that solves a problem for the customer, even when it is done by means of a physical product to which the customer gets access (Lusch and Vargo 2012; Bocken et al. 2014).

There are many examples of products made into services, such as the iPhone Upgrade Program and Filippa K's sharing-economic model for the rental of fashion wear that customers would otherwise have had to purchase. Companies that sell products can also apply service-logic to enhance their value creation by offering additional services. Many firms now aim to sell more robust and durable products that can be repaired, but this runs the risk of reducing profitability because they end up selling fewer products to each customer. To remain profitable, the companies must recoup this revenue by selling additional services to their customers (see, e.g., Mont 2002; Tukker 2004). Apple is thus far from alone in developing a business model in which services are an important component.

Rolls Royce, for instance, offers its products such as aircraft engines as a service rather than a product (see, e.g., Ng et al. 2012). Hence, the company retains ownership of the product while its customers use it, and at any given time offers maintenance on the engines. Rolls Royce commits to keeping the aircraft engines in operation at all times, and the payment model is such that the customer pays for the time the engine is running, for the duration of the contract. Such a change in the company's offering usually requires a new business model. With regard to the profitability, the challenge with such a service-based business model is that it may be more expensive than a business model in which the company "waves goodbye" to the product when the customer buys it. Instead, this business model requires that Rolls Royce has staff who can provide the necessary service that follows from such a value proposition, even after the customer has started using the product. This requires an entirely different set of resources and competences than did the traditional business model, and it implies that the company must capture value in a different way than through conventional sales transactions.

The Sharing Economy as Service-Logic

In the next chapter, we will explore the circular economy, wherein a basic idea is that waste is simply resources gone astray (e.g., Stahel 2016). However, resources can go astray long before they end up in the scrap heap. For example, a drill is used on average only 13 minutes of its lifetime; our cars stand still on average 23 hours a day and when they are used, they are less than half full; and many people have houses, apartments and rooms available all or part of the time. These drills, cars and rooms, and similar excess resources, are often referred to as "structural waste". This is of course not waste in the traditional sense, but it constitutes a form of waste in the sense that these are idle, yet valuable, resources. Therefore, the energy, resources and waste resulting from the production of even more similar objects could have been avoided if we had utilized the objects that already exist more efficiently (cf. McDonough and Braungart 2002).

This is the point of departure for the sharing economy, which has taken the world by storm in recent years (Belk 2014; Botsman and Rogers 2010). There is of course nothing new in people sharing their resources, or in people renting out items they do not use—whether houses, cars or smaller products. Especially in the United States, car sharing has long been commonplace. In recent years, however, the supply of such services has exploded in line with new technological solutions making them possible (e.g., Sundararajan 2013). Numerous technological platforms, or apps, have emerged and challenged the established players in the industry. The most famous services are perhaps Uber, which competes with taxis; Airbnb, which competes with hotels; and eBay, which sells all conceivable new and used products in an online marketplace.

The defining characteristic of these sharing-economic services is that they effectively bring together people who have excess resources and those who have a need for using those resources and a willingness to pay for it (Gansky 2010; Stephany 2015). An important prerequisite for an efficient sharing economy is trust between the parties in the transaction (Walter 2017). This is most often solved by the functionality of giving transaction partners a score or assessment after the transaction. Such assessment allows users to know whom they can trust and whom they should avoid. The transaction costs of using such services are decreasing, and as more people use the services, their peers are more likely to adopt the services as well. Sharing services thus serve as third-party entities linking together those who have resources to spare and those who would like to access them. Thereby, such services create a marketplace where consumption takes place through access to resources, without all consumers needing ownership of the resources.

An app seems to appear for any business opportunity related to shareable resources. The new app Tise facilitates the reuse of fashion clothing; TimeRepublik allows people to share their time with others, and Shyp connects customers who have items they want transported with those who have available vehicles. All these online platforms make it possible for people to make resources they do not use accessible such as their time, space in their cars, houses, ski equipment or drills they might have to spare.

The sharing economy is booming, but it is no stranger to controversy. This particularly applies to the question of workers' rights and taxation related to such services (Sundararajan 2016). Uber has, for example, been in the spotlight regarding labor law, and Airbnb has been criticized for the effects of its service on housing prices in densely populated urban areas. Thus, the social footprint of the sharing economy is ambiguous, but there can obviously be environmentally beneficial aspects of consuming in a way that allows more people to use the same resources. For sharing to take place under proper conditions, such markets need regulation in line with other markets. Currently, developments are happening so fast that legislative efforts are lagging behind, which implies that companies aiming to create sharing platforms must be aware of such possible negative aspects.

However, there are not just negative social side effects of the sharing economy. Not at least in a global perspective, these business models have great potential. Although sharing services are most prevalent in Europe and the United States, they have also started to gain a foothold in poorer parts of the world (see, e.g., Karnani 2007). In these markets, there is precisely a great need for products that people cannot afford to buy on their own. An example of a service remedying this is Hello Tractor, which gives farmers in developing countries access to tractors. Through a simple SMS-based system, farmers are given access to rent equipment that can increase their productivity considerably, without having to invest in expensive tractors that obviously stand idle for much of the time. In this way, such sharing services can also have a positive social footprint, not at least in those markets known as the "bottom of the pyramid".

7.2 Access to Everything

Did you know that nearly 1.2 billion people lack access to electricity? In addition, globally, more people have access to mobile phones than to toilets. In 2011, this inspired the founders Kristian Bye and Marius Andresen to start the company Bright Products. The aim was to bring the solar lamp SunBell, which K8 Industrial Design had already designed, to market. The lamp does not only provide light, it can also be used to charge mobile phones, and it can be installed and adjusted to many different types of use. Sveinung met the founders in 2013, right after the company had developed the first prototype of SunBell. It did not take long before a foundation headed by Sveinung invested in Bright, and he joined its board of directors.

Bright attracted early interest from the United Nations, which today is the company's largest customer and SunBell is still its main product. However, the company has developed more products and services that can solve even more problems in the markets where it operates. People at the bottom of the pyramid have great need for several important products and services that they often cannot afford or access (e.g., Prahalad 2012). This includes financial services, healthcare, electricity and education. However, the spread of mobile phones has given poor people access to services they could previously only dream of, precisely because services in banking and finance, electricity, health, entertainment and education are increasingly offered through more accessible digital platforms (Karamchandani et al. 2011). This also provides new opportunities for companies aiming to establish themselves in markets at the bottom of the pyramid. Led by CEO Ingun Berget, Bright therefore entered into a collaboration with Angaza Design in Silicon Valley to use its design of a mobile-based technology that enables customers to pay in installments—a so-called pay-as-you-go (PAYG) payment model, which is increasingly prevalent in African and Asian markets (Guajardo 2016).

Such a payment model can thus give Bright access to markets wherein potential customers cannot initially afford to buy the product at its full price. These customers have money to spend on kerosene, coal and charging their mobile phones in expensive charging stations. However, even though they spend two to three dollars each day on such products and services, they still do not have enough money to buy quality products that can cost anywhere from 50 to up to 200 dollars. This is despite the fact that the products would have paid off for them in a relatively short time.

Bright Products, then, is in the midst of a redesign of its business model, and it experiments with various services and payment models in these markets. The company is also making improvements in environmental performance, for instance, by making changes to product design, production processes and waste management, and it might also be possible to develop business models based on leasing rather than selling. Bright cannot succeed with such changes on its own, and there are a number of alliance partners in these efforts, such as microfinance institutions, distributors, suppliers of technological solutions and designers. A key driver behind this is the service-logic that involves moving from thinking about the company through the lens of the products it offers, and instead emphasize how its offering increases the experienced value for the customer. This implies that Bright goes from being a company that sells solar-powered lamps and mobile chargers to become a company offering services related to energy and beyond.

Profit from Services

We increasingly take for granted the services we have available through our smartphones. However, a lot has happened in a very short time. For instance, how did a typical office desk look 15 years ago versus today? At the time, most offices had fax machines, books, calculators, pictures, stationery and various types of calendars. Some of these products are still there, but they increasingly face competition from software and smartphone apps. When digital (and analog) services replace physical products, it is often referred to as servitization (e.g., Kastalli and Van Looy 2013). This happens at all levels—from the physical calendars we used to have on our desks now being an app on your phone, to companies that previously bought trucks and other vehicles for their own use now using app-based platforms to pay for access to such vehicles from companies that own fleets of vehicles.

When applying service-logic to products in this way, it may lead us to end up owning fewer things overall. From a sustainability point of view, this is clearly advantageous. The need for transportation can be reduced when meetings are held via Skype or when 3D printers enable printing components or products where and when they are needed, rather than producing them in low-cost countries and transporting them across the planet. Similarly, there will be less waste when physical products are replaced by digital services, although we should not underestimate the ecological footprint of the server farms that support all business online (see, e.g., Le et al. 2010). We conduct more and more shopping online rather than in physical stores that need large inventories. In addition, an increasing number of business models that contribute to better exploitation of corporate resources are appearing such as the app Too Good to Go. In the Scandinavian markets, this app facilitates transactions between residential customers who can buy food that would otherwise be thrown away from restaurants and cafés that have surplus food from their operations.

Many services that used to imply that we met people are now automatized or digital. This is because in many cases we have gone from being consumers to being prosumers—we take part in producing (or co-creating) the products and services companies offer us (cf. Toffler 1981). We buy our airline tickets online, we check in our own luggage and we scan our electronic tickets before we board the plane. In this way, the airlines reduce their costs by leaving a lot of work to the customers, many of whom prefer the efficiency of "prosuming" the airline travel experience. When we assemble IKEA furniture, we also act as prosumers—we do part of the job that the furniture companies used to do for us. Many of the apps we use, for instance, the maps on our mobile phones and the online services we use to communicate with others, are free. Companies that have offered physical versions of such services must therefore rethink their value propositions, while the companies that offer free services must develop business models that enable them to capture value in other ways (Anderson 2009). Examples of value capture strategies are integration of advertisements into the service or selling data about customers to companies that have use for such data.

When the Internet Enters Our Things

Technology in general and Internet technology in particular are important common denominators for the emergence of business models based on service-logic. The development of Bright Products from a product-based to a service-based company is intimately tied to this technological development. Elon Musk has said that he wants to send 4000 satellites into the skies, which in turn can provide worldwide access to WiFi. In that case, the so-called Internet of Things (IoT) will become even more widespread and important than it already is. IoT is the network of physical objects that have built-in electronics, software, sensors and network connections, which render these objects able to collect and exchange data. In the context of big data, machine learning and artificial intelligence, such applications can even be able to learn what your needs are and thereby customize the services they offer. This means that your refrigerator can tell you when the milk has gone sour or that the lights in your house learn your habits and thereby adjust themselves accordingly. Such a system can also be remote-controlled by means of various applications and can thus be enriched with information from the increasingly large amounts of data collected in real time. Ultimately, such systems support smarter decisions that are constantly self-enhancing because they learn while being in use.

For instance, when Tesla had a problem with a low rear axle on its cars that were driving around on American roads, its engineers solved it by pushing a button on a computer in Tesla headquarters. The next time Tesla owners started their cars, the cars were raised the necessary number of centimeters automatically. This was done without the cars being called back to the Tesla shops, which many other carmakers had to do when encountering similar problems. Tesla can remotely control such changes since all its cars are connected to Tesla's servers. It is estimated that in the near future, IoT will be built into several billion objects, such as the solar lamps and house systems offered by Bright Products. This technology is already affecting the way we live, work and organize our cities, and the impact will become considerably stronger. For example, companies like Cisco and IBM are collaborating with governments around the world to develop so-called smart cities. The concept refers to cities that are designed in such a way that essential services are interconnected and can be coordinated automatically and in real time by means of sensors, big data and digital decision support systems. Such systems can allow public transportation to be planned in real time based on information about who is where and their movements at any given time. Similarly, it can allow for full control over water and energy consumption, waste disposal systems and so on. In this way, the various services in the city are becoming increasingly connected and will be able to automatically adapt to each other. Such planning has an obvious potential for successfully managing resources in smarter ways, thereby reducing overall resource consumption.

An important aspect of IoT is that it takes us from a world wherein products are static to a world wherein they serve as dynamic services that can be changed, upgraded and improved on as they are used. It also enables automatic customization of services through the application's learning of the user's preferences. Previously, when we bought products, we had to bring them to the manufacturer or other companies if we wanted to modify them. IoT provides infrastructure that enables the improvement of products in real time, as in the Tesla example. Thus, products and services can do a better and better job of solving our problems over time. An "intelligent refrigerator" that tells us when milk turns sour, and which maybe even orders new milk from the online store without asking us first, resembles a service more than a product.

Both Apple's iPhone Upgrade Program and Bright Products' new business model are stories of companies that move from being providers of products to become service providers aiming to solve the problems of its customers. As we have seen, the value propositions of these companies typically look different from those of their previous business models, and usually it necessitates other types of payment models for making their business models profitable. One important characteristic of such business models, however, is that they enable smarter use of resources. In this way, they play an important role in changing business from being linear to being more circular.

References

Anderson, C. (2009). *Free: The future of a radical price.* New York, NY: Random House.

Baines, T. S., Lightfoot, H. W., Benedettini, O., & Kay, J. M. (2009). The servitization of manufacturing: A review of literature and reflection on future challenges. *Journal of Manufacturing Technology Management, 20*(5), 547–567.

Belk, R. (2014). You are what you can access: Sharing and collaborative consumption online. *Journal of Business Research, 67*(8), 1595–1600.

Bocken, N. M., de Pauw, I., Bakker, C., & van der Grinten, B. (2016). Product design and business model strategies for a circular economy. *Journal of Industrial and Production Engineering, 33*(5), 308–320.

Bocken, N. M. P., Short, S. W., Rana, P., & Evans, S. (2014). A literature and practice review to develop sustainable business model archetypes. *Journal of Cleaner Production, 65*, 42–56.

Botsman, R., & Rogers, R. (2010). *What's mine is yours. The rise of collaborative consumption.* New York, NY: HarperCollins.

Dhebar, A. (2016). Razor-and-Blades pricing revisited. *Business Horizons, 59*(3), 303–310.

Gansky, L. (2010). *The mesh: Why the future of business is sharing.* London: Penguin.

Guajardo, J. A. (2016). Pay-as-you-go business models in developing economies: Consumer behavior and repayment performance. Available at SSRN.

Karamchandani, A., Kubzansky, M., & Lalwani, N. (2011). Is the bottom of the pyramid really for you. *Harvard Business Review, 89*(3), 107–111.

Karnani, A. (2007). The mirage of marketing to the bottom of the pyramid: How the private sector can help alleviate poverty. *California Management Review, 49*(4), 90–111.

Kastalli, I. V., & Van Looy, B. (2013). Servitization: Disentangling the impact of service business model innovation on manufacturing firm performance. *Journal of Operations Management, 31*(4), 169–180.

Le, K., Bilgir, O., Bianchini, R., Martonosi, M., & Nguyen, T. D. (2010, June). Managing the cost, energy consumption, and carbon footprint of internet services. In *ACM SIGMETRICS performance evaluation review* (Vol. 38, No. 1, pp. 357–358). ACM.

Lusch, R. F., & Vargo, S. L. (2012). *Service-dominant logic.* Cambridge: Cambridge University Press.

McDonough, W., & Braungart, M. (2002). *Cradle to cradle: Remaking the way things work*. New York, NY: North Point Press.

Mont, O. K. (2002). Clarifying the concept of product–service system. *Journal of Cleaner Production, 10*(3), 237–245.

Ng, I., Parry, G., Smith, L., Maull, R., & Briscoe, G. (2012). Transitioning from a goods-dominant to a service-dominant logic: Visualising the value proposition of Rolls-Royce. *Journal of Service Management, 23*(3), 416–439.

Prahalad, C. K. (2012). Bottom of the pyramid as a source of breakthrough innovations. *Journal of Product Innovation Management, 29*(1), 6–12.

Stahel, W. R. (2016). The circular economy. *Nature, 531*(7595), 435.

Stephany, A. (2015). *The business of sharing: Making it in the new sharing economy*. London: Palgrave Macmillan.

Sundararajan, A. (2013). From Zipcar to the sharing economy. *Harvard Business Review*, 1.

Sundararajan, A. (2016). *The sharing economy: The end of employment and the rise of crowd-based capitalism*. Cambridge, MA: MIT Press.

Toffler, A. (1981). *The third wave*. New York, NY: Bantam Books.

Tukker, A. (2004). Eight types of product–service system: Eight ways to sustainability? Experiences from SusProNet. *Business Strategy and the Environment, 13*(4), 246–260.

Walter, E. (2017). *Trust in the sharing economy. Can trust make or break a sharing enterprise?* Anchor Academic Publishing.

World Bank. (2015). Services, etc., value added (% of GDP). Retrieved May 11, 2015, from http://data.worldbank.org/indicator/NV.SRV.TETC.ZS.

Open Access This chapter is licensed under the terms of the Creative Commons Attribution-NonCommercial-NoDerivatives 4.0 International License (http://creativecommons.org/licenses/by-nc-nd/4.0/), which permits any noncommercial use, sharing, distribution and reproduction in any medium or format, as long as you give appropriate credit to the original author(s) and the source, provide a link to the Creative Commons license and indicate if you modified the licensed material. You do not have permission under this license to share adapted material derived from this book or parts of it.

The images or other third party material in this chapter are included in the chapter's Creative Commons license, unless indicated otherwise in a credit line to the material. If material is not included in the chapter's Creative Commons license and your intended use is not permitted by statutory regulation or exceeds the permitted use, you will need to obtain permission directly from the copyright holder.

8

The Circular Rather than the Linear Economy

To become more sustainable, companies need to go from traditional, linear business models based on "take, make and dispose" to circular business models based on reuse, resource efficiency, the sharing economy and closed loops. This can counteract resource depletion, reduce pollution and be a source of cost reductions, new revenue streams and better risk management for companies.

Fig. 8.1 The Circular Rather than the Linear Economy

8.1 The Future Goes in Circles

Imagine a world without garbage, wherein what we used to refer to as waste is the most important resource. Some would argue that we are already on our way there. Did you know that most of the materials in a HÅG chair are reusable? Already, in 1991, HÅG used recycled plastic from bottle caps and ketchup bottles in its office chairs. Today, the company also uses other types of plastic in its products (Fig. 8.1).

In 2015, the European Association of Plastics Recycling and Recovery Organisations named the HÅG Capisco chair "Best Recycled Product 2015". HÅG Capisco is made from 100 percent recycled plastic, and 90 percent of its aluminum parts are also recycled. These office chairs contain no environmentally harmful substances, and none of the parts are glued together. Moreover, the chair is composed of very few materials, so that it is easy to disassemble and recycle at the end of life, and it is thus easy to use the materials in new products.

HÅG is not alone in making these types of changes to its products and business models. During the past decade, a new, circular-economic reality has gradually emerged. This development implies companies gradually changing their business models from being linear to become circular (see, e.g., McDonough and Braungart 2010; Stahel 2016; Bocken et al. 2016). Global giants like Apple, Google and Phillips are redesigning their business models to become more circular. This includes building the so-called closed-loop supply chains, in which as few resources as possible disappear in the form of waste or emissions.

These companies are joining the movement from a linear economy that drains the planet of resources and generates large quantities of waste to a circular economy that ensures that resources are used repeatedly, thus preventing large amounts of resources going astray and becoming waste (e.g., Webster 2015). Circular-economic thinking is based on the idea of the economy being restorative and regenerative—that is, economic activities should strengthen rather than break down social and environmental resources (McDonough and Braungart 2010). This entails maintaining products and materials in the economy at as high a quality as possible over time so that they can be reused many times. This phenomenon is referred to as *upcycling*, rather than recycling, which emphasizes the attempt to retain high value of materials, components and products, rather than allowing them to deteriorate downwards in the value hierarchy (McDonough and Braungart 2013).

This transition can have large effects on economy, society and the environment alike. A study of seven European countries concluded that a transition to a circular economy has the potential of reducing each nation's greenhouse gas emissions by 70 percent and increasing employment by 4 percent (Ellen MacArthur Foundation 2015). Both the consultancy firm McKinsey and the think tank the Club of Rome have estimated that there is an enormous profit potential for companies that develop circular business models. However, it will require very significant changes and breaking with one of the most fundamental characteristics of the production of products and services: it requires moving from a linear to a circular economy.

From Linear to Circular Value Chains

The essence of circular-economic thinking is that we need to abandon the linear value chain, which is based on the logic of "take, make and dispose", and rather build circular value chains, in which materials are used repeatedly (Stahel 2016). On the one hand, this concerns resources in the biological cycle, such as water, biomass, gas and other natural resources. On the other hand, it concerns resources in the technical cycle, such as plastic, glass and other materials that do not occur naturally (e.g., Lacy and Rutqvist 2015). Companies can think circular and reuse resources in both cycles, and thus prevent resources that previously went to waste—whether water, energy or physical resources—from disappearing out of the circle.

Linear thinking has dominated since the beginning of the third industrial revolution, and it has led to growth and prosperity in many parts of the world. It is, however, also one of the reasons for our current sustainability problems because the linear model implies using resources in an unsustainable way and producing large quantities of waste that destructs

Fig. 8.2 A traditional linear value chain

the environment further. Much of this waste is even toxic and harmful in other ways, so that it is not possible to reuse it (Fig. 8.2).

The circular-economic paradigm suggests that there are at least three necessary responses to the problem. First, we need to use resources in a way and to an extent that does not exhaust resource stocks. Many resources are exploited at such a rate that they will ultimately be completely depleted. This includes many metals, minerals and fossil fuels, not to mention various fish stocks. A circular-economic model requires balancing the use of these resources, while facilitating the regeneration of such renewable resources (see, e.g., McDonough and Braungart 2010).

Second, companies must design products, services and processes in ways that lead to less use of scarce resources and facilitate the reuse thereof. Specifically, this means designing away externalities, for example, by creating products that are possible to disassemble and reuse at the end of life (see, e.g., Bocken et al. 2016).

Third, all products and materials must be maintained at as high a quality level as possible, so that they can actually be reused. Circulation economists argue that we must "upcycle" resources (McDonough and Braungart 2013). Traditional recycling is really "downcycling", which means that resources are gradually degraded until eventually becoming unusable. When a plastic bottle is recycled into a fleece sweater, the plastic resource is still on its way to the landfill. If the sweater is burned when it is worn out, it generates energy, but it can happen only once.

Upcycling, on the other hand, implies maintaining the value of the resource so that it can be used repeatedly. Could one, for example, make a plastic bottle that is possible to use many more times? Alternatively, could one make a bottle in which the plastic does not deteriorate in quality when it is recycled? Increasingly, car manufacturers design their cars in such a way that components from old cars can be reused in new cars with little refurbishing. Even the new ships in the Danish company Maersk are designed in this way so that the ships can be easily disassembled several decades from now, which solves the problem of illegal shipbreaking on the beaches of poor countries, which results in pollution and health risks for poor shipbreakers. In addition, it importantly enables the recovery of ship parts of high value. Finally, it allows for simple replacement of parts that can give the ship a longer product life.

Such changes involve a shift from the traditional thinking of "from cradle to grave" toward a mindset of designing products and services "from cradle to cradle" (McDonough and Braungart 2010). In total, these circular-economic ideas thus involve redesigning products, services and value chains in a manner that allows for the use and reuse of products and resources in smarter ways (Jørgensen and Pedersen 2018). This implies a new model for producing, consuming and, finally, recycling products and services, and so the cycle begins again.

In order to attain the benefits of a circular economy, it is vital that companies design profitable, circular business models. The design of such business models can be done on at least five different levels (Fig. 8.3). As we see from the circles in the figure, companies can rent out their products, which, for example, MUD Jeans and Filippa K do with clothes. They can also offer repair services; they can reuse either parts of or all of the products and resell them; they can refurbish and renew products and they can upcycle resources and materials and thus reuse them instead of extracting new, virgin resources.

The Two Fundamental Cycles

HÅG's business model is designed to create, deliver and capture value by taking advantage of business opportunities in the circular economy. The chairs are made from recycled materials, they are designed in a way that makes them durable and easily repairable, and when they are worn out, they can easily be disassembled and their parts reused in new chairs. An important characteristic of the chair design is precisely that it is easy to

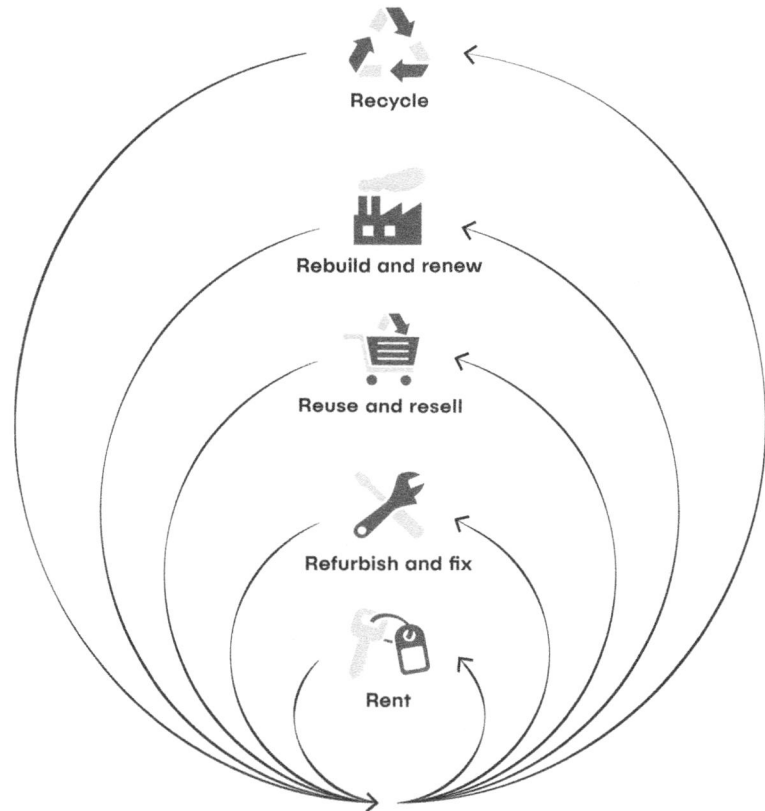

Fig. 8.3 Different types of upcycling in circular business models

disentangle the materials produced by naturally occurring resources and those that are processed from materials that do not occur naturally. These two types of resources must be treated differently and be possible to separate after the product's life span. Michael Braungart and William McDonough (2010) argue that resources should be seen as belonging to two fundamental cycles that reflect this distinction—the biological and technical cycles, respectively. These two cycles are illustrated below. It should be noted that any product will usually be made up of resources from both cycles (cf. Bocken et al. 2016).

The biological cycle comprises biological nutrients that regenerate continuously in natural cycles, such as cotton, plants, fungi and animals. In this cycle, waste, such as dead animals and plants, become food for bacteria and fungi, and thereby degrade into fertile soil through natural processes (i.e., composting). The technical cycle comprises materials such as plastics, glass and other resources that are not naturally generated in the biological cycle. Resources from this cycle therefore become waste that does not decompose naturally, and instead become waste if we do not create systems to reuse them (e.g., Webster 2015).

The vast majority of products consist of materials from both the biological and technical cycles. For example, the HÅG Capisco chair is made from metal and plastic parts from the technical cycle as well as wool from the biological cycle. When HÅG makes a point of the various parts of the chair not being glued together, it is precisely because it makes it easier to disassemble the chair after use. In this way, the cotton can be returned to the biological cycle, while the metals can be attributed to the technical cycle and, for instance, melted for repurposing. Some metal and plastic parts from HÅG chairs can be used directly in new chairs, thus being channeled right back into the technical cycle without requiring melting or similar repurposing. Other parts of the chair, like the cotton on the seats, are simply biodegradable. They are designed to be directly returned to nature, thus providing nourishment to the soil when they decompose (Fig. 8.4).

It is costly to recover and refine resources from both the biological and technical cycles. It requires water, transport and labor to produce cotton and aluminum, and it is a waste of scarce resources to compost cotton or melt aluminum if they instead can be reused in their existing form. For materials to be reused, they cannot be contaminated, they need to be produced in such a way that ensures durability, they must be easily reusable and it must be easy to disentangle, for instance, plastic, cotton and aluminum. A transition to a circular economy will therefore require large investments in new product design, new manufacturing processes and new activities, such as collection of old products and processing for reuse. Although the benefits of such a transition can be very large in the longer term, large transition costs should be expected in the shorter term.

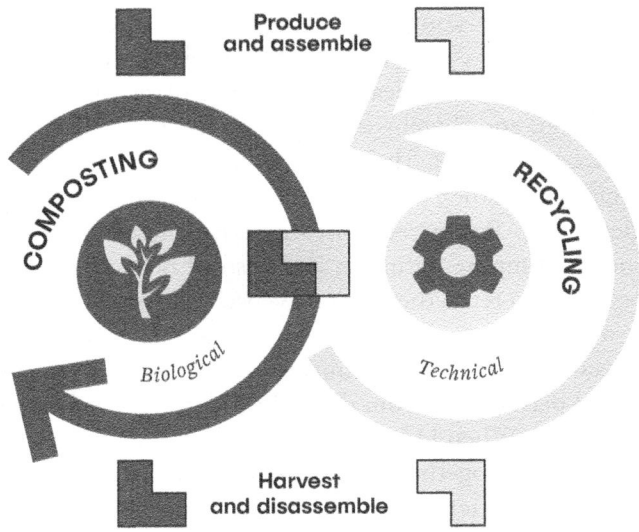

Fig. 8.4 The two basic cycles (based on McDonough and Braungart 2013)

8.2 Resources Astray

It is expected that by the year 2050, we will reach the point where there is more plastic than fish in the ocean, measured in weight (Ellen MacArthur Foundation 2017). The amount of plastic that floats in the ocean and assembles in increasingly massive garbage patches is very destructive to marine ecosystems.

The problem does not only exist at sea—there is also a huge plastic waste problem on land. However, more and more companies are finding ways to turn the plastic problem into an opportunity, and currently plastics from the oceans are used to make everything from carpets to shoes. This is also the concept of the Spanish clothing brand Ecoalf, which produces a full range of fashion apparel and bags made from old fishing nets and plastic bottles.

Using 235 grams of fishnets, Ecoalf makes one meter of yarn, which in turn is used to produce winter jackets and other products. Ecoalf is not capable on its own to conduct the entire process leading up to this.

Therefore, the company has established 18 joint ventures with other companies in order to collect waste, develop yarn and design and distribute its products. Ecoalf and its partners have thus developed a business model that enables the collection of waste and the production of new materials, and thereby novel and innovative ways of designing, producing, distributing and selling fashion clothes.

By using circular-economic thinking, Ecoalf and its allies turned the plastic problem into an opportunity. There are numerous business opportunities in the circular economy, and innovative companies can create value by recovering resources that have gone astray and putting them back into productive use.

Values at Stake

The circular model is characterized by being restorative and regenerative. It implies designing production processes and products in ways that strengthen rather than break down ecosystems and natural resources. This may be done by biodegradable products that nourish the environment rather than polluting it, and it may be done through the reuse of resources that in turn renders the exploitation of scarce virgin resources unnecessary (McDonough and Braungart 2010).

Upcycling of resources requires that materials, whether they come from the biological or technical cycle, maintain as high a value as possible for the longest possible time. Finished products typically have the highest value, while their parts and raw materials have a lower value. Finished products can for instance be used repeatedly, which requires business models that facilitate the repair, rental, sharing or reselling of products (Bocken et al. 2016; Jørgensen and Pedersen 2017). When this is not possible, companies can harvest the resources and reuse them or recycle them. An example is Norsirk, the Norwegian company that is responsible for the recycling of electrical and electronic waste. It has managed to attain a reuse of 97.5 percent of all components in stoves, for instance, thus keeping virtually all product components at a high level by enabling reuse.

Contaminated materials have the lowest value. Examples include materials that include asbestos, which can be included in neither the biological nor the technical cycle. A jacket from Ecoalf or an office chair from HÅG thus has a higher value than the constituent parts that go into making them. In order to maintain as high a value as possible, the products should be designed to last long. This may imply that companies offer repair services or sell the products on the secondary market. When the HÅG chair is worn out, its parts have a higher value than do materials for recycling. This implies maintaining the chairs at a higher level of value by designing for direct reuse of the parts.

The same applies to the biological cycle, in which the cotton fibers in chairs or in clothes have been planted, watered, harvested, transported and processed. This process is both energy- and resource-intensive, and we should therefore try to maintain the high value of the cotton once it is produced. Until it is worn out, it should be reused rather than buried in landfills. This of course depends on the cotton not being contaminated by toxins, in either production or use. And if the cotton is glued together with materials from the technical cycle, such as plastic, it will not decompose naturally. Regardless, we should wait as long as possible to lead the cotton back into the biological cycle. Used cotton should preferably be reused repeatedly as inputs in other products, such as insulation in car seats, for which many car manufacturers are using old, used socks. Only when the cotton is completely worn out should it be returned to nature.

As pointed out by Bocken et al. (2016), circular business models build on at least three strategies. First, closing the loop, that is, ensuring a flow of resources from post-use to production of new products. Second, narrowing the loop, that is, ensuring resource efficiency and the use of fewer resources per produced unit. Third, slowing the loop, that is, ensuring longer product lives by designing for longevity. Each of these three strategies on their own, but not at least in combination, can be the basis for significantly more circular business models.

Along the circular, closed-loop value chain, there are numerous business opportunities that innovative businesses can exploit (see, e.g., Lieder and Rashid 2016). Big companies are making their own systems in which they design long-lasting products and make money on additional services such as repair, upgrades and refurbishing. Some of these companies are now starting to rent rather than sell products, which implies that they regain access to the products after customers are done with them (see, e.g., Lacy and Rutqvist 2015). In that way, they can rent them out again or harvest their parts and thus get access to valuable resources. Big companies such as Apple, Renault and H&M, for instance, operate in this way.

Not all companies are big enough to conduct all activities that are necessary to succeed with a circular, closed-loop value chain. This opens for a variety of business models that can offer services along the value chain to help other organizations become more circular (cf. Bocken et al. 2016). For example, there are design agencies with expertise on circular product design, waste management companies that sell recycled materials as inputs into new products, technology companies that offer digital platforms for sharing and other types of consumption, companies that can facilitate the sale of used products on the secondary market and R&D organizations that can provide knowledge on how to recycle materials optimally to avoid excess energy and resource use. In other words, there are numerous business opportunities in facilitating the circular economy, for small and large companies alike. Many of the companies we use as examples in this book have done just this: Newlight Technologies recycles CO_2 to produce biodegradable plastic that Dell and other big companies use in their products. Interface redesigned its entire business model in a manner that included reusing waste as inputs in their carpets. Similarly, Norsk Gjenvinning provides services related to waste management and the smarter use of resources along the entire circular value chain.

It should be noted that not all sustainability challenges are necessarily best solved by means of circular solutions. Circular business models are particularly well suited to solve challenges related to product life cycles and resource scarcity more broadly. There are of course many other types of sustainability challenges that can be solved by means of other approaches that are not explicitly circular. However, generally speaking, the solutions offered by circular thinking imply increased cycling of materials, components and products, which is beneficial from a sustainability standpoint and which can reduce the footprint of products and services in many different industries. The three approaches outlined above—closing, slowing and narrowing the loop—together form a set of design strategies that can lead to considerably more sustainable business models.

Inspired by Nature

A prominent part of the circular economy is the idea that business should be in harmony with, and even reinforce, nature's own processes. A related development that is the basis for many exciting technologies and business models is products and production processes that imitate or copy mechanisms and elements from nature. This phenomenon is called biomimicry (see, e.g., Harman 2013). An example is the British company Skipping Rocks Lab, which has developed an alternative to plastic bottles. The company found inspiration in nature, after studying how plants collect liquid by means of membranes. This led to the design of Ooho!—a liquid packaging that is made from seagrass and other naturally occurring input factors. It looks like a small, spherical bottle, and it is not only an affordable alternative to traditional bottles, but it is also supremely biodegradable: It is actually edible!

The materials of which the bottle is made are reminiscent of an orange peel. When made thicker, the material can also be used to transport and store large quantities of other liquids. Such technologies thus have significant potential to be put to use for solving very different kinds of problems over time.

A comparable example is the US design and technology company Ecovative, which employs fungi to create a biological alternative to polystyrene. The world is flooded with polystyrene, which has significant adverse effects on the environment. The young founders of the company started experimenting with various forms of fungi and grew fungi in molds that made it possible to create packaging that is strikingly similar to polystyrene but biodegradable instead of environmentally harmful. After many years of experimenting with the technology, Ecovative has managed to make the product competitive on price, and it has companies like IKEA, Dell and Stanhope on its list of clients. The company also extended its product line with other products that use mushrooms as inputs such as insulation and floating docks.

These examples all illustrate some of the potential in biomimicry. There has been an explosion in business models built on such ideas, and we have probably only seen the beginning of this technology's utilization. It can be used to design and produce goods in ways that are less harmful and restorative rather than destructive to nature and ecosystems that are fully in line with the principles of the circular economy.

Unemployment Also Reflects Resources Astray

When speaking of the circular economy, it is easy to think of the environmental characteristics of business models. However, the ideas can also be used advantageously on human resources and the social dimension of business models. Ecoalf collects plastic waste, such as fishing nets, and uses it as an input factor in their products. In this way, the company also creates jobs for poor people in areas with a large surplus of plastic waste. Many so-called social entrepreneurs aim to solve social problems by creating jobs through which people are given the opportunity to help themselves (see, e.g., Peredo and McLean 2006; Short et al. 2009).

The Plastic Bank is built around such an idea. This company won Sustainia's Community Award in 2015 for its pioneering work with collecting plastic waste. David Katz and Shaun Frankson formed the company in 2013. They set out to contribute to alleviating two major problems: plastic pollution and poverty. They do this through a model that turns plastic into a currency, which enables poor and unemployed people to earn money by collecting plastic. The company provides incentives to poor people to collect plastic waste in Haiti and elsewhere. It pays collectors in cash or by vouchers that can be used to buy food and other essential products, or to charge their mobile phones or access similar services.

The Plastic Bank thus helps transform waste—it upcycles plastic from waste into new resources. In addition, The Plastic Bank creates valuable jobs for poor people who would otherwise not have been able to support themselves and their families. The CEO, David Katz, enthusiastically told us of his visions for the company when he visited our master course at NHH Norwegian School of Economics, and we had to take him on a long walk in the mountains of Bergen, Norway, to channel his exuberant energy. And David's enthusiasm is indeed contagious: On Facebook, people engage in campaigns to encourage companies into using plastic from The Plastic Bank. Lush Cosmetics has financed part of The Plastic Bank's activities in Haiti, and use plastic in the containers of Lush products. More recently, big companies such as Henkel and institutions such as the UN have partnered with the company The successful pursuit of many more large customers will be decisive for the business model of The Plastic Bank to be viable over time.

Social entrepreneurship involves using business tools to help solve societal and community-related problems. A defining feature of social entrepreneurship business models is that they primarily help solve a social or environmental problem, but that they use principles and tools from the business world (cf. Short et al. 2009). In this way, they align the desirable purposes of aid organizations and other non-profit organizations and the well-founded economic and organizational approaches that characterize modern companies. This can happen internally in established companies, as in the Norwegian outerwear company Stormberg, in which 25 percent of the workforce are people who are struggling to get into the labor market, for example, due to a history of drug problems and crime (Jørgensen and Pedersen 2015).

However, social entrepreneurship often takes place in smaller companies, in which the social dimension is at the core of the business model. This is, for instance, the case for Tyrili Climbing, for which Sveinung serves as the chair of the board. Tyrili is a facility that treats drugs addicts, but in Lillehammer, Norway, the organization also runs a climbing center—a commercial enterprise that sells climbing courses and climbing gear. Many people who use the climbing center are not aware that drug addicts in recovery largely run the center. The addicts learn how to run a company, they organize competitions and they serve as instructors for climbing students from the Norwegian College of Elite Sports. In this way, the organization creates value both for its own clients—the drug addicts—and for the many satisfied users of the center.

In Norway, the investment company Ferd and its owner Johan H. Andresen have actively promoted this type of social entrepreneurship. One of the companies in Ferd's portfolio is Monsterbedriften (Monsters Inc)—a social entrepreneur that conducts demolition services for the construction industry. In this company, most employees have a background from drug abuse and crime. Many social entrepreneurs are dedicated to bringing idle human resources back into productive activity, whether this includes former criminals, drug addicts or simply people who for various reasons have difficulty entering the labor market. In this way, social entrepreneurship also comprises a kind of circular thinking, in which excess and idle resources that have not been able to contribute to productive activity are brought back into the value chain (cf. Dentchev et al. 2016). This creates value both for the people who get to work and for the companies to which they offer their labor.

During a trip through Brazil in 2017, we encountered a unique social entrepreneurship business model that is based on a dual circular logic—it attempts to upcycle both human and natural resources. We were on foot through a colorful part of Rio de Janeiro called Lapa, when Refettorio Gastromotiva suddenly revealed itself to us. Originating from Milan, Italy, this social entrepreneur tries to solve two problems at the same time. At the core of its business model is the growing problem of poverty and hunger in Rio, tied to the substantial youth unemployment. The people behind Gastromotiva connected this to the problem of food waste in the more affluent parts of the city—from stores, restaurants and so on. Gastromotiva uses such discarded food close to its expiry date to cook three-course dinners for the poor in Lapa. "Why should they eat at a soup kitchen just because they are poor?", asked Mariana Vilhena Bittencourt, one of the managers at Gastromotiva. "And why shouldn't they eat at a beautiful location?" Gastromotiva's interior is indeed beautiful, and there are few complaints about the food—as one of Rio's leading chefs leads the kitchen every evening. Part of Gastromotiva's unique value proposition is that it has a rotation of top chefs cooking pro bono at the restaurant. Not only that, however—the chefs also contribute to Gastromotiva's in-house cooking school—another part of the value proposition, which is aimed at helping poor youth in Rio get jobs in the kitchens of hotels and restaurants in the city.

In this way, Gastromotiva contributes human and natural resources for societal benefit that would otherwise have gone astray. We were so inspired by our visit to this social entrepreneur that we set up an internship program for our business school students in Norway—allowing them to get hands-on experience contributing to build a sustainable business model for Gastromotiva. Currently, the company is funded by a set of global giants, including Coca-Cola and Carrefour. However, as Mariana pointed out to us on the busy day we visited the company: "We want to be self-sufficient. We want to build a sustainable business model that can survive and that we can scale." The company's quest to attain this is still ongoing, and their attempt to build a circular business model for this venture encapsules the challenge that many social entrepreneurs face.

The Circle is Not Closed

Ecoalf is just one of many companies that embrace the new, circular reality, and which has developed an ecosystem of partners that together offer products, services and jobs. Both research and anecdotal knowledge suggest that companies increasingly collaborate on green innovation projects, both with suppliers, NGOs, industrial networks, authorities and competitors. In this way, they try to find more sustainable solutions. One reason for this is that sustainability issues are complex and global in nature, and most companies realize that they cannot solve these problems on their own. Collaboration does not only happen among businesses—also consumers see that collaborative efforts can solve problems and lead to smarter consumption. Although we are slowly circling toward a more sustainable economy, much still remains before we have completely circular business models in place.

Not at least, many companies that aim to build circular and service-based business models using digital and knowledge-intensive technologies require a high degree of collaboration with stakeholders who can help with this expertise. The importance of such alliances to promote sustainable business is the topic of the next chapter.

References

Bocken, N. M., de Pauw, I., Bakker, C., & van der Grinten, B. (2016). Product design and business model strategies for a circular economy. *Journal of Industrial and Production Engineering, 33*(5), 308–320.

Dentchev, N., Baumgartner, R., Dieleman, H., Jóhannsdóttir, L., Jonker, J., Nyberg, T., & van Hoof, B. (2016). Embracing the variety of sustainable business models: Social entrepreneurship, corporate intrapreneurship, creativity, innovation, and other approaches to sustainability challenges. *Journal of Cleaner Production, 113*(1), 1–4.

Ellen MacArthur Foundation. (2015). *Growth within: A circular economy vision for a competitive Europe*. Cowes, UK: Ellen MacArthur Foundation.

Ellen MacArthur Foundation. (2017). *Beyond plastic waste*. Cowes, UK: Ellen MacArthur Foundation.

Harman, J. (2013). *The Shark's paintbrush: Biomimicry and how nature is inspiring innovation*. London: Nicholas Brealey Publishing.

Jørgensen, S., & Pedersen, L. J. T. (2015). *Responsible and profitable: Strategies for sustainable business models*. Oslo: Cappelen Damm Akademisk.

Jørgensen, S., & Pedersen, L. J. T. (2017). Towards smarter and more sustainable business models in retail. *Working paper*, NHH Norwegian School of Economics.

Jørgensen, S. & Pedersen, L.J.T. (2018). Towards smart and sustainable business models in retail. In N. Bocken, P. Ritala, L. Albareda, & R. Verburg (Eds.), *Innovation for sustainability: Business transformations towards a better world*. London: Palgrave (In press).

Lacy, P., & Rutqvist, J. (2015). *Waste to wealth: The circular economy advantage*. London: Palgrave.

Lieder, M., & Rashid, A. (2016). Towards circular economy implementation: A comprehensive review in context of manufacturing industry. *Journal of Cleaner Production, 115*, 36–51.

McDonough, W., & Braungart, M. (2010). *Cradle to cradle: Remaking the way we make things*. London: Macmillan.

McDonough, W., & Braungart, M. (2013). *The upcycle: Beyond sustainability—designing for abundance*. London: Macmillan.

Peredo, A. M., & McLean, M. (2006). Social entrepreneurship: A critical review of the concept. *Journal of World Business, 41*(1), 56–65.

Short, J. C., Moss, T. W., & Lumpkin, G. T. (2009). Research in social entrepreneurship: Past contributions and future opportunities. *Strategic Entrepreneurship Journal,* 3(2), 161–194.

Stahel, W. R. (2016). The circular economy. *Nature,* 531(7595), 435.

Webster, K. (2015). *The circular economy: A wealth of flows.* Coew, UK: Ellen MacArthur Foundation Publishing.

Open Access This chapter is licensed under the terms of the Creative Commons Attribution-NonCommercial-NoDerivatives 4.0 International License (http://creativecommons.org/licenses/by-nc-nd/4.0/), which permits any noncommercial use, sharing, distribution and reproduction in any medium or format, as long as you give appropriate credit to the original author(s) and the source, provide a link to the Creative Commons license and indicate if you modified the licensed material. You do not have permission under this license to share adapted material derived from this book or parts of it.

The images or other third party material in this chapter are included in the chapter's Creative Commons license, unless indicated otherwise in a credit line to the material. If material is not included in the chapter's Creative Commons license and your intended use is not permitted by statutory regulation or exceeds the permitted use, you will need to obtain permission directly from the copyright holder.

9

Alliances Rather than Solo-runs

No single organization can solve the big problems alone. Collaboration is therefore important for companies that want to develop sustainable and profitable solutions, and it is becoming more widespread, both within and across markets and sectors. To assess the sustainability efforts of companies properly, we must look at entire ecosystems of companies and their collaborative efforts for doing business more sustainably. Such collaboration requires that they are willing to open up their business models to each other and work together in ways that make the whole more than the sum of its constituent parts.

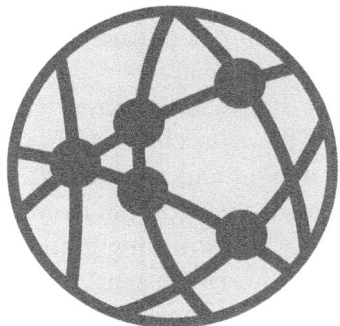

Fig. 9.1 Alliances Rather than Solo-runs

9.1 Unite and Collaborate!

The French car manufacturer Renault promotes itself with the slogan: "Recycle, Reuse, Renault". Renault is among the many companies collaborating with the Ellen MacArthur Foundation, which specializes in developing and implementing circular-economic solutions in companies. Circular-economic ideas are not new to Renault—the company actually began reusing engine parts in its cars already in 1949. Since then, the company has expanded the number of parts significantly. Currently, Renault works to redesign its business model to become more sustainable, which involves closing its value chain and implementing a circular business model. As part of this process, Renault has invested in new production facilities to move from a "take, make and dispose" model to a model of reuse and recycling. Moreover, the company has developed entirely new units that work to collect and process used parts for reuse. At Renault's plant in Choisy-le-Roi, near Paris, the company upcycles engines, transmissions and other components for resale. According to a report by McKinsey, this facility's recovery operations use 80 percent less energy, 90 percent less water and approximately 70 percent less oil and detergent waste, compared with the units that produce new components. The facility in Choisy-le-Roi also captures higher operating margins than does Renault overall (Fig. 9.1).

To attain these benefits, Renault has created joint ventures with several companies. Among them is a partner company that recycles steel and a recycling company that manages waste. Renault has established these alliances to access the resources, knowledge and competence of companies in this part of the value chain, so that it characterizes the way in which the company designs and produces cars. Renault collaborates with its suppliers to identify opportunities to create and distribute value along its entire value chain, thus making it attractive for other companies to join the collaboration. For instance, the company has helped a provider of cutting fluids to change its business model from a sales-based to a performance-based model. The change has led to a 90 percent reduction in waste from this supplier while reducing Renault's costs by 20 percent.

Between Competition and Collaboration

Researchers from MIT and a team from the Boston Consulting Group conduct an annual global survey in which they ask executives worldwide questions about sustainability-related issues. In 2015, the survey examined the role of collaboration in companies' sustainability efforts (see Kiron et al. 2015). While 90 percent of respondents believed that collaboration is necessary to become more sustainable, still less than 50 percent of companies say that they are actually engaging in such collaboration. This is perhaps embedded in the DNA of companies—they are intended to compete rather than to cooperate. Interestingly, there is increasing collaboration even between companies that are usually competitors (Brandenburger and Nalebuff 2011). Arguably, developing such collaborative willingness and competence will be important in trying to design more sustainable business models (see, e.g., Peloza and Falkenberg 2009).

As we have seen, Renault has made major changes in its business model to improve its sustainability performance and to attain the benefits of a circular economy. Not at least, the company has made changes in its organizational ecosystem, that is, its network of affiliated companies, including suppliers, distributors, customers, competitors, government agencies and so on. Successful alliances require investments, and such risky investments are not costless, even though the rewards can be big for those who succeed (cf. Das and Teng 2001). The challenge of collaboration is that it requires that different players with different objectives must come together and find mutually beneficial solutions. Collaboration also typically requires opening up the business model of the company and providing potential competitors with access to internal processes (see, e.g., Drechsler and Natter 2012). This is particularly true since such innovation projects often imply collaboration with companies that can simultaneously compete with the company in other markets.

It is naive to believe that such changes will take place without big and conscious efforts by the parties involved, especially since some of them will typically benefit more from the collaboration than will others. While barely 50 percent of companies report that they are collaborating on sustainability projects in the aforementioned survey, only about 60 percent thereof report being satisfied with their collaborations (Kiron et al. 2015). Meanwhile, alliances may be a virtue of necessity, especially for small- and medium-sized companies. However, large companies like Renault also have much to gain by solving problems together with others.

Companies are experts at solving problems profitably. However, they also create problems for society and the environment to varying degrees and in different ways. A car manufacturer solves the mobility problems of its customers, creates jobs, works to reduce emissions in line with regulations and customer expectations and pays taxes. The car manufacturer, however, also creates problems since cars pollute, people die in traffic, roads are clogged with ever more cars and large amounts of scarce resources are used to produce cars. A reasonable expectation must be that companies at least solve more problems than they create. In other words, they need to shed more light and less shadow and scale their solutions so that positive effects for the business, society and the environment increase.

The field of strategy devotes much attention to competition. The strategy literature has used metaphors from war and from "survival-of-the-fittest" biology. Moreover, its theories have focused on how companies can develop and leverage bargaining power to gain competitive advantage over suppliers, customers and other stakeholders. This knowledge is still important—a successful business model creates, delivers and captures value. However, a successful business model also involves collaboration with various stakeholders. As the father of stakeholder theory, R. Edward Freeman (1984) points out: a key role for leaders is to try to identify overlapping interests between the company and its stakeholders and to try to expand such overlap in a way that benefits both parties. The company can create greater value for customers, employees, suppliers and other stakeholders through collaboration, and it enables many types of innovation projects.

Above, we showed how Renault collaborates with a supplier of cutting fluids, which resulted in less reduced emissions and resource waste, and thus higher profitability for both partners. One could argue that companies compete to be the most attractive transaction partner, for example, in the market for skilled labor and vis-à-vis other important suppliers. It is easy to forget that companies must be attractive to all their transaction partners, and it is not sufficient to be an expert only at solving customers' problems. Companies do not necessarily attain profitable growth by being at war with their employees, suppliers, governments and other key stakeholders. It can therefore benefit companies to act as an ally, rather than as a competitor.

From Value Creation to Value Capture

In a simplified sense, we can compare value creation with baking a cake. Through collaboration in the supply chain, companies can improve their ability to satisfy the needs of both customers and suppliers. This would be the equivalent of baking a bigger cake. Customers who perceive the company as offering products and services that cater to their needs have better customer experiences and are therefore generally speaking willing to pay more for the products or services and to be more loyal. A supplier that perceives the company as more attractive to work with will perhaps be more willing to stretch to meet the company's needs. Employees may be willing to work more, be more loyal and even require less pay if they see the company as a great place to work (cf. Koys 2001; Harter et al. 2002; Frank 2004; Turban and Greening 1997). In addition, governments and regulators may be willing to invest in and facilitate education and infrastructure that benefit the company if they believe that the company creates considerable value to society and the environment. Collaboration can increase value creation for suppliers, companies, customers and other stakeholders, and thus the size of the cake increases as well. Companies that manage to build appropriate value-adding alliances can thereby improve their value capture by getting a slightly smaller piece of a much larger cake (Fig. 9.2).

Although alliances can increase the size of the proverbial cake of value creation, companies must of course also make sure to get a bargaining position that allows them to capture their fair share. Companies must

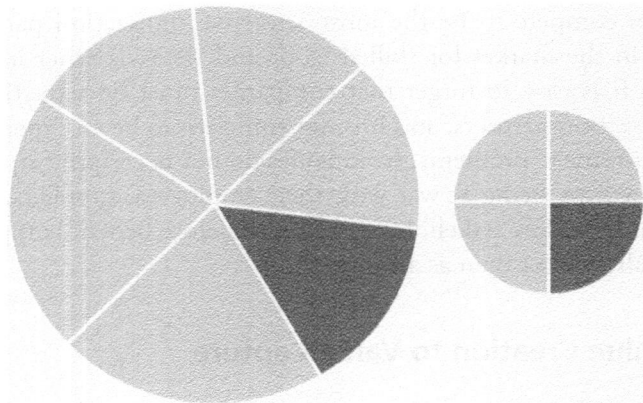

Fig. 9.2 A smaller part of a larger cake

therefore deal with a paradox: They must collaborate and compete at once. Managers face this reality continuously, regardless of whether sustainable business is the goal. When sustainability is part of the problem, however, it is perhaps even more important to collaborate since the complexity of the problems companies face requires complex competence, technology, inputs factors and other resources. This may require extensive alliances across both industry and sector boundaries.

9.2 Creating and Sharing Value

Who would have thought that it is possible to use the oil industry's surplus carbon dioxide (CO_2) to make fish feed? The innovative company CO2BIO does just that. By using CO_2 captured by the energy company Equinor at Mongstad in Norway, CO2BIO creates biomass that is rich in important Omega-3. There is a great shortage of Omega-3 in the oceans, and aquaculture completely relies on Omega-3 in its fish feed. This nutrient is also very important for the customers who eat the fish. At the same time, there is excess CO_2 in the atmosphere, and emissions from large companies exacerbate the problem. CO2BIO receives CO_2 free of charge from Equinor and leads it into a pipeline, wherein it grows algae. Water flows in the tubes, and the tubes are illuminated from all sides at all times, while water and CO_2 circulate in the pipes. In this way, algae grow and thus form the basis for the resulting fish feed that is rich in Omega-3. CO2BIO's business model helps solve two major problems at once: it reduces harmful greenhouse gases in the atmosphere while contributing nutritious fish feed for the aquaculture industry.

The technology used by CO2BIO is a type of biomimicry based on natural processes (see, e.g., Harman 2013). Currently, the project is still in the pilot stage. In other words, it is still an experimentation with new technology and a new business model. If CO2BIO manages to commercialize the product successfully, it can build a unique and advantageous business model. One of its main resources, CO_2, the company (for now) gets free of charge from Equinor's Mongstad operations. In the future, will perhaps companies with excess CO_2 emissions even pay CO2BIO to get rid of their emissions? On the customer side, the company may sell its product to companies in need of fish feed of high quality, which is an industry that is expected to grow significantly in the coming years. At the same time, however, various competitors using many different technologies are trying to capture this market with novel fish feed products.

CO2BIO would not have been able to implement this project on its own. Through cooperation and alliances with entities from the private and as public sectors as well as from academia and research institutions, the company has gained access to potential customers, knowledge, raw materials and capital. Interestingly, the parties in the alliance are also competitors in other markets. For instance, fish-farming companies like Marine Harvest, EWOS, Lerøy Seafood and Grieg Seafood are among the partners and shareholders of the project. In addition, various academic institutions such as the University of Bergen and UniResearch are central to the project.

There are several interesting characteristics of the CO2BIO business model related to how it aims to solve sustainability issues. Firstly, the business model is a collaborative model in which several organizations join forces to solve a problem that each of them could not successfully solve on their own. Secondly, one of the partners—Equinor, which provides the "raw material" of CO_2—helps to create parts of the problem that CO2BIO aims to solve. The project, after all, makes use of Equinor's

CO2 emissions. Rather than attempting to minimize its emissions problem by producing less, or otherwise reduce its emissions, Equinor thus finds a solution in a collaborative innovation project. The project turns Equinor's problem into a solution for another company. In order to solve the big problems we face, this kind of collaboration across organizational boundaries and business models will probably be necessary.

CO2BIO is located in a Norwegian industrial park, and the use of such parks for building circular collaborations has great potential and shows good results. This business model is often referred to as industrial symbiosis, and one of the most exciting examples in Europe is arguably the Danish industrial park Kalundborg Symbiosis. This industrial park was established already in 1959, but during the 1970s and 1980s, the first steps were taken toward making it into the eco-industrial park it is today. The concept behind Kalundborg Symbiosis is that waste and surplus resources from all companies are important inputs for other companies in the park. That is, the industrial park is based on a circular model, not for each individual company but for the park as a whole (see, e.g., Ehrenfeld and Gertler 1997; Jacobsen 2006). For instance, Gyproc uses the emissions from Dong Energy as input for making plasterboard; agricultural operators use the organic waste from Novozyme as fertilizer; and Asnæs Power Station uses excess water from Equinor's operations. In addition, excess energy from the industrial park generates heat and lighting for households in the vicinity of the industrial park, thus literally shedding light also on the nearby community. This symbiosis has also reduced Kalundborg's CO2 emissions by 275,000 tons a year and the saving and reuse of three million cubic meters of water every year.

The Company as a Coalition of Stakeholders

In our conversations with executives and other managers in companies, we often find that many of them are preoccupied with customers. This makes sense of course, and there is nothing wrong with being concerned with the company's customers. The company is after all reliant on them, seeing how they pay for the company's products and services. As we will see below, however, there are numerous other key stakeholders that also greatly affect companies' ability to align sustainability and profitability in their operations (see, e.g., Berman et al. 1999). In companies' work with an effective network strategy, it is therefore crucial to understand the interaction between companies and other stakeholders in its environment.

In an expanded view, companies can be seen as a coalition of stakeholders. Some of these stakeholders are formally transaction partners with the company, as customers, employees or other kinds of factor suppliers. Such partners provide something of value to the business—be it time, money or products and services—and they naturally expect something in return. Companies thus depend on them, and the dependence may be mutual. Other stakeholders are not in formal transactions with the company. Such entities are often called institutional (or external) stakeholders, and although they may not affect the company directly, they can still greatly affect the company indirectly, for example, by influencing the company's reputation. NGOs, media organizations, lobbyists and various opinion makers are examples of such stakeholders, which can influence the company's standing in the marketplace, without being in a formal relationship with the company at all (cf. Mitchell et al. 1997).

Figure 9.3 gives an overview of various key stakeholders in the corporate environment, and we have placed the company in the middle. The total scope of stakeholders that companies have to deal with may be even greater than what the figure captures. However, these key stakeholders are relevant for almost any organization and will influence its functioning and performance:

- Customers, who buy the company's products or services, whether they are end users (B2C) or other companies (B2B)
- Employees, who offer their competences and efforts to the company and the local community of which these employees often part
- Partners and competitors, which influence how successful the company's strategies are in the market through various interactions with the company
- Investors, who own the company and offer the necessary capital to finance its activities

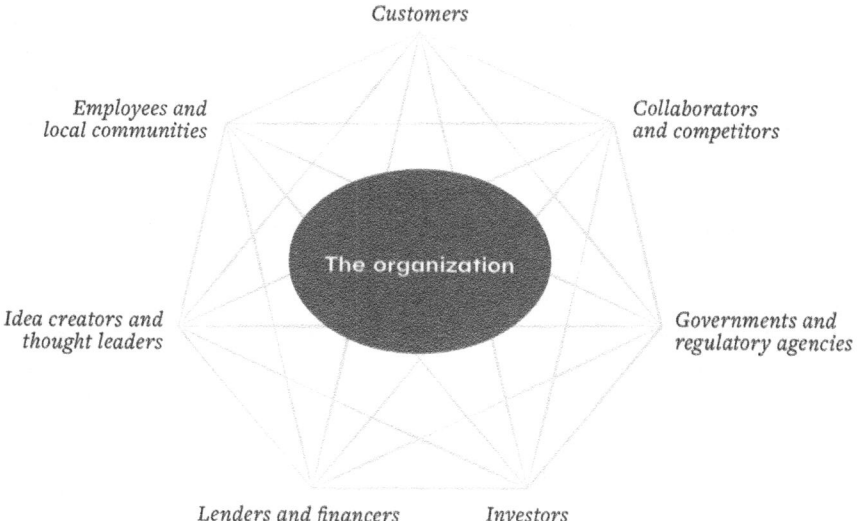

Fig. 9.3 The organization and its stakeholders

- Lenders, which cover short-term and long-term capital needs through loans
- Governments and regulatory agencies, which make and enforce laws and regulations relating to corporate activities
- NGOs, which speak the voice of the interests of society and the environment
- Idea generators and thought leaders, such as media and academic organizations, which create and spread ideas and beliefs that affect the company's reputation and performance.

Seeing the company as a coalition of stakeholders involves understanding it as an organism that depends on the support of key stakeholders contributing to its activities and to achieving its objectives. In different ways and to varying degrees, stakeholders influence the ability of the company to achieve these goals (Mitchell et al. 1997; Freeman 1984). In a stakeholder perspective, there may be at least two reasons to build stronger ties to such partners. The first, and most fundamental, is that partners may be important to the success of a project. CO2BIO has, for instance, probably been highly dependent on the research expertise of scientists in UniResearch, who have been involved in developing the technology that allows CO2BIO to develop its product. In addition, there is another reason to enter into alliances, namely, that it provides access to knowledge, technologies and insights to which the company might not otherwise had access (see, e.g., Mowery et al. 1996). When competitors like Marine Harvest, Lerøy Seafood and Grieg Seafood all join the CO2BIO alliance, this can also in part be because they see it as too risky to stand on the outside, in the event that the project becomes successful. There can thus be varied motives for entering an alliance or a joint innovation project (Varadarajan and Cunningham 1995). Different organizations will consequently enter with different levels of commitment and varying levels of gain from their participation, with respect to the goals they have set.

There is an ongoing trend in the direction of opening up companies and business models in more than one sense. So-called open innovation is increasingly prevalent, and such processes aim to drive innovation by drawing on external ideas, perspectives and voices (Chesbrough 2006). It may include letting customers influence product development, in the way that computer game developers and toy manufacturers like LEGO have done for a long time. It can also involve engaging in innovation projects in networks with other companies, research institutions and other actors, which in different ways can integrate in the project and benefit thereof. However, even in the design of companies' business models, companies are increasingly inclined to organize in ways that integrate other organizations in their value chains. This creates an interdependence between them that gives companies incentives to attend to each other's interests over time.

When Renault decides to go into joint ventures and long-term collaborations with companies from completely different industries, it reflects the fact that the company sees them as crucial for succeeding with a circular business model that can be profitable over time. Likewise, CO2BIO's business model would hardly have been possible without the fruitful interaction with organizations both upstream and downstream in its value chain, as well as knowledge partners who can contribute to the company's ambitious innovation project on which its business model is built. In sum, this is about finding new ways to create, deliver and capture value, both alone and in collaboration with others. In doing so, companies can achieve results they would not have achieved on their own. In the next topic, we turn to the challenge of prioritizing the right kinds of results.

References

Berman, S. L., Wicks, A. C., Kotha, S., & Jones, T. M. (1999). Does stakeholder orientation matter? The relationship between stakeholder management models and firm financial performance. *Academy of Management Journal, 42*(5), 488–506.
Brandenburger, A. M., & Nalebuff, B. J. (2011). *Co-opetition*. New York, NY: Crown Business.
Chesbrough, H. W. (2006). *Open innovation: The new imperative for creating and profiting from technology*. Cambridge, MA: Harvard Business Press.
Das, T. K., & Teng, B. S. (2001). Trust, control, and risk in strategic alliances: An integrated framework. *Organization Studies, 22*(2), 251–283.
Drechsler, W., & Natter, M. (2012). Understanding a firm's openness decisions in innovation. *Journal of Business Research, 65*(3), 438–445.
Ehrenfeld, J., & Gertler, N. (1997). Industrial ecology in practice: The evolution of interdependence at Kalundborg. *Journal of Industrial Ecology, 1*(1), 67–79.
Frank, R. H. (2004). *What price the moral high ground? How to succeed without selling your soul*. Princeton, NJ: Princeton University Press.
Freeman, R. E. (1984). *Strategic management: A stakeholder approach*. Boston, MA: Pitman.
Harman, J. (2013). *The Shark's paintbrush: Biomimicry and how nature is inspiring innovation*. London: Nicholas Brealey Publishing.
Harter, J. K., Schmidt, F. L., & Hayes, T. L. (2002). Business-unit-level relationship between employee satisfaction, employee engagement, and business outcomes: A meta-analysis. *Journal of Applied Psychology, 87*(2), 268.
Jacobsen, N. B. (2006). Industrial symbiosis in Kalundborg, Denmark: A quantitative assessment of economic and environmental aspects. *Journal of Industrial Ecology, 10*(1–2), 239–255.
Kiron, D., Kruschwitz, N., Haanaes, K., Reeves, M., Fuisz-Kehrbach, S. K., & Kell, G. (2015). Joining forces: Collaboration and leadership for sustainability. *MIT Sloan Management Review, 56*(3), 1–31.

Koys, D. J. (2001). The effects of employee satisfaction, organizational citizenship behavior, and turnover on organizational effectiveness: A unit-level, longitudinal study. *Personnel Psychology, 54*(1), 101–114.

Mitchell, R. K., Agle, B. R., & Wood, D. J. (1997). Toward a theory of stakeholder identification and salience: Defining the principle of who and what really counts. *Academy of Management Review, 22*(4), 853–886.

Mowery, D. C., Oxley, J. E., & Silverman, B. S. (1996). Strategic alliances and interfirm knowledge transfer. *Strategic Management Journal, 17*(S2), 77–91.

Peloza, J., & Falkenberg, L. (2009). The role of collaboration in achieving corporate social responsibility objectives. *California Management Review, 51*(3), 95–113.

Turban, D. B., & Greening, D. W. (1997). Corporate social performance and organizational attractiveness to prospective employees. *Academy of Management Journal, 40*(3), 658–672.

Varadarajan, P. R., & Cunningham, M. H. (1995). Strategic alliances: A synthesis of conceptual foundations. *Journal of the Academy of Marketing Science, 23*(4), 282.

Open Access This chapter is licensed under the terms of the Creative Commons Attribution-NonCommercial-NoDerivatives 4.0 International License (http://creativecommons.org/licenses/by-nc-nd/4.0/), which permits any noncommercial use, sharing, distribution and reproduction in any medium or format, as long as you give appropriate credit to the original author(s) and the source, provide a link to the Creative Commons license and indicate if you modified the licensed material. You do not have permission under this license to share adapted material derived from this book or parts of it.

The images or other third party material in this chapter are included in the chapter's Creative Commons license, unless indicated otherwise in a credit line to the material. If material is not included in the chapter's Creative Commons license and your intended use is not permitted by statutory regulation or exceeds the permitted use, you will need to obtain permission directly from the copyright holder.

10

Results Rather than Indulgences

The important thing is to solve the problems we face—not who does it or what looks good. In order to address the important issues properly, prioritization is key. This means giving priority to material sustainability issues, which in turn requires fruitful communication with the company's stakeholders in a way that convinces them that the company is taking appropriate and effective steps toward more sustainable business models.

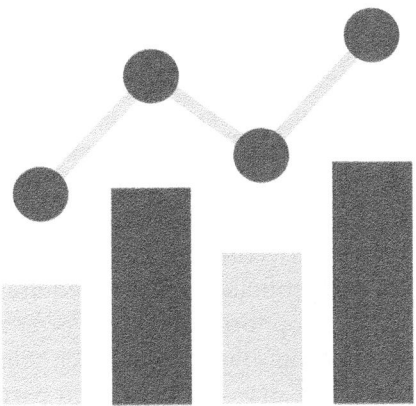

Fig. 10.1 Results Rather than Indulgences

10.1 With an Eye on the Ball

Do you buy ugly food? Every year, citizens in the European Union throw more than 88 million tons of food that could have been eaten, which is equivalent to more than 170 kg per person (Stenmarck et al. 2016) (Fig. 10.1).

By some estimates, we throw away approximately 42 percent of all the food we buy, and the greenhouse gas emissions, water consumption and the overall environmental impact associated with food production are enormous. Food waste is a global problem, and in response to this problem, the French retail chain Intermarché initiated the campaign "Inglorious Fruits and Vegetables". It started selling smoothies made of misshapen fruit and vegetables, accompanied by colorful and eye-catching posters depicting the weird ingredients. Customers liked the taste as well as the idea, and the company consequently developed the concept further so that customers were offered the "ugly" fruits in the store at a 30 percent discount. During the first two days alone, Intermarché sold tons of ugly fruit and vegetables, and the campaign received great attention worldwide.

Through this clever campaign, Intermarché succeeded with several things at once: It managed to change customers' ingrained habit of steering away from ugly food products. It managed to reduce food waste in its stores. Thus, it also reduced its costs related to managing food waste and, instead, sold the products at a lower, but still acceptable, price. Not at least, it received considerable positive publicity and attention around the campaign and its message.

Intermarché turned the problem on its head when it began to promote and sell products with imperfections. If companies are to succeed with aligning sustainability and profitability, it will require also looking at the sustainability problem as an opportunity (e.g., Porter and Kramer 2011). This may allow for developing solutions and technologies that can solve problems the company itself may not have been part of creating in the first place. Newlight did this when it realized that it could use excess CO_2 in the atmosphere to produce plastic. Interface did it when it addressed its own shadow and changed its production processes in a way that also reduced costs. Norsk Gjenvinning did it when it conducted an extensive turnaround and cleanup in its own backyard, to get rid of the troubled conditions in its supply chain.

In the last few decades, the majority of companies around the world have put corporate social responsibility (CSR) on their agenda. Part of the criticism directed against the CSR phenomenon is that it has often been about acting in ways that look good or that give stakeholders what they ask for (see, e.g., Visser 2011). This is not always the same as implementing impactful changes in business models to promote social and environmental performance (Eccles and Serafeim 2013). In particular, there has been considerable conflation between CSR initiatives that actually relate to the company's core business and those that are more peripheral, such as various types of philanthropy (e.g., Burke and Logsdon 1996). For companies that are committed to creating real change and that aim to align sustainability and profitability, it is essential that sustainability efforts are oriented to creating the right kind of results, rather than being a form of indulgence that does not really influence the business model (Khan et al. 2016).

The Road to Being Sustainable and Profitable

Much research has been conducted on the question of how to align sustainability and profitability (see, e.g., Khan et al. 2016; Kang et al. 2016; Eccles et al. 2015; Flammer 2015; Edmans 2011; Margolis et al. 2007; Orlitzky et al. 2003; Waddock and Graves 1997). However, a fundamental problem is that this stream of research often compares apples and oranges. First, many studies disregard the distinction between efforts aimed at promoting corporate social and environmental performance in ways that are tied to core business and efforts that are more peripheral to the company's strategy and operations (cf. Khan et al. 2016). Second, many studies have failed to distinguish between the types of efforts and practices that characterize companies that succeed in becoming more sustainable and those that do not.

We previously mentioned a study conducted by Robert G. Eccles and his colleagues (Eccles et al. 2014), which sheds light on the relationship between sustainability and profitability. The study builds on previous research, which has suggested a small but positive difference between more and less sustainable (or responsible) companies and that investments in sustainability have a positive but diminishing effect on financial performance. The study by Eccles and his colleagues is perhaps the single study that so far has presented the strongest evidence for a positive relationship between sustainability and profitability. Moreover, it reveals the organizational characteristics of these companies that set them apart from others. To dig deeper into the underlying mechanisms of the relationship between sustainability performance and financial performance, it is important to have insight into the efforts and practices that companies can employ in practice. Let us take a closer look at them.

Simply put, achieving profitability involves increasing revenues, reducing costs or both. By extension, this applies to the relationship between sustainability and profitability. For sustainability efforts to pay off, they must affect the company's bottom line by influencing revenues and costs directly and/or indirectly. Some efforts have a direct effect on the bottom line, for example, when Intermarché manages to sell ugly fruits and vegetables that the company would otherwise have had to pay to dispose of. Other efforts have a more indirect impact on the company's performance. For example, this is the case if competent workers choose Intermarché as an employer because of the positive attention to the campaign, and that Intermarché in turn uses this expertise to perform better. In Fig. 10.2, we show various effects of this type. We distinguish between efforts influencing the upside positively and efforts that reduce the downside. Furthermore, we distinguish between efforts that have a direct influence and those that have an indirect influence on the company's performance.

Figure 10.2 illustrates how sustainability efforts can promote profitability by contributing to higher revenues and/or lower costs. We denote the indirect upside intangible assets, and it shows that sustainable companies, for example, can improve their reputation and increase trust and

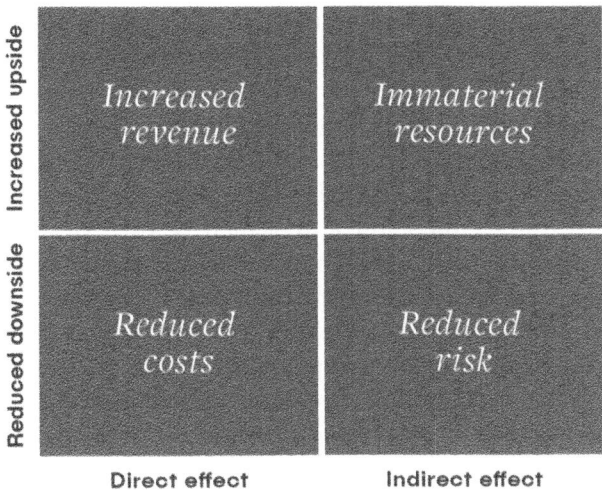

Fig. 10.2 How sustainability influences the company's performance (based on Esty and Winston 2009)

confidence among its key stakeholders, which in turn may translate into better performance. Sustainability efforts can influence the indirect downside by potentially reducing the company's risk, which can lead investors or lenders to give favorable financing conditions. This can, for instance, be due to a more circular business model that reduces the company's supply risk for key resources and input factors.

These four effects—higher revenues, lower costs, increased access to intellectual resources and reduced risk—may perhaps not belong in distinct categories. A better reputation can influence customers' inclinations positively and reduced risk could lead to lower interest rates on loans, thereby reducing costs in the short term. However, by differentiating between upside and downside effects, and between direct and indirect effects, it becomes easier for decision makers to see how investments in sustainability may also have effects beyond direct influence in the short term. Presumably, the most important effects will emerge over time—for example, increased trust could in turn make a company more attractive to collaborators, employees, investors and other stakeholders (Jørgensen et al. 2018).

Intermarché has reaped several of the benefits mentioned above. After the launch of the ugly fruit and vegetables campaign, the company experienced both an increase in the upside effects and a reduction in the downside effects. Ugly food became surprisingly popular with customers, and perhaps the most important effect was the massive media coverage worldwide. This also led supermarkets on several other continents to imitate the campaign, which in turn gave Intermarché even more attention. From a pure cost perspective, Intermarché reduced its costs associated with food waste and waste management. Finally, it succeeded in selling products that would otherwise end up in landfills, and, by its own account, the company claims that the number of customers in its stores increased by almost 25 percent in this period. However, perhaps the most striking consequence of the campaign—not at least in a sustainability performance perspective—is that the company has been successful in changing consumer behavior: While customers were previously not willing to eat ugly food, Intermarché found a clever way to stimulate greener consumption habits among its customers. This is a powerful opportunity for companies, and such mechanisms can obviously be used to encourage more sustainable consumption (see, e.g., Lehner et al. 2016).

The ugly food of Intermarché is a clear example of how sustainability efforts—in this case, reduced food waste—may cause financially advantageous consequences for a company. Such "low-hanging fruit" (!) cannot necessarily be found in all industries, but companies in any industry should be able to identify some opportunities to align sustainability and profitability in their operations. As the story of Intermarché shows, there are some important steps on the road to aligning sustainability and profitability. First, to identify material sustainability problems in the current business model: What types of light and shadow does the company cast through its current operations? Second, to map the stakeholders in the company's surroundings on which it depends. Which interests are at stake and which of them must be taken into account in the design of the business model? And finally, to find ways of assigning resources to sustainability efforts that are valued by stakeholders in such a way that they either directly or indirectly affect the company's revenue, costs, intangible resources or risk in a desirable manner. The process we describe here, however, can become costly if the company does not prioritize in a fruitful way. A characteristic of the most successful companies is that they are able to prioritize in appropriate ways in their sustainability efforts, which we will consider in the following.

10.2   Prioritize What Matters

How do you know if the resources you have allocated to sustainability efforts lead you toward the goals you have set?

We live in a globalized world, but some companies are more global than are others. Every single day, more than 2.5 billion people around the world use one of Unilever's products. If you have a cup of Lipton tea, wash your hands with Dove soap, cleanse your ears with Q-tips or treat yourself to a bowl of ice cream from Ben & Jerry, you have used one of Unilever's many brands. This company is almost as present in American supermarkets as in small local markets in Southeast Asia. Unilever has set a goal of improving the health, diet and nutrition of one billion people by the year 2020. The company also stated a very ambitious target to halve the environmental impact of its products. It thus aims to succeed with so-called green growth, which implies increasing productivity and solving social issues while reducing its environmental impact. These objectives are embodied in Unilever's corporate strategy, which is named the "Sustainable Living Plan".

Dedicated work lies behind this strategy, whereby Unilever systematically considers which problems to solve, for whom and why. In these analyses, Unilever maps what is important both for its own profitability and for the interests of its stakeholders. Such analyses are often called materiality assessments. To assess materiality involves identifying salient social and environmental issues that the company faces and prioritizing them with regard to their importance from economic, social and environmental standpoints. The key is therefore to draw awareness to the issues that are so important that they cannot be ignored and that can influence the decisions of the company's stakeholders (see, e.g., Eccles et al. 2012). Investors make the decision of whether to invest in the company; customers decide whether to buy the company's products and services; employees decide if they want to work for the company and so on. Generally, companies must take great care in addressing material sustainability issues, while they may place less emphasis on those that are less material (Khan et al. 2016). This may seem like a trivial point but, in practice, many companies prioritize sustainability efforts that relate to core business to a very low degree. Instead, they may imitate other companies' sustainability efforts regardless of their relevance and salience for the company's business model or choose to focus on "low-hanging fruit" with little impact. Figure 10.3 illustrates what a materiality assessment looks like, with issues that are important for stakeholders on one axis and those that are important for the company on the other.

As shown in the figure, such an analysis makes it is possible to rank and prioritize sustainability issues. In the bottom left corner, we find

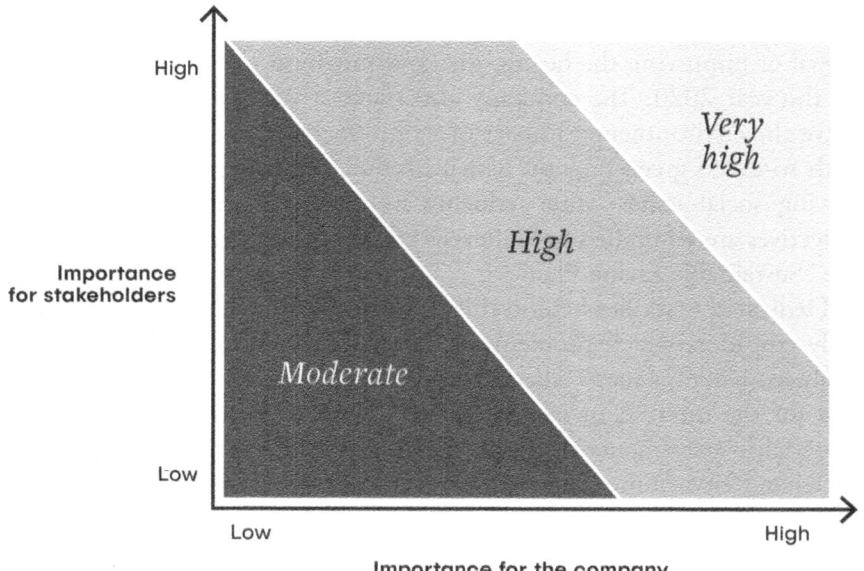

Fig. 10.3 Which issues are material—for the company and for its stakeholders?

moderately important sustainability issues. Issues further up and to the right in the diagram are gradually more important, and companies will typically try to prioritize issues that are ranked as high or very high. Such an analysis is not about asking whether improving sustainability performance makes companies become more profitable but about what kinds of sustainability efforts that may promote profitability. The first question is which efforts should be undertaken. The second question is how to know whether the resources allocated to sustainability efforts lead toward attaining the goals set by the company and if stakeholders appreciate the efforts.

It should be noted that the company and its stakeholders might have different perceptions of the reality of sustainability issues facing the company. For example, there is apparently still widespread fear of antibiotics in farmed salmon among the customers of such products. Numbers put forward by fish-farming companies, however, suggest that antibiotics are largely eradicated in farmed fish and have been for a long time, while problems such as fish lice and escapes from fish farms are considerably more urgent sustainability issues to address. Seen from the companies' perspective, then, its customers are perhaps worried about the wrong problems and should instead demand that companies address problems like fish lice and fish escape. This also suggests how working with materiality assessments can be valuable for other reasons than prioritization. The case of antibiotics in fish farming suggests that the fish-farming companies have not succeeded in communicating to customers that the antibiotics problem is largely resolved. Thus, they can take further steps to inform customers about this, for the benefit of both parties.

Unilever uses materiality assessments extensively. In its corporate strategy, Unilever has identified 191 issues, such as animal welfare, workers' pay and greenhouse gas emissions. These issues are distributed within 38 topics, such as climate change and fair trade. The 38 subjects are moreover distributed across five major focus areas: (1) improving health and well-being, (2) reducing environmental impact, (3) enhancing livelihoods, (4) responsible business practices and (5) wider sustainability topics. Within each of these five focus areas, the company can prioritize the issues that will likely lead to the most desirable results by solving problems with which stakeholders are concerned and that are to the benefit of the company.

Is It Profitable to Solve the Most Important Problems?

You might ask if materiality analyses are worthwhile conducting. An interesting study conducted by a group of Harvard researchers led by George Serafeim shows that such analyses may have substantial value (see Khan et al. 2016). The study digs deeper into what kind of sustainability efforts promote financial performance by differentiating between more and less material sustainability issues. The study categorizes the sustainability efforts of a wide range of companies in accordance with a materiality assessment based on the Sustainability Accounting Standards Board (SASB) standards. This enables the researchers to compare companies with respect to their priorities based on materiality and assess how these priorities in turn influence financial performance. The study reveals that the key is to allocate resources strictly to sustainability efforts that relate to material sustainability issues.

This implies that companies that invest in solving material sustainability issues experience greater positive financial performance effects than do both those that do not make such investment and those that invest in solving both material and immaterial issues. This has two aspects: First, it shows that solving the actual problems that influence stakeholder interests is what is rewarded in the market. Second, it shows that the amount of resources allocated to sustainability efforts is not the key. Rather, what matters is how these funds are actually used. There are many good intentions in dealing with social and environmental issues, but to solve the actual problems, resources must be used in a focused and smart manner on the material issues. Moreover, in order to identify and manage these problems, it is necessary that the company constantly monitors and engages with stakeholders and strictly prioritizes the most material issues.

An example of a company using materiality assessments in this way is Aker BioMarine, a Norwegian biotech innovator and Antarctic krill-harvesting company with a global presence. The company is the world's leading supplier of krill products, which are Omega-3-rich and used for human and animal nutrition purposes. The company has worked with integrating sustainability into the company's business model, and materiality assessments were central to this work. The basis for the sustainability strategies, however, were the UN Sustainable Development Goals (SDGs). The company selected four of the 17 SDGs as its strategic priorities:

- End hunger, achieve food security and improved nutrition and promote sustainable agriculture
- Ensure healthy lives and promote well-being for all at all ages
- Ensure sustainable consumption and production patterns
- Conserve and sustainably use the oceans, seas and marine resources for sustainable development

The selection of these goals as strategic priorities thus gave the company, and its sustainability director Cilia Holmes Indahl, further direction in the assessment of material sustainability concerns that allowed for integrating appropriate sustainability efforts into the business model of the company, in a way that aligned financial and sustainability-related objectives.

Let Sustainable Business Flourish!

For sustainability efforts to promote corporate financial performance, they must lead to two things at once. On the one hand, they must help the company cast less shadow and/or shed more light, whether because the company reduces its own externalities, or because it helps other companies reduce theirs. On the other hand, they must promote the company's financial performance by directly or indirectly increasing revenues or reducing costs in the shorter or longer term.

There are several ways companies can succeed with this. First, a company can offer new or improved types of value to its customers, which may lead customers to prefer its products or services. Second, the company can attract resources that would otherwise not have been available to it, such as employees, investors or partners who are attracted by the company's sustainability profile. Third, the company's sustainability efforts can render it able to perform value-adding activities that it could otherwise not have carried out, which can be a consequence of attracting new and valuable resources or partners. Fourth, the company can take advantage of opportunities in product markets that otherwise would have been inaccessible, for example, by attaining a position in the market or a reputation that makes the company more competitive. This all involves expanding the opportunity space of the company to the extent that well-designed sustainability efforts can lead to the company to exploit new business opportunities or enhance its position for exploiting existing business opportunities.

There are numerous scientific studies that support such mechanisms and that suggest that more sustainable companies can achieve unique competitive advantages. First, highly qualified employees are increasingly attracted to companies they perceive to be more sustainable, and they are often even willing to work for relatively lower wages (see, e.g., Koys 2001; Harter et al. 2002; Frank 2004; Turban and Greening 1997). Other studies show that the responsible companies have fewer capital constraints (Cheng et al. 2014). This is interesting in the context of how financial markets are developing, for instance, as one of China's largest banks is now screening all corporate loan applications for climate risk. Furthermore, there is research showing that customers—whether they are companies or individuals—are more trusting toward companies they deem responsible, which in turn may promote economic activity and reduce transaction costs (Zsolnai 2004; Jørgensen et al. 2018; see also Bartling et al. 2013). In some product and service categories, customers prefer companies they perceive as being responsible, and under some circumstances may be more loyal to these companies (see, e.g., Sen and Bhattacharya 2001; McWilliams and Siegel 2000; Bollen 2007). A stronger stakeholder orientation is moreover associated with being more innovative (Flammer and Kacperczyk 2015).

In addition to this, companies that are in extensive contact with its stakeholders may develop greater capacity to absorb market changes at an early stage. This may in turn help promote their ability to innovate, and recent research suggests that there is a positive correlation between stakeholder engagement and innovation (Flammer and Kacperczyk 2016). A final driver for investment in sustainability is the expectation of future regulations. For companies that proactively and voluntarily reduce their shadows, there may be a first-mover advantage in the event of future regulations (cf. Nehrt 1998). These are all mechanisms through which sustainability efforts directly or indirectly may promote companies' financial performance. It should be noted that there are also several studies that indicate that these effects are smaller and even negligible. However, the conclusions depend highly on what is measured and what time horizon is assumed.

Whether you make an optimistic or more moderate estimate of the potential positive effects of sustainability efforts for companies, emphasizing results rather than indulgences and prioritizing material issues are both essential for companies that take sustainability seriously. What the knowledge about sustainability efforts and the consequences thereof also suggests is that companies should better adapt their efforts in line with what they are trying to achieve and for whom. This begs the question: What do the drivers of sustainability efforts imply for how to design the efforts?

To answer this question, it may be useful to distinguish between "push" and "pull" factors for companies' investments in sustainability efforts. These factors, respectively, reflect the negative aspects of the current business model, which "push" the company toward more sustainable solutions, and the positive aspects of an alternative, more sustainable business model, which are attractive enough to "pull" the company toward change. In Table 10.1, we distinguish between these two types of factors that can act as drivers of sustainability efforts. In addition, we provide examples of such forces, respectively, associated with product markets, factor markets, capital markets, the regulatory environment and the socio-cultural environment (see also Horbach et al. 2012).

As the overview shows, there may be many factors driving the company toward becoming more sustainable. How a company prioritizes in order to achieve desired results will be a function of the kind of company it is. For example, some companies will be more influenced by trends for sustainable lifestyles, as is the case within the food industry and in mobility services. Similarly, some companies, such as financial institutions and aquaculture companies, are significantly more exposed to regulations. In addition, some companies will benefit more from technological innovations that make it easier to make their business model more sustainable, such as companies that can use 3D printers to reduce the need for transportation in their supply chains.

Table 10.1 "Push" and "pull" factors in sustainable business model innovations

	"Push" factors	"Pull" factors
The product market	Competitors offer attractive products and services that are more sustainable.	Customers demand more sustainable solutions. Opportunity to differentiate.
The factor market	Key inputs become scarcer and thus more expensive. Demands from partners.	Highly qualified employees are attracted by the more sustainable companies. New technologies make it easier and less costly to become more sustainable.
The capital market	Requirements of owners and lenders.	Attracting long-term investors with an aversion to sustainability risk.
The regulatory environment	Threat of stricter regulations or taxation.	Achieving first-mover advantage by setting the sustainability standard in the industry.
The socio-cultural environment	Pressure from key stakeholder groups, thought leaders, and so on.	Trends for more sustainable lifestyles.

These drivers will to varying degrees influence different sectors and at different times. For example, considerable stakeholder pressures and demands from customers drove big food producers to remove palm oil from their products around 2014. In Norway, the retail company Norgesgruppen argued publicly for stricter environmental regulations of Norwegian companies. This was probably, in addition to a desire for a greener economy, also done in the knowledge that it would give the company a first-mover advantage vis-à-vis its competitors. After all, Norgesgruppen had already made substantial investments to become more sustainable. In addition, the diffusion of better and cheaper solar panels has made it easier for companies in sunny areas to utilize this technology to replace a portion of their energy consumption with renewable energy. How many of the factors in Table 10.1 are applicable for the individual company, and how strong they are, will influence which sustainability issues the company prioritizes and the kinds of efforts it in turn implements. This will also be crucial for the company's ability to align sustainability and profitability over time.

Unilever is present worldwide, and the same is true for its sustainability efforts. The company provides poor customers in Southeast Asia with access to hygiene products using decentralized sales networks in cooperation with local entrepreneurs. Unilever also initiates large water conservation and reuse measures, which it attempts to scale throughout its entire value chain. Moreover, the company transitions toward more sustainable forms of soy production in Latin America, where such production has been very ecologically harmful for a long time. Common to all the major and minor efforts implemented by Unilever, along its many value chains worldwide, is that the company has assessed the sustainability issues with regard to their materiality. Based on this, the company prioritizes the initiatives that have the greatest possible value along three dimensions: economic, social and environmental performance (cf. Elkington 1997). By doing so, the company strengthens its ability to be sustainable and profitable over time.

References

Bartling, B., Fehr, E., & Huffman, D. (2013). Institutions and trust: Does trust generate lasting improvements in economic outcomes? *Working paper*, The University of Zürich, Zürich.

Bollen, N. P. (2007). Mutual fund attributes and investor behavior. *Journal of Financial and Quantitative Analysis, 42*(3), 683–708.

Cheng, B., Ioannou, I., & Serafeim, G. (2014). Corporate social responsibility and access to finance. *Strategic Management Journal, 35*(1), 1–23.

Eccles, R. G., Ioannou, I., & Serafeim, G. (2014). The impact of corporate sustainability on organizational processes and performance. *Management Science, 60*(11), 2835–2857.

Eccles, R. G., Krzus, M. P., Rogers, J., & Serafeim, G. (2012). The need for sector-specific materiality and sustainability reporting standards. *Journal of Applied Corporate Finance, 24*(2), 65–71.

Eccles, R. G., & Serafeim, G. (2013). The performance frontier. *Harvard Business Review, 91*(5), 50–60.

Elkington, J. (1997). *Cannibals with forks. The triple bottom line of 21st century*. Oxford: Capstone.

Esty, D., & Winston, A. (2009). *Green to gold: How smart companies use environmental strategy to innovate, create value, and build competitive advantage.* London: John Wiley & Sons.

Flammer, C. (2015). Does corporate social responsibility lead to superior financial performance? A regression discontinuity approach. *Management Science, 61*(11), 2549–2568.

Flammer, C., & Kacperczyk, A. (2015). The impact of stakeholder orientation on innovation: Evidence from a natural experiment. *Management Science, 62*(7), 1982–2001.

Frank, R. H. (2004). *What price the moral high ground? How to succeed without selling your soul.* Princeton, NJ: Princeton University Press.

Harter, J. K., Schmidt, F. L., & Hayes, T. L. (2002). Business-unit-level relationship between employee satisfaction, employee engagement, and business outcomes: A meta-analysis. *Journal of Applied Psychology, 87*(2), 268.

Horbach, J., Rammer, C., & Rennings, K. (2012). Determinants of eco-innovations by type of environmental impact—The role of regulatory push/pull, technology push and market pull. *Ecological Economics, 78*, 112–122.

Jørgensen, S., Pedersen, L. J. T., & Skard, S. (2018). Does going green build trust? The relationship between sustainability efforts, perceived innovativeness and trust. *Working paper*, NHH Norwegian School of Economics.

Kang, C., Germann, F., & Grewal, R. (2016). Washing away your sins? Corporate social responsibility, corporate social irresponsibility, and firm performance. *Journal of Marketing, 80*(2), 59–79.

Koys, D. J. (2001). The effects of employee satisfaction, organizational citizenship behavior, and turnover on organizational effectiveness: A unit-level, longitudinal study. *Personnel Psychology, 54*(1), 101–114.

Lehner, M., Mont, O., & Heiskanen, E. (2016). Nudging—A promising tool for sustainable consumption behaviour? *Journal of Cleaner Production, 134*, 166–177.

Margolis, J. D., Elfenbein, H. A., & Walsh, J. P. (2007). Does it pay to be good? A meta-analysis and redirection of research on the relationship between corporate social and financial performance. Ann Arbor, 1001, 48109-1234.

Nehrt, C. (1998). Maintainability of first mover advantages when environmental regulations differ between countries. *Academy of Management Review, 23*(1), 77–97.

Orlitzky, M., Schmidt, F. L., & Rynes, S. L. (2003). Corporate social and financial performance: A meta-analysis. *Organization Studies, 24*(3), 403–441.

Sen, S., & Bhattacharya, C. B. (2001). Does doing good always lead to doing better? Consumer reactions to corporate social responsibility. *Journal of Marketing Research, 38*(2), 225–243.

Stenmarck, A., Jensen, C., Quested, T., Moates, G., Buksti, M., Cseh, B., & Scherhaufer, S. (2016). *Estimates of European food waste levels*. IVL Swedish Environmental Research Institute.

Turban, D. B., & Greening, D. W. (1997). Corporate social performance and organizational attractiveness to prospective employees. *Academy of Management Journal, 40*(3), 658–672.

Visser, W. (2011). *The age of responsibility: CSR 2.0 and the new DNA of business*. Hoboken, NJ: John Wiley & Sons.

Waddock, S. A., & Graves, S. B. (1997). The corporate social performance-financial performance link. *Strategic Management Journal, 18*(4), 303–319.

Zsolnai, L. (2004). Honesty and trust in economic relationships. *Management Research News, 27*(7), 57–62.

Open Access This chapter is licensed under the terms of the Creative Commons Attribution-NonCommercial-NoDerivatives 4.0 International License (http://creativecommons.org/licenses/by-nc-nd/4.0/), which permits any noncommercial use, sharing, distribution and reproduction in any medium or format, as long as you give appropriate credit to the original author(s) and the source, provide a link to the Creative Commons license and indicate if you modified the licensed material. You do not have permission under this license to share adapted material derived from this book or parts of it.

The images or other third party material in this chapter are included in the chapter's Creative Commons license, unless indicated otherwise in a credit line to the material. If material is not included in the chapter's Creative Commons license and your intended use is not permitted by statutory regulation or exceeds the permitted use, you will need to obtain permission directly from the copyright holder.

11

Three-Dimensionality Rather than One-Dimensionality

The bottom line is becoming three-dimensional. To achieve such results, the entire organization must be designed in a way that renders the company able to become sustainable and profitable. This requires setting the right objectives socially, environmentally and financially; it requires measuring and monitoring the right things and communicating them to those who need the information. Not at least, it requires rewarding individuals, groups and entities who are able to help the company become more sustainable. In such a way, the company can be designed to pull powerfully and consistently in the right direction.

Fig. 11.1 Three-dimensionality Rather than One-dimensionality

11.1 Take the Lead

Could you imagine dying on Mars? Elon Musk, the CEO of Tesla and SpaceX, has stated that he would like to do so. He has also said that if something is important enough to die for, you should pursue it. And with his recent high-profile effort to send a car spiraling into space, with a sign that says "Don't panic!" and David Bowie's "Space Oddity" playing on an endless loop on the stereo, Musk indeed appears to be successfully exploring space (Fig. 11.1).

A group of engineers founded Tesla in Silicon Valley in 2003 to prove that electric vehicles could outperform cars with combustion engines. The company has since revolutionized the automotive industry with its electric vehicles and has already innovated its business model so comprehensively that it has become something more than an ordinary car manufacturer.

Tesla produces and sells more and more cars, and it develops new models—most recently, it has made public its intention to produce a Tesla truck. The company's objective is to make cars gradually cheaper, so that Tesla in turn can realize its vision: to accelerate the world's transition to sustainable transportation. One of Musk's many ideas is the concept he calls the hyperloop. The hyperloop is comparable to a pneumatic tube, and supposedly allows for people being transported in velocity up to 1220 km/h. Musk and the engineers in one of his companies prepared and described this concept in a 57-page design document, which they distribute freely to anyone who is interested. Hyperloop Technologies is now working to realize the project, and it hopes to commercialize the concept around 2020.

Musk, who was also one of the founders of PayPal, started work on the project SpaceX already at the turn of the century. SpaceX develops, manufactures, sells and launches aerospace equipment. The company aims to enable people to live on other planets—hence Musk's desire to live (and die) on Mars. Musk is also one of the founders of the rapidly growing company SolarCity—the second largest supplier of solar power in the United States. Musk has revealed that he plans to integrate the business models of Tesla and SolarCity in order to tie together the companies' mobility services and energy solutions. Importantly, however, Musk must ensure the economic viability of his various ventures, as at the time of writing, many analysts ponder whether Tesla will indeed be able to survive financially.

Like many other prominent CEOs, Musk is also chairman of a foundation. The Musk Foundation aims to spread solar power to disaster areas. In addition, he serves in various roles for numerous other companies that deal with mobility, energy and innovation. In these ways, Musk has taken a leadership role in the shift toward a greener future—both by virtue of his formal roles and as a global thought leader. Thus, he contributes to creating awareness about problems as well as potential solutions, and he takes part in creating a perception that the solutions are realistic. This leadership role—which both Musk and other executives occupy both within and outside their own companies—is a key to making change happen.

There is no doubt that Elon Musk has financial ambitions for Tesla and SpaceX and that he is concerned about both growth and market share. At the same time, he communicates clearly that the social and environmental dimensions of all his projects are important. He is apparently successful at mobilizing employees at all levels to pull in the same direction toward ever more ambitious solutions for a more sustainable world. Research on companies that manage to combine sustainability and profitability suggests that commitment and anchoring of sustainability efforts at the highest level of the organization are critical to the success of mobilizing and motivating employees to comply with the sustainability vision (Eccles et al. 2014). It is not enough to have a triple bottom line that emphasizes financial, social and environmental performance (Elkington 1997). It must also be communicated to employees in a way that makes it credible, relevant and able to stimulate contribution from employees (Du et al. 2010; Strand 2013, 2014). This further requires designing the organization in a manner that supports these objectives with regard to organizational design and management control systems (Gond et al. 2012; Schaltegger 2011; Gulbrandsen et al. 2015). To succeed with truly three-dimensional performance, leadership and organizational design must facilitate it.

Take Me to Your Leader

In his book *The Innovator's DNA,* Harvard Business School professor Clayton Christensen (2013) asks what characterizes leaders who drive innovation. He concluded that leaders and their characteristics are of crucial importance for the ability of companies to innovate. Leadership involves creating support for the managers' and organization's objectives. Managers can, for instance, do this by making work meaningful to employees. Workers are not necessarily bound to obey orders or blindly let themselves be led by formal frameworks. This implies that voluntary action is an important, but often overlooked, concept related to leadership. In most cases, managers have power that could enable them to steer employees in a desired direction. However, management is not just about controlling, but rather, both the ability to lead and the ability to control are essential tools in a manager's toolbox.

Since both employees and other stakeholders have the freedom to choose, managers can only control these stakeholders' actions to a limited extent. This is particularly true in cases where the company breaks with its previous practices, such as when it tries to develop a more sustainable business model. A key challenge for managers is directing employees' attention toward performance along all three dimensions on which the company is measured.

Put simply, we can therefore say that good managers manage to stimulate collaboration by making targets meaningful (see, e.g., Shamir et al. 1993), but they also manage to control their employees through the formal structure of the organization. Working to improve sustainability performance can be perceived as meaningful for employees because of the characteristics of the objectives and the tasks involved in achieving them. For example, employees may find it rewarding or stimulating to work with new technologies to reduce emissions or with procedures that improve conditions for employees in the company's supply chain. However, to work toward such goals can also be experienced as meaningful if the target itself—that is, the vision that employees share and strive toward—has value for the individual employee (cf. Deci and Ryan 2000).

To work in a company like Tesla and SolarCity can thus provide employees with rewarding sustainability-related work. Meanwhile, employees can also find these companies' visions to contribute to a more sustainable future valuable and motivating. It is important to emphasize that the organization's objectives, vision and values refer to a desired future state that everyone in the company must be willing to work together to achieve. Leadership thus involves setting the course and trying to create support for the goals and to stimulate cooperation among employees and other important stakeholders to attain them.

Leadership at All Levels

The tales of visionary and dynamic leadership personalities like Elon Musk and Ray Anderson of Interface can perhaps make it easy to lose heart. Most managers may not have either the capabilities or the resources needed to be large-scale change-makers, and many people lack such aspirations. It is therefore important to remind ourselves of the many everyday heroes we meet. A good example is the head of a technical department in a municipality. He set new goals for his unit, inspired his employees, their administrative head and the political decision makers in the municipality to implement new and more sustainable fuel alternatives both in public transport and in the municipality's own fleet of vehicles. This is not a sustainable business model innovation, but rather a change in the way the municipality deliver its services. It should be noted that it is a major change for the municipality, however, and it requires many stakeholders with different interests and goals to work together to attain new sustainability goals.

We come across plenty of other examples: Chief sustainability officers who succeed in changing the purchasing policy in large companies. HR managers who significantly improve the health, safety and environment (HSE) practices of their company. Product designers who redesign products so that they become more resource efficient and environmentally beneficial. Managers of marketing departments who join forces with chief financial officers (CFOs) to find new ways of offering existing products in markets that have not previously had access to such products. We have filled our backpack of experiences of sustainable business through numerous conversations with managers in small and large organizations across the private, public and voluntary sectors. It is interesting and inspiring to see how minor changes, often initiated from the grassroots of the organization, can also lead to significant subsequent changes in the direction of the organization becoming more sustainable. The reason is perhaps precisely that when a change is made to the way value is created, delivered or captured in the organization, it also spills over to other parts of its business model and operations.

It is therefore misleading to talk about leadership as something that only happens from the top of the organization. Developing sustainable business models is a result of leadership at different levels in the company, and it is a result of stakeholders with different expertise and experience questioning the existing practice. Often it is necessary that leaders and stakeholders inside and outside the company jointly work to set a new course.

The leaders who succeed in doing this must be able to formulate new visions, goals and values and manage to create movement in the new direction. They succeed with this not only by being a "guiding light" that shows the way. Reaching new targets also requires designing the organization in a manner that supports this, especially with regard to management control systems and other key characteristics of organizational design that encourages and supports performance along all three performance dimensions. Elon Musk and the companies in which he is involved have not been success stories solely because of visionary leadership. To realize the ambitious projects they have initiated, Tesla, SpaceX and SolarCity are completely reliant on formal systems and structures to create movement. Their success is also a consequence of appropriate management control and organization, which facilitates the alignment of sustainability and profitability.

11.2 Building a Better World

LEGO has taught us that by using the right building blocks in the right ways, one can create anything. And it may appear that decision makers in the company have realized that this also applies to companies trying to become more sustainable.

In 2015, LEGO took a huge leap in that direction, when it announced that it would invest one billion Danish kroner to find sustainable materials for its products. To achieve this, the company has established a new unit—the Sustainable Materials Center, in which 100 people will work to replace the petroleum-based plastic that the company now uses to produce its world-famous LEGO blocks, with more environmentally friendly plastic. According to LEGO's CEO Jørgen Vig Knud Torp, this is an important step to attain the company's ambitions of using only sustainable materials by 2030. In 2018, LEGO announced that it would launch its first sustainable bricks, as all botanical elements such as leaves, bushes and trees in LEGO's collections will be made from plant-based plastic sourced from sugarcane, starting in 2018. Later on, these materials will also be used in other LEGO products.

These changes add to the company's existing sustainability performance, which includes a reduction in its carbon footprint, reductions in the size of the product packaging, as well as investments in the company's own wind power park. In 2014, LEGO also decided to exit its partnership agreement with Shell, which had lasted since the 1960s. This happened after a lengthy campaign Greenpeace had run against Shell. As such, the decision to change the input factors in the LEGO blocks is just a part of larger ongoing changes of the entire LEGO business model in a more sustainable direction. However, major challenges of course still remain—not at least related to consumption, waste and other shadowy sides of the major LEGO theme parks, which have expanded on several continents.

The new sustainable materials center will be located at LEGO's headquarters in Billund, Denmark, and will be represented at LEGO's various offices all over the world. According to the owner of the LEGO Group, Kjeld Kirk Kristiansen, the investment is part of the company's vision to create a positive footprint on the planet that future generations will inherit. It is also in line with the motto of his grandfather—LEGO founder Ole Kirk Kristiansen: "Only the best is good enough." In 2014 alone, more than 60 billion LEGO blocks were produced, and the footprint thereof is massive. In 2012, the company therefore started work to find new solutions to reduce both its social and environmental externalities and started collaborating with partners including World Wildlife Fund (WWF) to find ways to become more sustainable. This includes collecting products at their end of life. In order to succeed, however, LEGO must ensure that appropriate organizational design and management control systems support the three-dimensional objectives in its vision. This is necessary to attain the ambitious goals the company has formulated as part of its strategy.

Organizing for Sustainability

Designing organizations in a way that reflects and supports the company's financial, social and environmental dimensions is a comprehensive challenge. However, it is important to mobilize and help employees at all levels contribute to make the company more sustainable. It is not sufficient merely to formulate goals along all three dimensions—the company must moreover be designed in a way that enables employees to act in accordance with those goals. Figure 11.2 illustrates four organizational characteristics that are particularly important for promoting simultaneous goal attainment along all three performance dimensions.

1. Assignment of authority and accountability within the organization and placement of suitable competence in the right places in the organization
2. Contact with stakeholders inside and outside the organization
3. Development and monitoring of control systems and performance indicators
4. Development of appropriate incentive structures

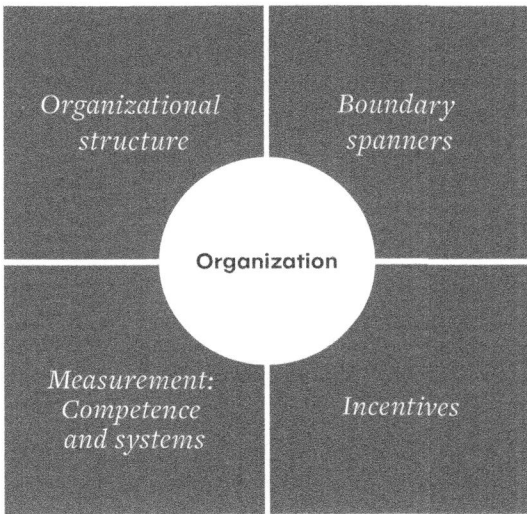

Fig. 11.2 Four elements of organizing for sustainability

The Structures That Support

To avoid reducing sustainability to a theme for celebratory speeches and a decoration on corporate websites and annual reports, it is important that those who are responsible for sustainability efforts gain real influence in the company. This is clearly the case in LEGO. The company formed a separate department with a solid budget and a dedicated manager who will be a part of the company's executive management.

One of the most important features of any organizational design is giving certain people the right to make decisions about resources in the company, as well as the corresponding accountability. These decision rights determine the opportunities they have to make independent choices and implement activities with the necessary resources (Foss et al. 2012).

LEGO's decision to create the new center places both authority and accountability to implement these changes with its managers. There is no doubt that these managers will deal with core business—they are after all redesigning the LEGO block! If LEGO is able to transition away from oil-based plastic, it may positively influence its reputation and strengthen its competitive advantage. However, it is not the public relations department that is tasked with these sustainability efforts, although LEGO's sustainability practices also relate to such aspects of the company. Instead, the sustainability center will be located in the heart of the company's activities. In this way, the project is built into the core of the organization, making it more likely that those who work there can take the necessary steps to improve the company's sustainability performance.

Build a Bridge to Your Surroundings

No company is an island. To the contrary, every organization depends on numerous stakeholders in its environment, which contribute to the organization attaining its objectives. The so-called boundary spanners play a key role in this (Aldrich and Herker 1977). Boundary spanners operate in the critical area where the organization "flows into" surroundings. Boundary spanners communicate with stakeholders but can also drive innovation projects that include individuals, groups or entities outside the walls of the organization. For instance, LEGO engages its customers in innovation activities, wherein they are encouraged to give suggestions for new products and product lines.

The boundary spanner has two primary roles. The first is to collect and process information that the company can benefit from in its decisions. The second is to represent the company in the external environment, for example, by carrying out stakeholder dialogue or building legitimacy among stakeholders. This work supports the company's risk management and contributes to knowledge gathering that can be valuable for business development and innovation (Aldrich and Herker 1977; Seuring and Gold 2013).

Being in touch with stakeholders in this way has an accountability side ("who are affected by the company's activities, and what does that mean for the company?") and an opportunity side ("who is able to influence the company's activities, and what does that imply for the company?"). Through its open innovation work, LEGO has in particular exploited the opportunity side, but through changes in its relationships with partners such as Shell, as well as new collaborations with Non-Governmental Organizations (NGOs) like WWF, the company also addresses responsibility issues. For instance, LEGO works closely with its suppliers to try to reduce the shadow side of its supply chain.

Better Dashboard, Better Management

A key challenge in any organization is to monitor and manage performance. This involves developing useful performance indicators, which reflect the degree to which the company is attaining its goals. In addition, it requires systematic collection of data for these indicators and adjusting the course accordingly. This is a challenge that is difficult enough even when the company operates with only one performance dimension—the financial. Taking triple bottom line performance seriously, however, makes it significantly more difficult (see, e.g., Perrini and Tencati 2006; Schaltegger 2011).

Real performance management of social and environmental performance implies measuring and keeping track of the externalities that require monitoring and follow-up (Epstein and Roy 2001). A major challenge in this context is to develop appropriate indicators for social and environmental performance and to collect data related to them (Keeble et al. 2003; Gulbrandsen et al. 2015). In addition, it is difficult to compare across the three performance dimensions in order to steer the company's activities in a direction that takes into account all three dimensions and the relationship between them.

An important trend in companies' sustainability efforts is to put in place suitable key performance indicators—the so-called KPIs. These essential management tools can improve decision-making but are also important for external reporting purposes (Perrini and Tencati 2006). Increasingly, companies are reporting their social and environmental performance, either in sustainability reports or in the so-called integrated reports (Eccles and Krzus 2010; Etzion and Ferraro 2010). We are thus already moving toward a world in which investors and other stakeholders can rely on this type of non-financial information (see, e.g., Serafeim 2015).

Measuring and managing social and environmental performance, however, require employees with the skills to identify existing KPIs or develop new KPIs that relate to these dimensions. There are a number of standardized measures of this kind, including the Global Reporting Initiative (GRI) framework or the FutureFit framework, but companies are increasingly also customizing measures and indicators used in combination with standardized indicators in order to manage particularly important aspects of their performance better. As negative social and environmental externalities will largely be unique to the individual company (or at least the industry), it will usually be convenient to use a combination of standardized measures that are relevant across companies (such as CO_2 emissions and the like) and customized measures targeting the company's specific sunny and shadowy sides (Eccles et al. 2012).

Walk It Like You Talk It

A final feature of organizational design of importance in trying to become more sustainable is the incentives used to promote this behavior in the company. To succeed with this, the company can develop an incentive system that promotes sustainable behavior and disincentivizes socially and environmentally detrimental behaviors (Kiron et al. 2012; Eccles et al. 2014; Gulbrandsen et al. 2015). This is not limited only to financial incentives, such as salary, bonuses and so on. It may also involve organizational incentives, such as which behaviors the organizational culture stimulate; social incentives, such as social norms or various forms of pressure to conform; and moral incentives, such as shared beliefs about what is the right thing to do within the organization (Jørgensen and Pedersen 2011).

Any organizational member has limited time and resources and in prioritizing between many different tasks in their daily work, employees will emphasize tasks they perceive as most important. A major source of information for individuals about what is important and what to prioritize is whether there are positive or negative incentives tied to particular goal attainment or the lack thereof. This may involve specific financial bonuses tied to social or environmental goals. In organizational terms, it may involve promotions or other benefits for employees who perform especially well along these dimensions. For organizational and social incentives, it is particularly relevant how people talk of and see these types of objectives in the organization.

Using incentives to promote sustainability can be very powerful, and research shows that companies performing particularly well with regard to sustainability typically have corresponding financial incentives for managers who are responsible for such outcomes. However, this type of instrument should be used with caution in order to avoid crowding out employees' intrinsic motivation to achieve social and environmental goals. There is, however, reason to believe that tying incentives to non-financial performance can promote employee motivation for such goals since it can strengthen the employees' experience of contributing to something bigger than the company's profitability (Pedersen 2013).

The international aluminum giant Alcoa is a company that has received attention for its management control system for sustainability (see, e.g., Epstein and Buhovac 2014). This company was an early mover in identifying key KPIs, setting concrete goals, designing measurement systems, tying executive remuneration to sustainability-related goal attainment and transparently reporting on its performance and the implication for executive pay. The company identified its key shadowy sides and set goals for improving each of them, which it in turn made public on the company website and in annual reports. Subsequently, the company measured these KPIs and tied a significant part of executives' performance-based pay to the attainment of the sustainability-related goals. The progress toward attaining those goals, and for which goals managers were more and less successful, is made public, and the company also reports on the concrete implications for performance-based payment. This allows stakeholders to monitor the company's self-reported goals, performance and progress, and thus stimulates the company to be more transparent while it incentivizes and commits managers to perform in accordance with the expectations such an approach creates.

Move the LEGO Blocks Around

LEGO's new organizational design stems from a new goal and a new vision for the company. Both the owners and the management want to make the company sustainable. The company has put in place many measures already, and now it is being implemented with regard to the core product and the way it is produced. LEGO has assessed its own practices with regard to environmental sustainability, and the company understands that it must set new goals to align its own interests with planetary and societal boundaries. The company's organizational design is changed, a new department is created with a new manager who becomes part of executive management, employees are hired and the company engages with stakeholders inside and outside the organization, all of which is part of the efforts toward achieving LEGO's ambitious sustainability goals. In this way, LEGO builds an organization that is equipped to strive for social, environmental and financial objectives simultaneously, and thus it moves in the direction of aligning sustainability and profitability.

References

Aldrich, H., & Herker, D. (1977). Boundary spanning roles and organization structure. *Academy of Management Review, 2*(2), 217–230.

Christensen, C. (2013). *The innovator's dilemma: When new technologies cause great firms to fail.* Cambridge, MA: Harvard Business Review Press.

Deci, E. L., & Ryan, R. M. (2000). The "what" and "why" of goal pursuits: Human needs and the self-determination of behavior. *Psychological Inquiry, 11*(4), 227–268.

Du, S., Bhattacharya, C. B., & Sen, S. (2010). Maximizing business returns to corporate social responsibility (CSR): The role of CSR communication. *International Journal of Management Reviews, 12*(1), 8–19.

Eccles, R. G., Ioannou, I., & Serafeim, G. (2014). The impact of corporate sustainability on organizational processes and performance. *Management Science, 60*(11), 2835–2857.

Eccles, R. G., & Krzus, M. P. (2010). *One report: Integrated reporting for a sustainable strategy.* Hoboken, NJ: John Wiley & Sons.

Eccles, R. G., Krzus, M. P., Rogers, J., & Serafeim, G. (2012). The need for sector-specific materiality and sustainability reporting standards. *Journal of Applied Corporate Finance, 24*(2), 65–71.

Elkington, J. (1997). *Cannibals with forks. The triple bottom line of 21st century*. Oxford: Capstone.

Epstein, M. J., & Buhovac, A. R. (2014). *Making sustainability work: Best practices in managing and measuring corporate social, environmental, and economic impacts*. San Francisco, CA: Berrett-Koehler Publishers.

Epstein, M. J., & Roy, M. J. (2001). Sustainability in action: Identifying and measuring the key performance drivers. *Long Range Planning, 34*(5), 585–604.

Etzion, D., & Ferraro, F. (2010). The role of analogy in the institutionalization of sustainability reporting. *Organization Science, 21*(5), 1092–1107.

Foss, N. J., Pedersen, T., Pyndt, J., & Schultz, M. (2012). *Innovating organization and management: New sources of competitive advantage*. Cambridge: Cambridge University Press.

Gond, J. P., Grubnic, S., Herzig, C., & Moon, J. (2012). Configuring management control systems: Theorizing the integration of strategy and sustainability. *Management Accounting Research, 23*(3), 205–223.

Gulbrandsen, E. A., Jørgensen, S., Kaarbøe, K., & Pedersen, L. J. T. (2015). Developing management control systems for sustainable business models. *Beta: Scandinavian Journal of Business Research, 29*(1), 10–25.

Jørgensen, S., & Pedersen, L. J. T. (2011). Organizing for responsibility. In O. Jakobsen & L. J. T. Pedersen (Eds.), *Responsibility, deep ecology & the self: Festschrift in honor of Knut J. Ims*. Oslo: Forlag1.

Keeble, J. J., Topiol, S., & Berkeley, S. (2003). Using indicators to measure sustainability performance at a corporate and project level. *Journal of Business Ethics, 44*(2), 149–158.

Kiron, D., Kruschwitz, N., Haanaes, K., & von Streng Velken, I. (2012). Sustainability nears a tipping point. *MIT Sloan Management Review, 53*(2), 69–74.

Pedersen, L. J. T. (2013). Systems of accountability and personal responsibility. In P. Gooderham, K. Kaarbøe, & H. Nørreklit (Eds.), *Managing in dynamic business environments: Between control and autonomy*. Cheltenham, UK: Edward Elgar.

Perrini, F., & Tencati, A. (2006). Sustainability and stakeholder management: The need for new corporate performance evaluation and reporting systems. *Business Strategy and the Environment, 15*(5), 296–308.

Schaltegger, S. (2011). Sustainability as a driver for corporate economic success: Consequences for the development of sustainability management control. *Society and Economy, 33*(1), 15–28.

Serafeim, G. (2015). Integrated reporting and investor clientele. *Journal of Applied Corporate Finance, 27*(2), 34–51.

Seuring, S., & Gold, S. (2013). Sustainability management beyond corporate boundaries: From stakeholders to performance. *Journal of Cleaner Production, 56,* 1–6.

Shamir, B., House, R. J., & Arthur, M. B. (1993). The motivational effects of charismatic leadership: A self-concept based theory. *Organization Science, 4*(4), 577–594.

Strand, R. (2013). The chief officer of corporate social responsibility: A study of its presence in top management teams. *Journal of Business Ethics, 112*(4), 721–734.

Strand, R. (2014). Strategic leadership of corporate sustainability. *Journal of Business Ethics, 123*(4), 687–706.

Open Access This chapter is licensed under the terms of the Creative Commons Attribution-NonCommercial-NoDerivatives 4.0 International License (http://creativecommons.org/licenses/by-nc-nd/4.0/), which permits any noncommercial use, sharing, distribution and reproduction in any medium or format, as long as you give appropriate credit to the original author(s) and the source, provide a link to the Creative Commons license and indicate if you modified the licensed material. You do not have permission under this license to share adapted material derived from this book or parts of it.

The images or other third party material in this chapter are included in the chapter's Creative Commons license, unless indicated otherwise in a credit line to the material. If material is not included in the chapter's Creative Commons license and your intended use is not permitted by statutory regulation or exceeds the permitted use, you will need to obtain permission directly from the copyright holder.

12

RESTART Before It is Too Late

Johnny and Richardson—two athletic men who knew every back-alley in Port-Au-Prince—were waiting in the arrival hall at the Toussaint Louverture International Airport. Sveinung and Rannei Johanne, his then 18-year-old daughter, had just landed after a colorful flight on a plane that was so small that even though they sat on isle 3, they were in the middle of the plane, and even though they sat together, both of them had a window seat. Johnny and Richardson were hosts working for The Plastic Bank—the company Sveinung and Rannei Johanne were visiting, and their temporary role as "bodyguards" was not just for show. This was an unstable time in Haiti—a place where instability is the rule rather than the exception. However, the level of tension was even higher than normal, as the 120-day period of the interim president, Jocelerme Privert, had expired. The president had lost public confidence but did not intend to let go of power. There was political turmoil, and chaos on the streets—violence had escalated, and just a week before Sveinung and his daughter arrived in Port-Au-Prince, a Swedish tourist was shot in broad daylight.

The local management team from The Plastic Bank, with Sephora Pierre-Louis as their natural leader—had notified Sveinung that they needed the protection that the two men could offer. Upon arrival, they sat in a car with dark-tinted windows and sped up toward The Plastic Bank's headquarters on the island. This company, which we have discussed earlier in the book, had become widely known for its innovative business model that made plastic into a currency for poor collectors of plastic. On an invitation from the founder, David Katz, Sveinung traveled to Haiti to study the company's business model up close. Not at least, he wanted to understand more about how such a business model could work in the unstable and chaotic context of Haiti in the year 2016.

We started the book with the story of our stopover in Rwanda, where it is forbidden to bring plastic into the country. Prohibition of some kinds of plastic has since been introduced in many other countries, and the plastic problem that The Plastic Bank is trying to solve has worsened worldwide. This has also resulted in increased attention to the problem. It is extremely hot in Haiti, and people have to buy water in bottles or in bags. Every day, five million small plastic bags of water are consumed in the country and most of the bags are discarded on the ground. The renovation system does not work, and streets, rivers and canals are therefore inundated with plastic bottles, plastic bags, polystyrene and other waste. People burn waste on the streets, and from the mountains around the city, one can see many small and large bonfires at any time. In Haiti, The Plastic Bank has developed 30 recycling stations where people can trade plastic for cash, charging of their cell phones or other services. Approximately 3500 people currently collect plastic, and the goal of The Plastic Bank is to establish 200 such recycling stations in various locations in Haiti—also beyond the metropolis of Port-au-Prince.

People in Haiti are entrepreneurial—they get up early and walk a long way to work and feed their families. Early in the morning, people get together on the streets to sell bananas, used shoes, car parts and all other imaginable products and services. By turning plastic into a currency and making it possible for people to trade plastic for money and other services, The Plastic Bank is creating value for many people. Moreover, the company thus helps plastic from ending up in the sea every time it rains. The vision is to establish this business model in many countries, with Asia as the next stop, where the problems related to plastic and poverty are substantial. In preparation for its entry into the Asian market, The Plastic Bank is also collaborating with IBM in order to build a blockchain-based bank for the poor—thus getting one step closer to become an actual "bank", as indicated by the company's name.

One of the challenges to succeed is to get the major companies in the world to buy and use recycled—or rather upcycled—plastic. The current low oil prices imply that the production of virgin plastic is cheap, which in turn reduces the demand for recycled plastic. Companies therefore need customers to pay more for shampoo bottles, sunglasses and clothing that are made by Social Plastic. For the time being, companies rely on customers and other stakeholders agreeing to pay a premium for Social Plastic, while The Plastic Bank continues to reduce its costs and create economies of scale in order to be cost-effective. Still, The Plastic Bank is driving down the costs associated with its production and has managed to secure many large contracts in recent years. For instance, in late 2017, the company entered into a comprehensive contract with the German chemical and consumer goods company Henkel, which intends to use Social Plastic-branded materials in its products.

In order to make its operations more efficient, The Plastic Bank is trying to make plastic collectors in Haiti cooperate. As a pilot project, the company has just established three cooperatives in which eight collectors work together. In this way, the collectors are able to collect more plastic, and they may get better bargaining power vis-à-vis those who buy the plastic. Sveinung and Rannei Johanne went to meet two of these cooperatives to see how they worked. In blazing sunshine, in an environment still characterized by the major earthquake that killed over 200,000 people in 2010, a group of collectors worked in the shadow of ragged blankets that they had hung as protection. A woman with a large pipe in her mouth removed the labels on the bottles, while another washed the bottles. A third person sorted the different types of plastic in big bags, while four others were out collecting bottles.

All of them lived in the same area, where children played and slept between large sacks of plastic. Few people can read, write or do simple mathematics. Therefore, each cooperative has an accountant who keeps track of how much each member contributes, not to mention how much the cooperative will get when delivering the plastic to the recycling stations. The Plastic Bank runs an intensive training program and empowerment is a key consideration. There was consequently particular support and encouragement for the young accountants to complete high school. They were on job rotation so that they shared the tasks of the team, and Sephora and her colleagues worked with training the members of the cooperative as well as the rest of the collectors.

The Plastic Bank collaborates with companies that tear up the bottles mechanically and distributes plastic to customers all around the world. There is hard work at all levels in the organization, from the collectors on the ground to the executives who engage with the major companies that are buyers of its plastic. When Sveinung and Rannei Johanne experienced the operations of the company up close, the pollution problem and the extreme poverty in Haiti seemed overwhelming. At the same time, business models of this kind provide hope that companies can make a difference, both locally and globally. However, that requires many RESTARTs of business models—at the top, the middle and the bottom of the pyramid.

12.1 It is Not Going to Be Easy

What is striking about The Plastic Bank and its ambitious and demanding project in Haiti is that it illustrates the difficulty of addressing global sustainability challenges. Haiti can almost serve as a "worst case" example on the triple bottom line. The country's economy is in ruins. Social distress and instability undermine the country's ability to rebuild country properly and create security risks for companies and other organizations contributing to the reconstruction. Environmental destruction and pollution are on the increase because of infrastructural and institutional failure. This all implies that it is very difficult to do business in Haiti. Yet many companies face this reality in trying to contribute to a greener economy. This is the case whether they are working at the bottom of the pyramid or simply working with a global supply chain that involves doing business in these markets. The companies involved know firsthand that the social and environmental problems they face in these markets are complex and comprehensive. They will not be solved overnight, and any single company will not solve them.

Leaders in business, politics and civil society are increasingly arguing that a so-called green transition toward more sustainable business is imperative. However, most of them also acknowledge that it will be no walk in the park. This is in line with the research led by Lord Nicholas Stern and his colleagues, who published The New Climate Economy Report (Richardson et al. 2009). Their conclusion is that green growth is possible, but it will require major transformation of business models and patterns of production and consumption. This will also imply that many current business models will disappear and many existing companies will not be able to transition successfully, and consequently not survive. And maybe there are companies and business models that we will be better off without, from the point of view of sustainability. After all, this is innovation in a nutshell—old ways of doing things that served us well for a long time eventually become replaced by something better.

In this book, we have looked at many apparent success stories of green transition: companies that have both the ability and the willingness to implement extensive changes to their business models, in ways that allow them to solve the problems they face while giving them advantages in the markets in which they operate. However, let us not fool ourselves into thinking that such changes or any positive consequences thereof come easily. On the contrary, the changes are demanding and their resulting benefits are not self-evident.

12.2 Ready, Set, RESTART!

The good news is that all companies can get started and experiment their way toward more sustainable business models. If we succeed with the green transition, it will happen as a sum of numerous small movements in companies worldwide, in combination with major technological and behavioral shifts that push us in the same direction. Often, the first step—to start the RESTART—may be the hardest. Many of the examples in this book illustrate—as we have seen in many other companies—that movements toward sustainability often spread like ripples in water, both within the company and in the industry.

There is perhaps not a single company described in this book that is truly sustainable. Some of them are however on their way to *becoming more* sustainable—on the path toward green growth. Some companies have to patiently experiment their way to profitability. Facebook made very little money for a long time, and analysts doubted the company's business model. Spotify is still struggling to make its streaming services profitable, despite considerable growth. We need to be patient with companies that are trying to change their business model in order to align sustainability and profitability—the path toward success is made up by trial and error, and the course needs to be adjusted continuously.

During the week in which we wrote this section of our book manuscript, sustainability investments flowed all over Europe: Google acquired the entire power production of the Norwegian wind power company Norwegian Wind Energy. The financial giant Deutsche Bank divested all its coal investments. A Dutch brewery launched a new type of beer brewed on rainwater, while Belgian researchers presented a technology that makes it possible to make beer from urine. Finally, new numbers were published that showed that more than 20 countries have succeeded in increasing their gross domestic product while at the same time cutting greenhouse gas emissions. All those things happened within a week, and more and more weeks were like that—an indication that the green transition is gaining momentum.

Many large and small steps in the right direction are thus taken all the time, but we need many more. We need change to take place much faster, and we need all the companies that are currently sitting quietly in the boat to start rowing. Hans Bruyninckx, the head of the European Environment Agency, said recently that there is no such thing as being "somewhat sustainable". Companies must become more sustainable, and increasingly sustainable, so that they may eventually become truly sustainable. Importantly, we need them to do so in ways that are compatible with profitability. In other words, it is time for a RESTART.

Reference

Richardson, K., Steffen, W., Schellnhuber, H. J., Alcamo, J., Barker, T., Kammen, D. M., & Stern, N. (2009). *Climate change-global risks, challenges & decisions: Synthesis report.* Copenhagen: Museum Tusculanum.

Open Access This chapter is licensed under the terms of the Creative Commons Attribution-NonCommercial-NoDerivatives 4.0 International License (http://creativecommons.org/licenses/by-nc-nd/4.0/), which permits any noncommercial use, sharing, distribution and reproduction in any medium or format, as long as you give appropriate credit to the original author(s) and the source, provide a link to the Creative Commons license and indicate if you modified the licensed material. You do not have permission under this license to share adapted material derived from this book or parts of it.

The images or other third party material in this chapter are included in the chapter's Creative Commons license, unless indicated otherwise in a credit line to the material. If material is not included in the chapter's Creative Commons license and your intended use is not permitted by statutory regulation or exceeds the permitted use, you will need to obtain permission directly from the copyright holder.

Part III

Implications and Future Research

In the last part of the book, we outline implications for practical application and for future research. We first summarize the RESTART framework, before we present The Business Model RESTARTer—a process model for working with sustainable business model innovation in practice. We discuss avenues for future research based on the RESTART framework. Finally, we explore two case studies—one of the company Scanship and the other of the alliance between the companies Orkla and BIR. Thereby, we both apply the process model and explore further research opportunities in the extension of the framework.

13

A Recap of the RESTART Framework

In Part II of the book, we developed the RESTART framework and its seven constituent components. Each component sheds light on a major development toward enabling companies to become sustainable and profitable. In the following sections, we will draw implications of the framework, and we begin with its potential practical implications. However, as we will discuss further toward the end of the book, much more research is needed in order to investigate how companies can design and innovate more sustainable business models. The framework—in its current form—can at least serve as a platform for asking the right kinds of questions for companies aiming to align their sustainability performance and their business performance and for researchers interested in investigating such phenomena.

The seven chapters outlining the RESTART framework have explored the following propositions about the business models of the future, based on the RESTART framework:

…they will require frequent REDESIGN,
…which necessitates controlled EXPERIMENTATION.

>   …and be characterized by SERVICE-LOGIC
>   …based on ideas from THE CIRCULAR economy.
>   …which will make ALLIANCES even more important,
>   …in order to achieve the right RESULTS
>   …in a world where the scorecard is THREE-DIMENSIONAL.

At first glance, it might seem that not all seven components are, or will be, equally relevant for all companies. However, all companies will to a greater or lesser extent need to change their business model and will need the tools to think, articulate and act with regard to *redesign* of its business model going forward. To succeed, it is necessary to conduct controlled *experimentation* to identify and analyze what works and what does not. In many cases, sustainable business can be promoted by a *service-logic*, in which value creation and value delivery are oriented toward giving the customer access to what he or she needs, rather than offering it in the form of a product based on ownership. There is no company in the world that does not use energy, water and other natural resources or that does not generate to some extent excess resources and waste from their operations. To become more sustainable in a way that is compatible with financial performance, it can be helpful to think in terms of *the circular economy* in designing the way resources are acquired, processed, used and ultimately reused. Solutions of the type that promote service-logic and circulation will often require that businesses enter into *alliances* with other entities that may enable them to create and deliver value in this way. In order to set the right objectives and to prioritize efforts that can both promote real sustainability and align this with profitable growth, it is essential to emphasize *results*, in the sense of addressing the right externalities and the material sustainability issues, which are related to core business and critical for corporate strategy and performance. To succeed in achieving these goals, the entire organization must be designed in a way that reflects *three-dimensionality*, which implies that social, environmental and financial objectives are reflected in organizational design, leadership and management control systems (Fig. 13.1).

In the following chapters, we outline implications of this framework, both for practical application and for future research. First, we account

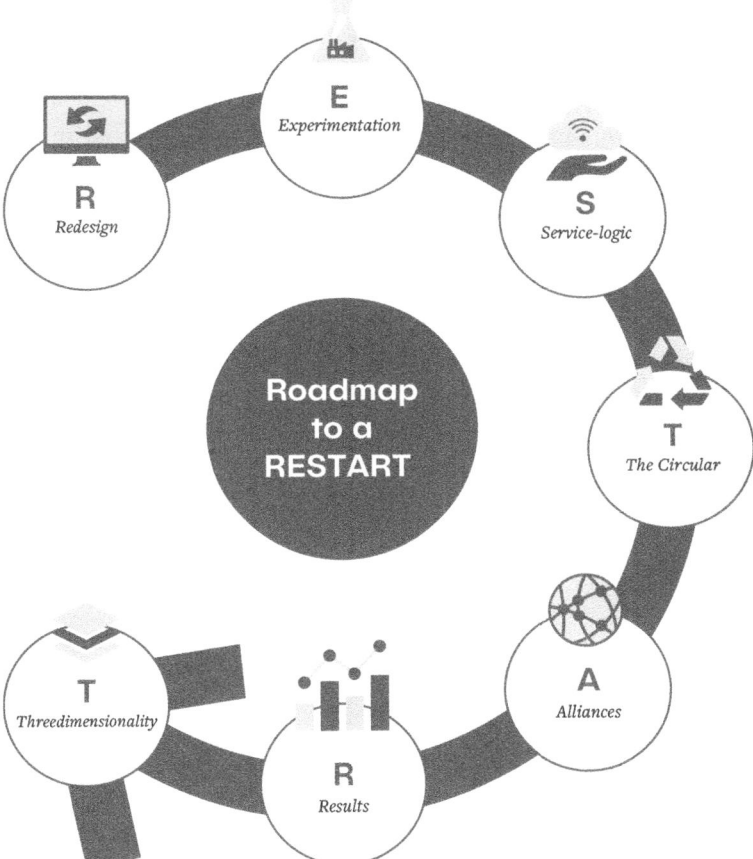

Fig. 13.1 A roadmap to RESTART

for *The Business Model RESTARTer*—a process model for working with sustainable business model innovation in practice. Thereafter, we outline implications for future research based on each of the seven components of the framework. Finally, we present two case studies that build on the framework, of the company Scanship and the alliance between the two companies BIR and Orkla, respectively.

Open Access This chapter is licensed under the terms of the Creative Commons Attribution-NonCommercial-NoDerivatives 4.0 International License (http://creativecommons.org/licenses/by-nc-nd/4.0/), which permits any noncommercial use, sharing, distribution and reproduction in any medium or format, as long as you give appropriate credit to the original author(s) and the source, provide a link to the Creative Commons license and indicate if you modified the licensed material. You do not have permission under this license to share adapted material derived from this book or parts of it.

The images or other third party material in this chapter are included in the chapter's Creative Commons license, unless indicated otherwise in a credit line to the material. If material is not included in the chapter's Creative Commons license and your intended use is not permitted by statutory regulation or exceeds the permitted use, you will need to obtain permission directly from the copyright holder.

14

A Process Model for Sustainable Business Model Innovation

In this chapter, we take one step further toward exploring how to build on the insights from the RESTART framework when attempting to conduct a sustainable business model innovation in practice. Like any innovation process, this will require considerable change in the organization, which implies that there are considerable management and leadership challenges involved. It requires a willingness to enter "the dark room of innovation", and an ability to ask the right questions once you are inside the dark room, which may allow you to find the light switch. For this purpose, we have developed "The Business Model RESTARTer", a process model that can serve as inspiration and guidance in such a change process.

We have argued that in the future, companies will have to redesign their business models more often. This book's point of departure was that three major trends drive this need for continuous business model innovation: first, the comprehensive sustainability problem, which is both a threat and an opportunity for companies; second, the technological opportunity space related to digitalization and the fourth industrial revolution, which renders old business models obsolete and opens up for completely novel business models, and third, ongoing changes in

Fig. 14.1 Three trends driving the development of new business models

consumer preferences, lifestyles and consumption patterns that make new types of value creation both possible and necessary (Fig. 14.1).

The big question is how companies should go about designing new business models that take all of these three trends into consideration. As researchers, when we work with companies, one of our aims is to enable the managers from the company to develop questions that can be tested empirically and form the basis for simple pilot tests, A/B tests or experiments. Our collaboration with companies is part of the background that gave the spark to develop the RESTART framework outlined in Part II. Working with managers in innovation processes has also led us to believe that managers need a knowledge-based model to guide their innovation processes. *The Business Model RESTARTer* aims to be such a tool. This process model gives "a view from 30,000 feet" and intends to help managers ask the right questions at the right time and thus get closer to the light switch in the dark room of innovation.

We conceive of *The Business Model RESTARTer* as a reiterative process model in which we divide the sustainable business model innovation process into four phases (Fig. 14.2):

1. *Recognize* your business model—understanding the status quo and identifying the need for change
2. *Rethink* your business model—identifying opportunities, threats and possibilities for an improved business model
3. *Reinvent* your business model—hypothesizing, testing and deciding on a new business model
4. *Reorganize* your business model—implementing the new business model

The business model is the focal point of the RESTART framework developed in Part II, and therefore we have placed the business model in

A Process Model for Sustainable Business Model Innovation

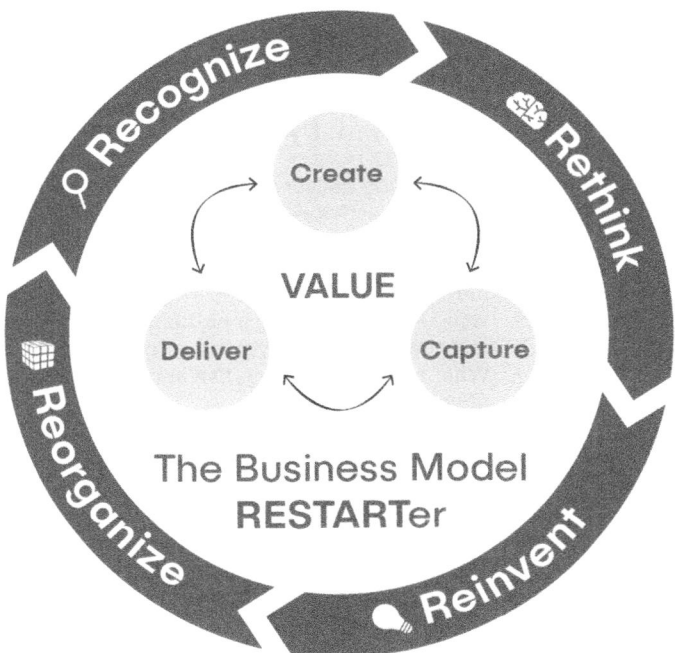

Fig. 14.2 The business model RESTARTer for sustainable business model innovation

the middle of the model. This is illustrated by the three gray circles that represent how companies create, deliver and capture value. The four phases, recognizing, rethinking, reinventing and reorganizing the business model, are illustrated in the quadripartite and cyclical arrow surrounding the business model. All four phases are related to the business model, and as we will discuss below, elements from the RESTART framework serve as important building blocks in the whole process from recognizing the current business model to reorganizing in order to facilitate the new one.

We propose that any innovation process needs to start with a *recognition* of the current business model and an identification of its shortcomings—its negative and positive externalities. The next phase is to *rethink* the business model. This includes an examination of the threats from novel business models from new and existing competitors and a thorough exploration of the current business model's failure to exploit the opportu-

Table 14.1 Questions to guide the four phases of the sustainable business model innovation process

(1) Recognize your business model	• Who are your target customers, what problems do they have, what products and services do you offer them and what is your value proposition to these customers? • How do you deliver value, that is, what are the key resources, activities and partners that allow you to deliver on your value proposition reliably over time? • How do you capture value, that is, what are your most important sources for revenue and cost? • What are your current ambitions? And what scope and time horizon do you have for growth? • What are the main negative and positive externalities of your business model?
(2) Rethink your business model	• Which jobs do customers really want to have done? • Which technological and societal trends and drivers influence your business model? • Who are the main players in your industry? • How can elements from the RESTART framework be an inspiration for sustainable business model innovation? • Is there a platform for change and a culture for a RESTART in your organization? If not: What are the main obstacles and how can you overcome them?
(3) Reinvent your business model	• What are your new ambitions? And what time horizons and scope for growth do you have now? • Who should your customers be? • What should your new value proposition(s) be, and how can value be delivered and captured in new ways? • What needs to be true for the new business model(s) to go to market? • How can you test and experiment with new business models?
(4) Reorganize your business model	• Is there a strong relationship between the new ways of creating, delivering and capturing value in your business model? • Are you organized to leverage your resources and facilitate value-creating activities? • Are you counting, incentivizing and communicating the things that really matter? • How are you preparing your business for a new RESTART?

nity space related to changes in markets, technologies and consumer preferences. These two first phases, *recognize* and *rethink*, can be understood as a problem formulation, while the purpose of the two next phases, *reinvent* and *reorganize*, is to develop and test new solutions and to integrate them in a new business model.

We will dig deeper into all of these four phases below. Before we do so, we outline some questions in Table 14.1 that we have found useful to ask in the different phases of such an innovation process.

14.1 A Closer Look at the Four Phases of the Sustainable Business Model Innovation Process

The Business Model RESTARTer is inspired by the business model innovation literature (e.g., Osterwalder and Pigneur 2010; Kaplan 2012; Gassmann et al. 2014; Morris et al. 2005; see also Foss and Saebi 2017; Zott et al. 2011) and the organizational change literature (in particular, Lewin 1947). Lewin's well-known model suggests that change processes have three phases, popularly summarized as *unfreeze—change—freeze*. By *unfreeze*, Lewin refers to making the organization ready to change, while *change* refers to the actual implementation of novel solutions and *freeze* (or refreeze) is ultimately about making the new features of the organization stick. In order to make impactful and lasting change, all three are necessary.

The first phase of a RESTART is to *recognize the current business model*, which is illustrated at the top left of Fig. 14.2. Such a recognition involves understanding how the company creates, delivers and captures value today. Moreover, this implicates examining the negative and positive externalities of the current business model. We have discussed these shadowy and sunny sides of the business model in the first part of the book, but it has also been a returning theme throughout the book—not at least in the discussion of what constitutes material sustainability concerns. Many of the managers we work with have an implicit understanding of their business models, and when we use this framework we put quite a lot of effort into making the managers examine their current business model(s) explicitly. When we work with entrepreneurs, who might only have an idea about a product or a service, we make them spend time on recognizing the existing business models in the market they want to enter.

The second phase is to *rethink the business model*, which is illustrated at the top right of Fig. 14.2. As noted above, this is still a part of what Lewin denotes the change, or unfreeze, process. One thing is to know the company's business model, another thing altogether is to analyze the company's ecosystem, including important technological and societal trends and drivers, stakeholders, competitors and other players. In addition, companies must assess the internal factors of relevance for the business model innovation process. In this stage, it is important to assess if there is a culture for a RESTART in the company and if there is a "burning platform" shared by the top management team and the board. If this is not the case, actions should be undertaken to ensure that important stakeholders are onboard and that there is a common understanding of problems that need to be solved with the current business model.

The third phase of the innovation process is to *reinvent the business model*, illustrated at the bottom right of Fig. 14.2. Albert Einstein supposedly said that if he had only one hour to save the world, he would spend 55 minutes defining the problem and only five minutes finding the solution. In other words, he would trust that the solution would come to him if he only understood what the problem really was. Thus, we can think of the two first phases as problem formulation and the third phase as finding the solution(s) to the problem. We often experience that truly novel and innovative solutions tend to emerge as a result of thorough problem formulation and that the questions that arise in phases one and two make managers view their organizations with fresh eyes.

In the reinvent phase, several elements from the RESTART framework are relevant, regarding the understanding of new business models (redesign), testing and piloting (experimentation), as well as specific ideas for new business models informed by the perspectives on service-logic, circular business models and alliances. Generally, the aim in this phase is to develop and test new ways of creating, delivering and capturing value, while at the same time reducing the shadowy sides and increasing the sunny sides of the business model. As we have discussed in this book, how this is done depends on, for instance, what industry the company is in, if it is possible to digitize and virtualize its products, if there is a demand from customers for more sustainable products and services, and so on.

One way of working with rethinking and reinventing the business model is to use the insights from the UN Global Compact, as we discussed using, for instance, the Aker BioMarine case in Part II. The UN Global Compact (UNGC) defines ten principles that can be understood as the minimal responsibilities of companies, that is, the fundamental values that business needs to integrate in their strategies and operations to ensure that they minimize the shadowy sides of their companies in the areas of human rights, labor, the environment and anti-corruption. The UN SDGs, on the other hand, can be used to explore the sustainability opportunities and the sunny sides of the business model, that is, "the upside" of sustainability. One cannot expect that one company can solve all of the 17 goals. However, after an assessment of the current business model and its negative and positive externalities, managers can use one or more of the SDGs as inspiration to find new ways of creating, delivering and capturing value. As shown in the case of Aker BioMarine, the company actively used the SDGs to prioritize which societal and environmental problems it could contribute to solving, given the nature of its business model. Similarly, other companies can examine their business models, their shadowy sides using the UNGC principles, and then explore opportunities to shed light by building on one or more relevant SDGs.

After new ideas are piloted and tested, and choices made regarding a new business model, the fourth phase is to *reorganize the business model*. Lewin called this step freeze or refreeze, and it involves making changes related to organizational design, leadership, management control and governance systems. The purpose is to rebuild the organization in a way that facilitates and supports the new business model and to make sure that the changes made are lasting and that the company does not revert to business as usual as soon as the enthusiasm for novelty fades. The insights from the three-dimensionality chapter in the second part of the book are particularly important and applicable in this phase.

14.2 Why the Business Model RESTARTer?

You might ask why we need a process model in addition to the RESTART framework. In the second part of the book, we discussed the seven components in RESTART. It is, however, not necessarily fruitful to follow R-E-S-T-A-R-T to the letter, starting the process with redesign and ending with three-dimensionality. It goes without saying that the first step of a sustainable business model innovation is not to redesign the business model. Such a redesign should definitely be the aim of the process, but successful redesign requires using input from the other six components in RESTART in order to understand how to create, deliver and capture value in new ways.

One could even argue that a better way to achieve a RESTART is to reverse the sequence of the letters, that is, perform a TRATSER rather than a RESTART. Following TRATSER to the letter would involve beginning the process with taking *three-dimensionality* seriously in order to define the new objectives and goals of the company, considering the financial, environmental and social dimensions. In turn, the process could continue with aiming for the right *results* by assessing stakeholders and materiality and thereby identifying how to become both sustainable and profitable by addressing mechanisms for increasing revenues and reputation and/or reducing costs and risk. Next, the analyses would continue based on insights related to how *alliances*, perspectives from *the circular economy* and *service-logic* could inform the prototype of a new business model. This new business model could be tested using insights on *experimentation*. Finally, based on these analyses, the company would be ready for a *redesign* of its business model.

14.3 Starting the RESTART

Our experience is that wise managers are able to jump back and forth in business model innovation processes and can thus use the different parts of the framework at different times depending on what kinds of problems they need to understand and solve. Companies will typically have different starting points for a RESTART, and as we discussed in the second part of the book, there are different pull and push factors that can drive a sustainable business model innovation process (see Table 10.1 in Chap. 10 on *Results rather than indulgences*).

One starting point for a company can be that it needs to become more circular due to new regulations or motivated by the possibility to reduce cost. If so, the discussions and analysis often start with understanding what a circular business model is, what embracing such a model would imply for the company, with which partners the company would need to collaborate or how it can use insights from service-logic to turn its products into services. Another starting point can be that the company's board or its investors demand materiality assessments, risk assessments or new KPIs that reflect the sustainability performance of the company. Increasingly, we see that such pressures meet managers in companies across all industries. The outcome of a materiality assessment might be that the managers understand that they need to redesign the company's business model to address stakeholder expectations, while new KPIs might similarly lead to a redesign of how the company delivers and captures value.

Other starting points for a RESTART can be new technologies, competition from new players in the market, new regulations, price increases or increased supply risks for important resources, and so on. Whatever the motivation for a sustainable business model might be, we propose that managers need to understand their current business model and the threats and opportunities related to it, which is the point of departure for how it can be changed in ways that improve both sustainability performance and business performance more broadly. *The Business Model RESTARTer* can be used as a way to structure such an innovation process, asking the right kinds of questions in pursuit of the right answers.

Visit our website www.JorgensenPedersen.no for more tips, videos and materials to use—either as a facilitator of a RESTART in your own company, as a consultant for others, as an entrepreneur mapping out existing business models in the market or a fellow researcher like us who needs a toolbox for working with companies in order to carve out researchable hypotheses that can be tested empirically. We will discuss such research projects in the following chapters, starting with a general discussion of avenues for future research, before we dig deeper into two business cases based on the RESTART framework.

References

Foss, N. J., & Saebi, T. (2017). Fifteen years of research on business model innovation: How far have we come, and where should we go? *Journal of Management, 43*(1), 200–227.

Gassmann, O., Frankenberger, K., & Csik, M. (2014). *The business model navigator: 55 models that will revolutionise your business.* Harlow, UK: Pearson UK.

Kaplan, S. (2012). *The business model innovation factory: How to stay relevant when the world is changing.* London: John Wiley & Sons.

Lewin, K. (1947). Group decision and social change. *Readings in Social Psychology, 3,* 197–211.

Morris, M., Schindehutte, M., & Allen, J. (2005). The entrepreneur's business model: Toward a unified perspective. *Journal of Business Research, 58*(6), 726–735.

Osterwalder, A., & Pigneur, Y. (2010). *Business model generation: A handbook for visionaries, game changers, and challengers.* London: John Wiley & Sons.

Zott, C., Amit, R., & Massa, L. (2011). The business model: Recent developments and future research. *Journal of Management, 37*(4), 1019–1042.

Open Access This chapter is licensed under the terms of the Creative Commons Attribution-NonCommercial-NoDerivatives 4.0 International License (http://creativecommons.org/licenses/by-nc-nd/4.0/), which permits any noncommercial use, sharing, distribution and reproduction in any medium or format, as long as you give appropriate credit to the original author(s) and the source, provide a link to the Creative Commons license and indicate if you modified the licensed material. You do not have permission under this license to share adapted material derived from this book or parts of it.

The images or other third party material in this chapter are included in the chapter's Creative Commons license, unless indicated otherwise in a credit line to the material. If material is not included in the chapter's Creative Commons license and your intended use is not permitted by statutory regulation or exceeds the permitted use, you will need to obtain permission directly from the copyright holder.

15

Avenues for Future Research

The point of departure for this book is the need for business model innovation that can lead to more business models that are both sustainable and profitable. In the first part of the book, we argued why such business models are needed, we discussed the overarching goal of aligning sustainability performance and financial performance and we illuminated the challenges related to succeeding with such business model innovations. In the second part of the book, we developed the RESTART framework that sheds light on seven characteristics that we propose will be important in the transition toward more sustainable business models. However, in order to enable such a green transition, much more knowledge is needed on the nature and characteristics of these kinds of business models. Moreover, we need knowledge of the mechanisms through which they may create value for stakeholders while ensuring that they restore and regenerate, rather than break down, societal and natural capital. Finally, we need empirical insight into the managerial, leadership-related and organizational capabilities and governance structures that can support the implementation of such business models.

In this chapter, we discuss avenues for future research on these issues. This book aims to contribute to the research agenda for sustainable business model innovation. For this reason, we have explored—both from the conceptual and empirical points of view—the nature and characteristics of such business models and how they might be designed and innovated. In these final sections of the book, we aim to articulate some of the implications the discussions in this book have for future research. What are the unanswered questions? Where is the fertile soil for empirical investigation? What might be valuable research designs and methodological approaches to shed more light on these issues? And where do we see the field going in the coming years?

15.1 Mind the Gap!

Issues related to corporate conduct and misconduct, in general, and corporate responsibility, in particular, have been studied for a very long time. Even Aristotle discussed the problems related to value creation for profits, which he coined "chrematisike" (see, e.g., Solomon 1992), but the roots of the current discussion of corporate responsibilities mostly arose in the twentieth century (cf. Carroll 2008). While there was some academic discussion about corporate responsibility with regard to corporate crime in the early 1900s, the conversation on corporate social responsibility began to converge on some of the issues still relevant today during the post-World War II period (see, e.g., Bowen 1953; Davis 1960; Katz 1960; Frederick 1960; Eells and Walton 1969). The seminal piece by Friedman (1970) and the equally important response more than a decade later by Freeman (1984) laid the foundations for the academic and practical discussion about the business case of sustainability that is still ongoing today.

As reviewed in the second part of the book, there is a comprehensive literature investigating the so-called business case for sustainability or in the language used in this book—the attempt to align sustainability performance and financial performance. One would arguably still consider this literature inconclusive—it depends on the time horizon measured (Wang and Bansal 2012), the way outcome variables are construed (see, e.g., Orlitzky et al. 2003; Waddock and Graves 1997) and even the context in which the empirical investigations are conducted (cf. Strand 2017; see also Eccles et al. 2015). The right question, perhaps, is not whether investing in sustainability pays, but rather through which mechanisms sustainability efforts may lead to improved business performance. In essence, it involves thinking about the relationship between business models and (positive and negative) externalities and how attending to the right externalities at the right time with the right means can translate into benefits for the company's product and/or factor markets (Jørgensen and Pedersen 2015). Sustainability efforts are not a one-size-fits-all phenomenon, and the heterogeneity in which sustainability issues are most important and which efforts are best suited to address them is crucial to corporate sustainability efforts in practice.

The perhaps most convincing attempts to study the relationship between sustainability and business performance are characterized by exactly such precision and focus. Examples include Khan et al. (2016), who study the relationship between companies' prioritization of more and less material sustainability concerns and financial performance; Edmans (2012), who investigates the link between social performance, job satisfaction and firm value; Flammer and Kacperczyk (2015), who demonstrate a positive relationship between stakeholder orientation and the company's innovativeness; and Kang et al. (2016), who manage to distinguish empirically between different mechanisms through which sustainability efforts translate into business performance.

Going forward, we believe that these are exactly the kinds of studies we need to proliferate. Focused empirical investigation of such mechanisms, ideally also with experimental interventions, can considerably further our understanding of what it takes to align sustainability performance and financial performance in practice. In the following, we aim to point out fruitful avenues for further research based on the framework developed in this book. In doing so, we share parts of our own research agenda, but we simultaneously invite all fellow researchers to join us in investigating these relationships. The research gap in corporate sustainability research is of course very comprehensive, and too far-reaching than what can be meaningfully outlined in this chapter. Therefore, our goal is mainly to outline the empirical investigations that can serve as a continuation of the work presented in this book, specifically on the phenomenon of sustainable business model innovation.

15.2 Research Designs and Methodologies

Our framework does not assume any specific research designs or empirical strategies. Corporate sustainability research is highly interdisciplinary and heterogeneous with regard to both theoretical and methodological approaches. As documented by Bass and Milosevic (2016), qualitative research designs have increased significantly in business and society research, and such research designs are arguably well suited to address numerous issues in sustainability research that are as yet ill-defined and "messy" phenomena from a definitional standpoint (see also Eisenhardt et al. 2016). Predominantly, however, there have been considerable amounts of studies using quantitative approaches, including studies of the business case, studies that investigate consumer behavior related to sustainability efforts, studies informed by moral and social psychology that investigate decision-making in sustainability efforts and so on (see, e.g., Lockett et al. 2006 for an overview).

In an inspiring "call to arms", Crane et al. (2018) reviewed the field of business and society research and made a broad distinction between "quants" and "poets". That is, they distinguish between the mainly quantitative research approaches of the "quants", the mainly qualitative research approaches of the "poets" and the mixed-methods approaches of the "quants and poets". Crane et al. (2018) look into the crystal ball with regard to future methodological development. They emphasize that future studies need to "respond to the real-world problems and challenges that lie ahead", that they need to be able to shed light on issues that "are systemic in nature" and therefore span across single cases and that there is "a need for more theoretically informed empirical research". In order to achieve such research designs, the authors argue that there is need for more mixed-methods studies, more research based on field data and more "adventurous and robust" action research.

As we will show in the following, we share many of the viewpoints proposed by Crane et al. (2018). As is evident from the present work, we are strong believers in research conducted in proximity to, and collaboration with, companies. Our own empirical efforts that underlie this work began with a series of qualitative studies in the mid-2000s, after which we conducted some surveys on broad samples of companies. Increasingly, however, we concluded that in order to properly investigate the sustainability efforts of companies, we needed an empirical strategy that allowed us to get closer to the phenomena we wanted to understand.

For this reason, we are currently in the process of conducting field experiments with existing corporate partners and planning new field experiments to investigate the phenomena and relationships discussed in this book. With many of these companies, we simultaneously engage in innovation processes, sometimes using the tools from *The Business Model RESTARTer*. This is because designing field experiments requires a very intimate understanding of the context in which the investigation takes place, and what are the most important relationships to be studied and outcomes to be measured. Field experiments are a specific subset of experimental studies that are characterized by being conducted in the field in which decision makers and organizational members actually carry out their choices and activities (cf. Harrison and List 2004). This allows for a unique combination of realism and control in empirical investigation (Levitt and List 2007). Not at least, field experiments are desirable due to the possibility of randomization in the field, which can allow for better identification of cause-and-effect relationships (see, e.g., Levitt and List 2009). Delmas and Aragon-Correa (2016) argued that such research designs are particularly suited to study "microanalyses of employee or consumer behavior as they relate to sustainability". However, as demonstrated by Chatterji et al. (2016), this methodological approach can also allow for interventions and investigations related to firm-level outcomes. As we will show below, we believe that many important phenomena discussed in this book can be successfully studied by means of field experimental designs—a relatively novel approach in the field of corporate sustainability research (cf. Delmas and Aragon-Correa 2016; Crane et al. 2018).

However, we do not believe that all phenomena in sustainable business model innovation are equally well suited for experimental studies. We share the enthusiasm of Crane et al. (2018) for action-based methods, and as shown in this book, we already work in research projects with companies in which we also serve as advisors and therefore "actors" in the empirical reality we are trying to map. In the case study on Scanship elsewhere in this book, this role is evident. However, a combination of empirical approaches—for instance, a combination of action-based research and field experiments developed as the culmination of such a process—seem promising in this regard. Importantly, it is necessary to move beyond mere description or accounts of companies' efforts to become more sustainable, which can be a limitation of some pure action-based studies.

Finally, we believe that there is considerable need for further qualitative work on many of the issues covered in this book. In particular, comparative case studies between different kinds of business models, different kinds of sustainability efforts and the fit of various sustainability efforts in different contexts (e.g., industrial, geographical and cultural) seem promising. Moreover, in-depth interview studies, observational studies and other approaches that can shed light on microprocesses of sustainability work can contribute important insights that are valuable for the attempt to design more sustainable business models, and—perhaps in particular—implementing them in practice in organizational settings.

In the following section, we try to formulate a specific research agenda for the seven components of the RESTART framework outlined in the second part of the book. We consider this agenda work in progress, and we invite all our colleagues to join us in implementing it in practice, using manifold empirical strategies, in various contexts and for different purposes.

15.3 A RESTART Research Agenda

As outlined in the second part of the book, we consider the seven components of the RESTART framework to be simultaneous developments and factors in the movement toward more sustainable business models. This implies that they are inter-connected, and we believe that in order to succeed with each of them in practice, more knowledge is needed.

With regard to *redesign*, there is already a considerable literature detailing the need for further research on business model innovation in general. For instance, Foss and Saebi (2017) emphasized the need for studies investigating four main issues: (1) defining and dimensionalizing the business model innovation construct, (2) identifying antecedents and outcomes of business model innovation, (3) investigating contingency and moderating variables and (4) mapping the boundary conditions of the concept (see also Zott et al. 2011). In a review that is one step closer to the scope of this book, Boons and Lüdeke-Freund (2013) formulated a research agenda for sustainable innovation. They argued that there is a need for more investigation of sustainable system innovations and their relation to business success (cf. Crane et al. 2018), as well as an investigation of the degree to which sustainable business model innovations actually deliver on sustainability-related outcomes.

Informed by these reviews and by our work on redesign thus far, we believe that future studies should investigate the mechanisms underlying successful sustainability improvements that contribute to, or enable, business model innovation. That is, what characterizes business models wherein sustainability improvements are central elements in the new business model that are value-enhancing for customers or other stakeholders? Moreover, we believe that piloting or A/B-testing—as carried out by companies that conduct business experiments (see, e.g., Anderson 2011; Davenport 2009)—can serve as the basis for potential field experiments that can compare the viability of rival business models during the "reinvent" phase (cf. the chapter on *The Business Model RESTARTer*). Implementing a new business model is a high-risk endeavor and using experimental methodology to test and compare business models prior to redesign seems a particularly high-value research contribution. However, a crucial challenge from the point of view of research design, in general, and generalizability of results, in particular, is that the experiment is designed in a manner that is not too specific to the case company in question.

This leads us to research opportunities related to *experimentation* itself. This implies studying the experimentation processes of companies and can provide insight into success factors in carrying out such efforts in practice. Bocken et al. (2017) conducted a study on how such experimental efforts aided the transition to circularity in an international clothing company. Crucial questions related to experimentation in practice include how to cultivate a culture for experimentation in a company as well as how to identify and design key performance indicators that can be measured by means of well-designed business experiments.

In addition, a particularly tempting proposition is to conduct a "meta-experimental" study, that is, to conduct an experiment on business experimentation. For instance, investigating two different approaches to business model experimentation, or two different uses of key performance indicators, could reveal success factors in carrying out such business experiments in practice. Qualitative and quantitative studies of barriers to such experimentation could also provide valuable insights.

Regarding the three components in the center of the framework—*service-logic, the circular economy* and *alliances*—there is of course considerable work done as well as plentiful calls for further research. However, for the present purposes, we emphasize the need for further research into how these three phenomena can be drivers of, or constituent parts of, more sustainable business models.

With regard to *service-logic*, there are exciting research opportunities tied to the boundary conditions of service-based business models for sustainability. Business models based on access or functionality rather than ownership (see, e.g., Bocken et al. 2014) are widely considered to be important to promote more sustainable consumption. An interesting question is what distinguishes products that consumers are willing to consume through such business models from the products that consumers still prefer to own, even when access-based models emerge. Such boundary conditions are important for understanding the scope and potential for such business models across product categories and industries. A second main theme that carries great promise is product-service systems, and in particular the potential for adding new services "on top of" the main value proposition when transitioning to a product-service system business model (see, e.g., Mont and Tukker 2006; Tukker and Tischner 2006). This issue is central to the financial viability of such business models and the ability of companies to sustain them over time.

With regard to *the circular* economy, many research efforts are needed to understand how circular business models can function and succeed as an alternative to linear, "business-as-usual" models. In fact, we have already commenced a couple of research projects aimed at investigating circular business models, one of which is introduced in the case study chapter on Orkla and BIR elsewhere in the book. The first main theme we see as promising relates to new distribution channels in the circular economy. The need for take-back of old products, materials and components, as well as the need for package-reducing solutions, such as "refilleries", are central to make the infrastructure of circular business model function (cf. Bocken et al. 2016). A central research question in this regard is what types of distribution channels are more and less attractive to customers and users and which are the barriers for adoption of such distribution channels.

A second, and highly important, topic for research in relation to circular business models relates to payment models. Anecdotal evidence suggests that one of the challenges for many circular business models thus far is to generate sufficient revenue over time, which, for instance, some leasing-based apparel business models (e.g., Filippa K) have experienced. Payment models are foundational to business models, and they need to be adapted to the characteristics of customers, markets and the competitive landscape. Thus, investigating various forms of payment models for different circular business models is likely to yield valuable insights for companies trying to unlock the profit potential in such business models.

A final promising research topic related to circular business models is to investigate the contingencies between different types of circular business models and the industries in which they are used. For instance, are there systematic differences in the viability of different circular business models—as an example, a leasing-based model versus a refurbishing-oriented model versus a sharing model—depending on the industry? Insights into the fit between business model design and industry characteristics seem a promising, although challenging, avenue for research.

With regard to *alliances*, there is also plenty of fertile ground for empirical investigation. As discussed by Kiron et al. (2015), CEOs all over the world state that collaboration for sustainability has become increasingly important for their companies, but at the same time, very few of them perceive their collaborative efforts to improve sustainability-related outcomes as being successful. As pointed out by Selsky and Parker (2005), cross-sector collaborations for social (and, one would add, environmental) purposes are increasingly widespread but pose particular challenges with regard to partnership design and implementation.

One promising avenue for research on this issue relates to the challenge of developing collaborative cross-sector business models at the bottom of the pyramid—a topic we have discussed previously in the book. Such a collaborative process involves the alignment of objectives across organizations, the leveraging of resources and capabilities of the different partners of the collaboration and the attempt to build a distribution channel for products and services in a market with considerable needs, but where infrastructural, human capital and financial conditions render distribution challenging. All of these issues are ripe for empirical exploration, and the knowledge gap with regard to business models for the bottom of the pyramid, and the collaboration that can enable such business models, is considerable. Moreover, the interrelated set of topics listed above is not only relevant in the specific case of business models at the bottom of the pyramid. The attempts to align the objectives of alliance partners in a collaboration for sustainability or the leveraging of resources across organizational boundaries in such alliances are more generally important topics for empirical investigation.

The latter two components of the RESTART framework—*results* and *three-dimensionality*—offer very interesting and potentially impactful research. As demonstrated by, for example, Eccles et al. (2015), organizational and governance characteristics related to management control systems are highly important for successful design and implementation of sustainability efforts. Not at least, the research on materiality assessments and strategic prioritization, which is steadily growing, has shown great promise (cf. Khan et al. 2016). In prior work, we have empirically investigated such characteristics of companies in the Norwegian setting (Gulbrandsen et al. 2015, 2017), and our findings reveal that, thus far, the systematic use of key performance indicators, incentives for sustainability performance and so on are quite limited.

With regard to *results*, future studies should continue the important work being done on materiality assessments. One interesting approach would be to investigate further the relationship between stakeholder management as conducted by means of materiality assessments on the one hand and the development and use of key performance indicators related to material concerns on the other. A related topic of potentially high value is the role played by chief sustainability officers and similar organizational roles in such work (see, e.g., Strand 2013), which could contribute to the understanding of organizational microprocesses underlying successful stakeholder management.

With regard to *three-dimensionality*, there are several interesting strands of potential research. One interesting approach from a management control point of view would be to investigate how companies generate and use relevant and timely information on sustainability performance in order to inform ongoing sustainability efforts. In an age of digitalization, it will be interesting to follow if—and, if so, how—the use of real-time information for decision-making purposes will emerge. There has been a lot of emphasis on sustainability reporting and accounting in recent years, but one would expect that new technologies for data management and analysis are likely to create novel forms of real-time information systems that may even replace conventional sustainability reporting systems, both for internal and external purposes.

A topic related to three-dimensionality that is fruitful for field experimental investigation is the use of incentives (financial or non-pecuniary) to stimulate sustainability performance at the individual, unit and corporate level. For instance, a study could build on an intervention whereby different incentive schemes were tested and compared to a control condition absent of incentives. Such empirical investigation could provide valuable insights into the specific and differential effects of various incentive schemes for sustainability performance, which could be valuable in corporate attempts to drive such performance. Finally, comparative case studies and other empirical designs could also provide valuable insights into different organizational designs for driving sustainability performance—both in the specific case of how sustainability work is integrated in the organization (separate unit vs. embedded approach) and with regard to how the work itself is organized.

15.4 An Ocean of Opportunities

In the preceding sections, we have given an overview of a vast set of research opportunities in the vaguely defined field that comprises research on sustainable business model innovation. While this overview only scratches the surface of the possibilities for exciting research, it at least points out a set of potentially fruitful ways to empirically explore the RESTART framework developed in the second part of this book.

A final note on this overview is related to the rapidly changing opportunity space that follows from ever-increasing amounts of data combined with increasingly powerful statistical methods based on deep learning and so on. It is argued by many that we are entering an "inductive revolution", meaning that the traditional hypothesis-developing and -testing approach of research will be replaced by methods whereby algorithms explore vast amounts of data to find patterns and relationships that can provide valuable insights (see, e.g., Sullivan and Zutavern 2017). For most researchers, it is hard to envision how such a future of empirical investigation will look, what it will imply for the role of the researcher and what constitutes good research questions. However, we are confident that such developments will also shape the future of corporate sustainability research.

More generally, attempting to do research, teach and write about sustainable business model innovation in the age of digitalization is like drawing a map of a landscape that changes quickly and continuously. For this reason, we expect—and hope—that this overview of avenues for future research will have a relatively short half-life. Regardless, we hope that our account of research opportunities reviewed here can stimulate interesting research projects and—perhaps even more importantly—further research ideas not yet conceived.

References

Anderson, E. T. (2011). A step-by-step guide to smart business experiments. *Development and Learning in Organizations: An International Journal, 25*(6). https://www.emeraldinsight.com/doi/full/10.1108/dlo.2011.08125faa.011.

Bass, A. E., & Milosevic, I. (2016). The ethnographic method in CSR research: The role and importance of methodological fit. *Business & Society*. https://doi.org/10.1177/0007650316648666.

Bocken, N., Miller, K., Weissbrod, I., Holgado, M., & Evans, S. (2017). Business Model Experimentation for Circularity: Driving sustainability in a large international clothing retailer. *Economics and Policy of Energy and the Environment (EPEE)*.

Bocken, N. M., de Pauw, I., Bakker, C., & van der Grinten, B. (2016). Product design and business model strategies for a circular economy. *Journal of Industrial and Production Engineering, 33*(5), 308–320.

Bocken, N. M. P., Short, S. W., Rana, P., & Evans, S. (2014). A literature and practice review to develop sustainable business model archetypes. *Journal of Cleaner Production, 65*, 42–56.

Boons, F., & Lüdeke-Freund, F. (2013). Business models for sustainable innovation: State-of-the-art and steps towards a research agenda. *Journal of Cleaner Production, 45*, 9–19.

Bowen, H. R. (1953). *Social responsibilities of the businessman.* New York, NY: Harper & Row.

Carroll, A. B. (2008). A history of corporate social responsibility: Concepts and practices. In A. Crane et al. (Eds.), *The Oxford handbook of corporate social responsibility* (pp. 19–46). Oxford: Oxford University Press.

Chatterji, A. K., Findley, M., Jensen, N. M., Meier, S., & Nielson, D. (2016). Field experiments in strategy research. *Strategic Management Journal, 37*(1), 116–132.

Crane, A., Henriques, I., & Husted, B. W. (2018). Quants and poets: Advancing methods and methodologies in business and society research. *Business & Society, 57*(1), 3–25.

Davenport, T. H. (2009). How to design smart business experiments. *Harvard Business Review, 87*(2), 68–76.

Davis, K. (1960). Can business afford to ignore social responsibilities? *California Management Review, 2*(3), 70–76.

Delmas, M. A., & Aragon-Correa, J. A. (2016). Field experiments in corporate sustainability research: Testing strategies for behavior change in markets and organizations. *Organization & Environment, 29*(4), 391–400.

Eccles, R. G., Ioannou, I., & Serafeim, G. (2015). The impact of corporate sustainability on organizational processes and performance. *Management Science, 60*(11), 2835–2857.

Edmans, A. (2012). The link between job satisfaction and firm value, with implications for corporate social responsibility. *The Academy of Management Perspectives, 26*(4), 1–19.

Eells, R. S. F., & Walton, C. C. (1969). *Conceptual foundations of business.* Homewood, IL: R.D. Irwin.

Eisenhardt, K. M., Graebner, M. E., & Sonenshein, S. (2016). Grand challenges and inductive methods: Rigor without rigor mortis. *Academy of Management Journal, 59*(4), 1113–1123.

Flammer, C., & Kacperczyk, A. (2015). The impact of stakeholder orientation on innovation: Evidence from a natural experiment. *Management Science, 62*(7), 1982–2001.

Foss, N. J., & Saebi, T. (2017). Fifteen years of research on business model innovation: How far have we come, and where should we go? *Journal of Management, 43*(1), 200–227.

Frederick, W. C. (1960). The growing concern over business responsibility. *California Management Review, 2*, 54–61.

Freeman, R. E. (1984). *Strategic management: A stakeholder approach*. Boston, MA: Pitman.

Friedman, M. (1970, September 13). The social responsibility of business is to increase its profits. *New York Times Magazine*.

Gulbrandsen, E. A., Jørgensen, S., Kaarbøe, K., & Pedersen, L. J. T. (2015). Developing management control systems for sustainable business models. *Beta: Scandinavian Journal of Business Research, 29*(1), 10–25.

Gulbrandsen, E. A., Jørgensen, S., & Pedersen, L. J. T. (2017). Sustainability practices and performance in Norwegian knowledge-intensive service companies. *Working paper*, NHH Norwegian School of Economics.

Harrison, G. W., & List, J. A. (2004). Field experiments. *Journal of Economic Literature, 42*(4), 1009–1055.

Jørgensen, S., & Pedersen, L. J. T. (2015). *Responsible and profitable: Strategies for sustainable business models*. Oslo: Cappelen Damm Akademisk.

Kang, C., Germann, F., & Grewal, R. (2016). Washing away your sins? Corporate social responsibility, corporate social irresponsibility, and firm performance. *Journal of Marketing, 80*(2), 59–79.

Katz, W. G. (1960). Responsibility and the modern corporation. *Journal of Law and Economics, 3*, 75–85.

Khan, M., Serafeim, G., & Yoon, A. (2016). Corporate sustainability: First evidence on materiality. *Accounting Review, 91*(6), 1697–1724.

Kiron, D., Kruschwitz, N., Haanaes, K., Reeves, M., Fuisz-Kehrbach, S. K., & Kell, G. (2015). Joining forces: Collaboration and leadership for sustainability. *MIT Sloan Management Review, 56*(3), 1–31.

Levitt, S. D., & List, J. A. (2007). What do laboratory experiments measuring social preferences reveal about the real world? *Journal of Economic Perspectives, 21*(2), 153–174.

Levitt, S. D., & List, J. A. (2009). Field experiments in economics: The past, the present, and the future. *European Economic Review, 53*(1), 1–18.

Lockett, A., Moon, J., & Visser, W. (2006). Corporate social responsibility in management research: Focus, nature, salience and sources of influence. *Journal of Management Studies, 43*(1), 115–136.

Mont, O., & Tukker, A. (2006). Product-service systems: Reviewing achievements and refining the research agenda. *Journal of Cleaner Production, 14*(17), 1451–1454.

Orlitzky, M., Schmidt, F. L., & Rynes, S. L. (2003). Corporate social and financial performance: A meta-analysis. *Organization Studies, 24*(3), 403–441.

Selsky, J. W., & Parker, B. (2005). Cross-sector partnerships to address social issues: Challenges to theory and practice. *Journal of Management, 31*(6), 849–873.

Solomon, R. C. (1992). Corporate roles, personal virtues: An Aristotelean approach to business ethics. *Business Ethics Quarterly, 2*(3), 317–339.

Strand, R. (2013). The chief officer of corporate social responsibility: A study of its presence in top management teams. *Journal of Business Ethics, 112*(4), 721–734.

Strand, R. (2017). *Strategic management in the era of cooperation: Toward a theory of scandinavian cooperative advantage*. Unpublished manuscript, University of California-Berkeley.

Sullivan, J., & Zutavern, A. (2017). *The mathematical corporation: Where machine intelligence and human ingenuity achieve the impossible*. New York, NY: PublicAffairs.

Tukker, A., & Tischner, U. (2006). Product-services as a research field: Past, present and future. Reflections from a decade of research. *Journal of Cleaner Production, 14*(17), 1552–1556.

Waddock, S. A., & Graves, S. B. (1997). The corporate social performance-financial performance link. *Strategic Management Journal, 18*(4), 303–319.

Wang, T., & Bansal, P. (2012). Social responsibility in new ventures: Profiting from a long-term orientation. *Strategic Management Journal, 33*(10), 1135–1153.

Zott, C., Amit, R., & Massa, L. (2011). The business model: Recent developments and future research. *Journal of Management, 37*(4), 1019–1042.

Open Access This chapter is licensed under the terms of the Creative Commons Attribution-NonCommercial-NoDerivatives 4.0 International License (http://creativecommons.org/licenses/by-nc-nd/4.0/), which permits any noncommercial use, sharing, distribution and reproduction in any medium or format, as long as you give appropriate credit to the original author(s) and the source, provide a link to the Creative Commons license and indicate if you modified the licensed material. You do not have permission under this license to share adapted material derived from this book or parts of it.

The images or other third party material in this chapter are included in the chapter's Creative Commons license, unless indicated otherwise in a credit line to the material. If material is not included in the chapter's Creative Commons license and your intended use is not permitted by statutory regulation or exceeds the permitted use, you will need to obtain permission directly from the copyright holder.

16

Case Study: A RESTART for Scanship

> *"Maybe the company name is the 'red herring' holding you back from discovering business opportunities in other industries?"*, Lars Jacob asked rhetorically at a strategy seminar with the executive team in Scanship Holding ASA (henceforth referred to as Scanship).

Consultants from an international consulting firm facilitated the workshop, which took place in 2017. The purpose of the session was to *rethink* Scanship's business model. After the workshop, Scanship decided to change the heading on its website from "A complete system for wastewater treatment systems" to "World leading solutions for cleaner oceans". This might not seem like a big step, but for more than ten years, Scanship had primarily delivered waste management and wastewater purification systems to the cruise ship industry, which also dominated its mindset when thinking about business opportunities. Changing the description of its operations in this way signaled both internally and externally that the company had redefined the problem it was designed to solve.

Moreover, the new phrase conveyed that Scanship were—and are—in the middle of what can be called a process of sustainable business model innovation. In this still ongoing process, the company expands horizontally into other industries, such as aquaculture. This process will perhaps not stop with solutions for cleaner oceans, as we will see in the following. Scanship is in fact also exploring land-based solutions for water purification and waste management systems. And who knows, perhaps the ongoing innovation process will lead the company to take on a completely new name—a name that does not give associations to ships and the shipping industry?

Later in 2017, Henrik Badin, the CEO of Scanship, told us that the discussions before, during and after the strategy seminar had fundamentally changed their view of what the company was and why it existed. "We have always thought our work was important", Badin said, "but now we really know why we get up early every morning and hurry off to work!". He added a story that might have been coincidental, but that he interpreted because of their shift in mindset. "Following the change of how we presented our business on our website, we were contacted by Sir Richard Branson's new cruise company Virgin Voyages. At the time, we had already entered into contracts with the Italian shipbuilder Fincantieri to equip the Virgin Voyages newbuilds with Scanship clean ship systems. However, the new entrant in the cruise industry wanted to do more to substantiate their sustainability efforts".

Branson and McAlpin's vision is to disrupt the cruise industry, and Virgin's motto is "Changing business for good", which also includes a goal of substantially reducing its environmental impact. In an interview with the industry magazine Cruise Business Review late in 2017, McAlpin told about Virgin's new partnership with two Scandinavian companies that would help achieve Virgin's environmental goals: the Swedish company Climeon and the Norwegian company Scanship. Both Climeon and Scanship provide services and technologies, McAlpin said, that can make Virgin's new cruise ships much more sustainable. Climeon has developed technology that turns heat into electricity, and there is a lot of wasted heat onboard ships. Scanship was invited to become a partner because of its new waste to energy technology microwave-assisted pyrolysis (MAP). In the interview, McAlpin especially highlighted this technology that is currently under development. This technology uses microwaves to transform carbon-based waste into energy sources as syngas, biofuels, charcoal and heat. The technology produces a substantial amount of energy that will reduce onboard fuel consumption, and with the production of charcoal, carbon is captured that either can be landed as a valuable product for soil enrichment known as "terra preta" or further used to produce hydrogen gas for fuel cells. Virgin Voyages will integrate both Climeon's and Scanship's technologies in its new ships, and by doing so, the company seeks to substantially mitigate the shadowy side of its ships.

We will return to Scanship's new MAP technology and the opportunities it may create in different industries also beyond the cruise industry. We got involved with Scanship and the processes described above in early 2017. The company's executive team invited us to participate in a research project to explore new business opportunities and to develop prototypes of business models and test them in the field. In the following, we will give a snapshot of the status of this research project in light of the RESTART framework and the process model for sustainable business model innovation. Thereby, we will give a glimpse into ongoing research on sustainable business model innovations in practice, largely based on the framework developed in this book.

16.1 Business Opportunities on the Floating City

Did you know that a cruise ship carrying 5000 people has the same footprint as a land-based town with a population of 30,000, and that by turning the food waste, garbage and sludge from the wastewater purification process from these ships into fuel, each ship can reduce their fuel costs by about 1 million USD a year? And did you know that wastewater from the fishery industry can be rinsed and dried and sold as organic fertilizer instead of polluting the ocean? This was news to us when we first met Henrik Badin and Narve Reiten, the CEO and Chairman of the board of Scanship, respectively. Enthusiastically, they told us about the shadowy sides of the cruise industry and of aquaculture and how Scanship was working to turn these problems into business opportunities.

Historically, Scanship did this by using its technology in different kinds of waste management systems to the cruise industry. Recently, however, the company has set out to enter new industries. In the pipeline is also a groundbreaking technology called MAP, which Virgin Voyages, as well as many other cruise lines, is eagerly awaiting. Ships and other autonomous sites like ports, islands, airports and offshore platforms use MAP. The technology enables them to turn carbon-based waste, such as food, sewage, paper, cardboard, plastics, wood, oils and mixes, into flammable gas, bio-oil and phosphorus-rich charcoal. These materials can in turn be used for fertilizer and heating purposes. Moreover, the MAP technology will capture carbon in the activated charcoal, which means that it will give Scanship's customers a substantial reduction in their carbon footprint.

The MAP technology was still in development when we first met Badin and Reiten early in 2017, and the management team was in the process of designing collaborative business models that could help them create, deliver and capture value in different industries. We should note that neither Badin, Reiten nor the company was new to the idea of conducting ambitious turnarounds. Scanship is a Norwegian company and it was listed on the Oslo Stock Exchange in 2014. In 2017, its share price increased by a stunning 352 percent, which is in stark contrast to the situation in late 2008 when the company went bankrupt. Only days after the bankruptcy, Badin and a handful of other top managers bought what remained of the company's assets and managed to turn it around. Today, Scanship delivers advanced technologies for processing and purifying wastewater, food waste, solid waste and bio sludge. Its main activities include designing, engineering and producing solutions for waste management and wastewater purification to markets worldwide. Currently, the core market for these technologies is the cruise industry to which Scanship delivers systems to the yards for new-build constructions and to existing ship-owners for fleet upgrades.

There are approximately 400 cruise ships in the world, and Scanship is the industry leader in advanced wastewater purification (AWP). Every second cruise ship delivered to the market in the period from 2014 to 2020 is equipped with Scanship AWP. During this 7-year period, Scanship AWP will have been installed on 42 of 75 newbuilds globally. Scanship is a supplier to most major cruise liners, and the business opportunity upon which the company's business model is based is the fact that modern cruise ships generate substantial amounts of wet and dry waste that need to be properly treated. Scanship's technology processes this waste into recyclables, clean flue gas and treated wastewater. The company's headquarter is in Lysaker, Norway, and the group has offices in Tønsberg, Norway, Davie, Florida and Gdynia, Poland.

Reiten and his partner Bård Ingerø bought approximately one-third of the company's stock in 2017, and Reiten soon became the Chairman of the board. When we first met Badin, he had already read our Norwegian practitioner-oriented book *RESTART*. He said that Scanship was already in the middle of "restarting" its business and that the company was looking for ways to redefine what the company was and by exploring different kinds of environmental problems it could solve. However, he added that this was not Scanship's first big change. Ever since they established the company, the managers had redesigned its business model several times. Badin explained how the biggest challenge they had faced from a business model standpoint perhaps was to convince the cruise industry of the value of its technology. In order to unlock this door, several changes had been necessary in how the company created and delivered value for its (potential) customers.

16.2 Solutions for Cleaner Oceans

"You have to remember", Badin later told us, "that when we restarted this company almost 10 years ago, not many people talked about the circular economy, global warming and the plastic problem in the oceans". Today, however, this has changed drastically, and now customers, regulators and the cruise industry itself are starting to understand that the industry's footprint can be—and must be—reduced. Earlier, the tendency was to comply with regulations enforced by International Maritime Organization (IMO) Marpol and the port states in which ships operated, even though these regulations in many situations were considered a minimum. In the company's first years, leading up to the bankruptcy in 2008, the technology was more difficult to sell as it was more advanced than what the regulations required.

In recent years, there has been a shift, as the different ship-owners are starting to compete on environmental initiatives driven by increased focus on corporate responsibility, more media attention and public awareness. This has been driving demand for shipboard environmental technology. Today, Scanship serves more than a third of the approximately 400 cruise ships in the world, and new contracts are lined up. "Our challenge now", Badin and Reiten said, "is to increase the pull from this industry and to develop technologies like the MAP that can do an even better job for the customers". At the same time, the company was trying to design business models that could do similar jobs in other markets Scanship is now targeting such as aquaculture.

One important barrier for Scanship is regulation, and therefore the company relies on influencing lawmakers. With some exceptions, it is still legal to dump wastewater and food waste in the so-called territorial waters, that is, 12 nautical miles from the shore. An example of a protected area is the shore of Alaska, which is protected by environmental regulation, but there is still a long way to go before regulation facilitates full-scale adoption of greener solutions. One of the drivers for change in the cruise ship industry has been the growing pressure from other stakeholders, not at least local communities, the media and NGOs. One example is a report published by Friends of the Earth (FoE) in 2012, which revealed the following figures for the amount of waste generated by a large cruise ship on a one-week voyage (cf. Friends of the Earth 2012):

- 800,000 liters of human sewage
- 15,000 million liters of gray water (water from sinks, baths, showers, laundry and galleys)
- 95,000 liters of oily bilge water
- Up to 44,000 liters of sewage sludge
- More than 400 liters of hazardous wastes

Keep in mind that this is in addition to the solid waste that each ship generates, including leftovers from about 25,000 meals a day, given that the cruise ship has 5000 people on board. Excess food is typically grounded up and discharged as a slurry into the ocean, often together with plastic and other forms of litter. Food waste discharged in this manner lowers oxygen and creates acid and a nutrient imbalance in ocean waters.

FoE also regularly publishes a sustainability report card for cruise ships. In such report cards, it ranks the 17 major cruise lines and their initiatives in sewage treatment, air pollution control, water treatment and other criteria. In the 2016 report, Disney Cruise Line is the top scorer with an A-, while Cunard, Holland America, Norwegian and Princess Cruises share the second place with a C. Yet, it is unclear to what degree the scores in such ratings translate into stakeholder action—customers choosing whether or not to buy a cruise, investors choosing whether or not to invest in the company, regulators assessing the need for regulation, and so on. However, it seems clear that negative attention toward the cruise industry is on the increase, which makes it likely that companies will act in ways that can improve this image.

16.3 Toward Uncharted Waters

The cruise industry is not big enough to allow for continuous growth for a technology provider such as Scanship, however. Therefore, to enable continued growth, Scanship has now entered the aquaculture industry and land-based applications. The intensive production of Nordic salmon and other seafood has increased the need for water purification and residue treatment. The basic business opportunity related to this industry is to treat the water in the fish tanks in a way that minimizes water consumption and reduces the negative environmental impact. This process creates sludge that needs to be handled properly to allow for more sustainable fish farming. Scanship identified an opportunity in this challenge and has now entered into an alliance with different partners in the industry in order to produce organic fertilizer that is highly demanded in Asian markets. The aquaculture company Skretting, the waste management company IVAR and the organic waste treatment company HØST are its alliance partners in this project. Scanship's technology dries the aquaculture sludge for this purpose and thus commercializes waste from the aquaculture sector together with its alliance partners.

Scanship's systems can also be used in land-based operations, for which the company provides a variety of industrial applications for waste processing and water purification. The technologies can also be used for several purposes by municipalities and other governmental entities, for instance, in wastewater treatment plants and waste-handling facilities. The Scanship wastewater technology is installed in many municipalities in the Nordic region to remove nutrient and organic matter. Also, it has delivered two larger waste management systems in the Jamaican airports Norman Manley in Kingston and Sangster in Montego Bay. These waste management systems include garbage recycling equipment and waste incinerators, processing all waste from arriving airplanes and terminals.

16.4 Restarting Scanship: Practical Challenges and Research Opportunities

The many examples outlined in the preceding paragraphs are illustrations of the ways in which Scanship attempts to develop new business models that are complements to its main business model in the cruise industry, while simultaneously "tweaking" the existing business model to function even better. As summarized after presenting the RESTART framework, one could argue that, in practice, a RESTART should perhaps rather be structured in the opposite direction—as a TRATSER. In many ways, one could argue that Scanship has gone through such a process. Scanship is trying to make cruise line companies take *three-dimensionality* seriously—to consider their footprints, but at the same time realize how reducing the footprints is possible to align with financial objectives. The value proposition of the company is based on a thorough understanding of what are the material concerns in the industries it aims to serve—food waste, energy usage and other forms of pollution on cruise ships, as well as sludge in the fish farming industry. In this way, it can identify the *results* managers in these companies aim for—or at least should be aiming for. Scanship's core value offerings are based on *the circular economy* since they build on upcycling various forms of waste and they employ *service-logic* in their attempt to turn their technologies into convenient bundles of services for their customers. And, in particular in the case of aquaculture, the company enters into *alliances*. These alliances allows it to deliver value in ways it could likely not have done on its own. Finally, based on these characteristics and the company's identification of new market opportunities, it aims to conduct systematic business *experimentation* in pursuit of these market opportunities. This was in fact partly why Scanship first contacted us. The company wanted us to take part in the design of such experiments that could eventually contribute to a *redesign* of the company's business model, as well as the development of new business models in new markets.

This journey is far from complete, and even though Scanship has achieved a lot to move the company—and its customers—in a greener direction, the company is still navigating difficult waters. Among the challenges it faces is achieving profitability in the experimental business models in new markets, especially since the "burning platform" for adopting such solutions is still not as clear in, for instance, aquaculture as in the cruise industry. In addition, the relative inertia of regulators when it comes to imposing regulations that would be drivers of adoption for technologies offered by Scanship is also a challenge for the company's growth in these markets.

In collaboration with the managers of the company, we are currently in the process of planning empirical studies that can provide knowledge-based input for addressing some of the challenges the company—and companies offering similar solutions—is facing. At the time of writing, this work is very much in progress, and we are still to decide what are the most important issues to be studied empirically, both with regard to being crucial for the success of the company's business model and providing valuable insights to the scientific literature. We therefore end this chapter as a "cliffhanger", by outlining two of our concrete research ideas here. This is an illustration of how we are approaching these issues empirically.

One of the potential research projects is tied to the end consumer in the cruise industry, who in an indirect sense can exert important influence on the competitiveness of Scanship's technologies. An important question in this regard is whether waste management and pollution issues are at all material from the point of view of consumers. That is, do these issues at all influence the consumer's choice of cruise? Part of the problem in this regard is that consumers have little knowledge about, and ability to envision, the environmental impact of the cruise ships, beyond the evident emissions from the funnels atop the ships. Inspired by recent "artefactual" field experiments (cf. Harrison and List 2004) using virtual reality (VR) technology to visualize and make salient various aspects of a product or service, we are exploring the possibility to carry out such VR experiments on cruise travelers. Prior to a cruise or during the cruise, consumers could be exposed to the green technologies aboard the ship and how they lead to the avoidance of waste and pollution in the waters. By comparing consumers subject to such an intervention to consumers in a control condition who are instead shown VR videos of the cruise without such emphasis on environmental dimensions, we could in turn investigate a potential influence on important outcomes such as attitudes, willingness to buy, willingness to pay or experiential dimensions of the actual cruise. It could be added here that a similar design could be used in the setting of fish farming as well, and it would even be possible to conduct comparative analyses across the two sectors. Such research designs would provide important insight into how sustainability improvements in value delivery that are not necessarily possible for consumers to observe can influence consumers' experience and thus the relative attractiveness of the offering.

A second research opportunity relates to the strategic alliances Scanship has entered into, for instance with Skretting, IVAR and HØST for the aquaculture project. As discussed in the chapter on avenues for future research, there is a need for further research on such cross-sector collaborations that include both sustainability-related and financial objectives for all alliance partners. There are several possibilities for empirical investigation in such an alliance, but we are particularly intrigued by the question of how to design a value capture model that allows for successful business modeling on the part of all business partners. This is a main challenge in strategic collaborations—how to design an alliance that benefits all partners and that—as far as possible—aligns their different objectives and priorities. Several different research designs could be applicable in such a project, including a case study combining qualitative and quantitative data sources as well as simple experiments comparing various payoff structures under different versions of the value capture model.

Such a study could contribute valuable knowledge on designing value capture models across organizational boundaries in such cross-sector collaborative business models.

References

Friends of the Earth. (2012). *Cruise ship report card*. Washington, DC: Friends of the Earth.
Harrison, G. W., & List, J. A. (2004). Field experiments. *Journal of Economic Literature, 42*(4), 1009–1055.

Open Access This chapter is licensed under the terms of the Creative Commons Attribution-NonCommercial-NoDerivatives 4.0 International License (http://creativecommons.org/licenses/by-nc-nd/4.0/), which permits any noncommercial use, sharing, distribution and reproduction in any medium or format, as long as you give appropriate credit to the original author(s) and the source, provide a link to the Creative Commons license and indicate if you modified the licensed material. You do not have permission under this license to share adapted material derived from this book or parts of it.

The images or other third party material in this chapter are included in the chapter's Creative Commons license, unless indicated otherwise in a credit line to the material. If material is not included in the chapter's Creative Commons license and your intended use is not permitted by statutory regulation or exceeds the permitted use, you will need to obtain permission directly from the copyright holder.

17

Case Study: A Circular Business Model for Orkla and BIR?

> *Since we depend on plastic packaging, we also have a part to play in the plastic problem. Can we reduce our plastic footprint by making our customers refill their plastic containers with our products instead of throwing them in the bin after a single use? Or is it a better option for our customers to return their containers so we can reuse them? And who could we collaborate with in order to get hold of discarded containers? If we use more recycled plastic, will this help in reducing the chance of whales full of plastic waste stranding on the shores while suffocating from plastic?*

Bård Bringsrud Svensen, the Sustainability Innovation Manager at Orkla Home & Personal Care, bombarded us with questions. And we bombarded him back. We were walking through the streets of Bergen vigorously discussing questions such as will customers be willing to deliver their plastic containers if they are given a discount on their next purchase? What kinds of technologies are necessary to make this happen in practice? Before Bård had left town for his flight back to Oslo, we had even discussed drone-delivered refill of cleaning products and many other futuristic distribution solutions to Orkla's problem: How to design a circular business model for an industry giant.

As fate would have it, around the same time as our walk with Svensen, we received a phone call from Steinar Nævdal—the CEO of the waste management company BIR. It is owned by the municipalities in the Bergen region in Norway, and it had already positioned itself as an innovative and digitally oriented player in the waste management industry, for instance, with its early adoption of an underground waste system beneath the city streets of Bergen, as well as high-tech scanning systems for waste. Nævdal had long noticed the emergence of circular thinking in business, and he thought that his company, with its dual competence in waste management and digital systems, should be in a pole position to facilitate the circular transition.

The co-occurrence of these two conversations with Svensen and Nævdal made us realize that this might be, as Humphrey Bogart said in Casablanca, "the beginning of a beautiful friendship". That is, there might be potential for an unusual alliance between the consumer products giant Orkla, the waste management company BIR and two researchers on sustainable business model innovation from the world of academia. This sparked a collaborative research project in which we build on the RESTART framework and the Business Model RESTARTer process model outlined above for developing hypotheses and experiments together with the two companies. In this case study, we shed light on this collaborative effort and emphasize how we extend and apply the frameworks from this book in practice, in a manner that can have both business-related and scientific outcomes.

17.1 Orkla and Its Ecosystem

Svensen, Orkla's sustainability innovation manager, is an engineer who has worked with innovation and product design his whole career. When he contacted us, he had just been assigned the responsibility for sustainability innovation in one of the largest divisions of Orkla—Orkla Home & Personal Care. On its webpage (www.orkla.no), Orkla describes itself as follows:

Orkla is a leading supplier of branded consumer goods to the grocery, out-of-home, specialised retail, pharmacy and bakery sectors. The Nordic and Baltic regions and selected countries in Central Europe are Orkla's main markets. The Orkla Group also holds strong positions in selected product categories in India. Orkla's Branded Consumer Goods business comprises the Orkla Foods, Orkla Confectionery & Snacks, Orkla Care and Orkla Food Ingredients business areas. Orkla also has operations organised under the Orkla Investments business area, consisting of its investment in and Jotun (42.5% interest), in addition to Hydro Power and financial assets. Orkla ASA is listed on the Oslo Stock Exchange and its head office is in Oslo, Norway. As of 31 December 2016, Orkla had 18,154 employees. The Group's turnover in 2016 totalled NOK 37.8 billion.

Orkla Home & Personal Care is a part of Orkla Care, one of the biggest business units in Orkla. Orkla Home & Care holds a leading position within home detergents and personal care products and competes with international corporations such as Unilever, Procter & Gamble and Colgate-Palmolive. Unilever is perhaps the corporation in this industry that has been most successful in branding itself as sustainable, but in January 2018, Orkla's efforts to become more sustainable were also noticed. At the World Economic Forum annual event, Orkla was unveiled as one of the 100 companies included in the Corporate Knights Global 100 list of the world's most sustainable companies. However, neither Unilever nor Orkla have solved all the problems related to their substantial shadowy sides. One of the most important negative externalities in these industries is related to the use of plastic in product design and packaging, which is turning into a big headache for companies and consumers alike.

In Norway, one incident in particular fueled the public conversation about the environmental consequences of plastic usage. It happened early in 2017, when a whale was found stranded off the coast of Norway—its stomach full of 30 different types of plastic bags. According to a recent report from the World Economic Forum, at least 8 million tons of plastic already ends up in the ocean annually. It is the equivalent of a full truck of waste every minute. Many of the plastic items in the oceans are branded with famous brand names, and according to Terje Lislevand, a zoologist who examined the stranded whale in Norway, many of the labels were in

Danish and English print. He added that the whale's intestines were probably blocked up by plastic, which would cause severe pain. This incident and the attention it received in Norwegian media put pressure on all companies that are seen as part of the plastic problem. Also, from a consumer point of view, this incident also seemed to make everyone more aware how consumption translates into concrete environmental problems that we collectively need to address.

When we met Svensen, he said that Orkla had been aware of the negative effects of the use of plastic for a long time and that they had been working on finding solutions to reduce these effects and related externalities in Orkla's business model for a long time. Svensen still had many questions regarding the way forward for Orkla Home & Personal Care's business model. Sustainability was a large part of the problem, but at the same time, Svensen explained that factors such as increased competition from international brands and ongoing and expected changes in the retail industry because of the fourth industrial revolution were also central to their concerns. To make matters worse, the younger generations of consumers are generally less brand loyal and more willing to switch than their parents and grandparents. This implies that Orkla constantly needs to reposition itself to stay competitive. "We're not just becoming more circular, more sustainable", said Svensen. "This is also a matter of maintaining our profitability—now and in the future".

17.2 BIR: From Waste Manager to Circular Business Partner?

When we received the phone call from Nævdal—CEO of the BIR Group (BIR)—it was because he, his management team and the board had decided that BIR should take on a leading role in the transition from a linear to a circular economy. As a municipal entity, BIR is responsible for collecting, transporting and handling household waste, as well as industrial and hazardous waste in the regional municipalities. However, it also offers waste solutions for business. The BIR Group is Norway's second largest company in this industry with 417 employees, and in 2016, it had a turnover of NOK 736.7 million.

The first well-known innovation project in BIR was its underground vacuum system for waste collection in Bergen, which has since been imitated by waste management companies elsewhere in the world. It is a closed, pipe-based system for collecting waste. It works almost like a giant vacuum cleaner that sucks waste from the waste collection points to central containers. Moreover, BIR has invested quite heavily in a digital waste identification system called BOSS ID (in English, WASTE ID). This system gives each user her own identity, and the customer's access to the waste system is controlled by a Radio Frequency Identification (RFID) key. In this way, BIR gets access to data about the customers, the customers pay directly for usage and BIR collects and manages valuable information about the flow of waste in its value chain. Thus, the potential for building further services based on this data can be considerable in the longer term, while in the shorter term, it allows for the optimization of BIR's operations.

We brought ORKLA and BIR together so that they could attempt to rethink their operations jointly and to see whether there might be benefits from seeing their business models in tandem. After all, massive amounts of Orkla plastic ends up in BIR's containers every year. Svensen had told us that Orkla had already come a long way in rethinking their operations, but that its managers were looking for partners who could offer solutions that the company could not provide on its own. Given BIR's innovative approach toward circular thinking, we thought that the two companies could innovate together. At the Norwegian Waste Management Conference in fall of 2017, we therefore jointly launched a research project on circular business models with particular emphasis on plastic packaging.

17.3 Recognize—Rethink—Reinvent—Reorganize

Together, we embarked on a problem formulation process about the future of circular business models, with Orkla as the main case. As it happened, Orkla had recently launched a new brand and product portfolio series that would in part cannibalize on its well-known soap and detergent products. The series is called KLAR—a word that in Norwegian can mean "clear", "transparent", as well as "ready". The product line is vegan, its formulations are sustainable, of course free from microplastics, and packaged in 100 percent recycled plastic. The KLAR concept was chosen as an initial case for our research project, which implied that the manager responsible for the development of the brand and the product portfolio, Anne Marheim Støren, became an important part of our research project.

The case of sustainable cleaning products is particularly interesting for many reasons. First, it is a product category most, if not all, households rely on. Importantly, however, there had scarcely been any sustainable products in this category and to the extent that there had been, customers generally did not seem to trust their quality. Since these products constitute a low involvement and habit-based product category, we were particularly intrigued by the challenge of working with a company like Orkla to investigate how consumer behavior and habits could be changed to embrace more sustainable solutions. This made it necessary to understand several aspects of consumer behavior related to such products: the barriers and drivers of adoption, the beliefs about effectiveness and the preferences for or against such products and the decisive characteristics and messages that could drive consumers to change from less sustainable to more sustainable products.

We based our work process on the three phases in the Business Model Restarter, and at the time of writing, we are still somewhere in between rethinking and reinventing. In the early phases of the process, we ran workshops with the two companies and crowdsourced the viewpoints and ideas of a group of innovators at the Innovation Festival 2017 in Åndalsnes, Norway. There, we hosted an interactive workshop wherein participants generated and discussed ideas for the future distribution of home care products. At a workshop with BIR and Orkla at the end of 2017, however, a shortlist of sub-projects to be pursued further was developed. We facilitated this work in close collaboration with business developer Tore Totland and Anders Waage Nilsen, two freethinking individuals whose help BIR had also enlisted when embarking on this journey. Together, we designed the four sub-projects, and we began thinking more concretely about how empirical studies could be derived from each of the projects.

The different groups of project members from BIR, Orkla and the academic institutions generated four problems to be solved along a circular chain. In order to solve the problem of plastic circularity in practice, at least four challenges must be overcome: First, in order for circularity to function for plastic products, the products must be designed and manufactured in a manner that makes them recyclable (cf. Bocken et al. 2014). A project group was formed to address this challenge, which at least initially is more a technical and practical process than a research project, although there might be opportunities for scientific studies at a later stage. Second, once products are distributed to stores, knowledge of consumer behavior in the store and at home is essential. Here, a project group was formed to design lab and field experiments on consumer behavior related to the choice of an explicitly "green" product series such as KLAR—a strand of literature already rich on interesting findings. Moreover, there was a clear intention to dig deeper into the life of the product after consumers brought it home—a topic that could be investigated by groups of master students, for instance.

Third, in order to connect the business models of Orkla and BIR, the third sub-project related to the systems, solutions and incentives for getting consumers to return the packaging after the product had been discarded. A project group with both practitioners and academics was tasked with developing ideas for such systems and to envision testable solutions in the field. Fourth, in the more practical end, a group was formed for investigating the question of how collected plastics could be "led back to" Orkla, so that yesterday's KLAR containers could become the Orkla packaging of tomorrow.

By forming these four groups and commencing the work in each four of them, the innovation process starts leaning from a rethink phase to a reinvent phase. That is, as ideas are generated and in due course tested scientifically or through various forms of A/B tests or pilots by the companies, opportunities for actually changing the business models of the companies emerge. Thus far, we have mostly been explicit about how

Orkla's business model might change. But what about BIR? What are the characteristics of a successful outcome for such a company in a process like this? Will BIR need to change its business model in a way that involves differentiated payment from companies that either would like to purchase generic recycled materials versus, for instance, recycled materials that are in fact based on its own prior goods being returned and recycled? Or should BIR be paid not for waste management but for waste avoidance, as the company Norsk Gjenvinning also asked itself, as detailed in the case in Part II of the book?

It is too soon to tell where the project with Orkla and BIR will end up, and what will be the outcomes for the partners involved. The preceding description, however, attempts to account for a messy innovation process in which there are explicit desires from all partners to run scientific studies, in general, and experiments, in particular, in order to reveal some of the factors that can help companies achieve more circular business models. The remainder of the story will have to be told another day.

17.4 Restarting Together: More Cake for All?

We have argued that alliances such as the one described above can increase the value created for all players and may even have beneficial outcomes for society and the environment. By no means, however, do we believe that succeeding with such alliances is an easy task. Fortune favors the bold, some say, and it is at least our impression thus far that by embarking on this unusual and ambitious collaboration with players from different industries as well as academics with other objectives, time horizons and mindsets, BIR and Orkla have opened doors to new ways of thinking about how they create, deliver and capture value.

Reference

Bocken, N. M. P., Short, S. W., Rana, P., & Evans, S. (2014). A literature and practice review to develop sustainable business model archetypes. *Journal of Cleaner Production, 65*, 42–56.

Case Study: A Circular Business Model for Orkla and BIR? 229

Open Access This chapter is licensed under the terms of the Creative Commons Attribution-NonCommercial-NoDerivatives 4.0 International License (http://creativecommons.org/licenses/by-nc-nd/4.0/), which permits any noncommercial use, sharing, distribution and reproduction in any medium or format, as long as you give appropriate credit to the original author(s) and the source, provide a link to the Creative Commons license and indicate if you modified the licensed material. You do not have permission under this license to share adapted material derived from this book or parts of it.

The images or other third party material in this chapter are included in the chapter's Creative Commons license, unless indicated otherwise in a credit line to the material. If material is not included in the chapter's Creative Commons license and your intended use is not permitted by statutory regulation or exceeds the permitted use, you will need to obtain permission directly from the copyright holder.

References

Adner, R. (2006). Match your innovation strategy to your innovation ecosystem. *Harvard Business Review, 84*(4), 98.

Aldrich, H., & Herker, D. (1977). Boundary spanning roles and organization structure. *Academy of Management Review, 2*(2), 217–230.

Anderson, C. (2009). *Free: The future of a radical price*. New York, NY: Random House.

Anderson, E. T. (2011). A step-by-step guide to smart business experiments. *Development and Learning in Organizations: An International Journal, 25*(6).

Anderson, R. (2002). Mid-course correction: Toward a sustainable enterprise. *Journal of Business Administration and Policy Analysis, 30*, 415.

Andries, P., Debackere, K., & Looy, B. (2013). Simultaneous experimentation as a learning strategy: Business model development under uncertainty. *Strategic Entrepreneurship Journal, 7*(4), 288–310.

Atkinson, A. B. (2015). *Inequality*. Cambridge, MA: Harvard University Press.

Baines, T. S., Lightfoot, H. W., Benedettini, O., & Kay, J. M. (2009). The servitization of manufacturing: A review of literature and reflection on future challenges. *Journal of Manufacturing Technology Management, 20*(5), 547–567.

Bales, K. (2016). *Blood and earth: Modern slavery, ecocide, and the secret to saving the world*. Spiegel & Grau.

Banerjee, A. V., & Duflo, E. (2011). *Poor economics: A radical rethinking of the way to fight global poverty*. New York, NY: Public Affairs.

Barney, J. B. (2001). Resource-based theories of competitive advantage: A ten-year retrospective on the resource-based view. *Journal of Management, 27*(6), 643–650.

Bartling, B., Fehr, E., & Huffman, D. (2013). Institutions and trust: Does trust generate lasting improvements in economic outcomes? *Working paper*, The University of Zürich, Zürich.

Bass, A. E., & Milosevic, I. (2016). The ethnographic method in CSR research: The role and importance of methodological fit. *Business & Society*. https://doi.org/10.1177/0007650316648666.

Belk, R. (2014). You are what you can access: Sharing and collaborative consumption online. *Journal of Business Research, 67*(8), 1595–1600.

Berman, S. L., Wicks, A. C., Kotha, S., & Jones, T. M. (1999). Does stakeholder orientation matter? The relationship between stakeholder management models and firm financial performance. *Academy of Management Journal, 42*(5), 488–506.

Bocken, N., Miller, K., Weissbrod, I., Holgado, M., & Evans, S. (2017). Business Model Experimentation for Circularity: Driving sustainability in a large international clothing retailer. *Economics and Policy of Energy and the Environment (EPEE)*.

Bocken, N. M., de Pauw, I., Bakker, C., & van der Grinten, B. (2016). Product design and business model strategies for a circular economy. *Journal of Industrial and Production Engineering, 33*(5), 308–320.

Bocken, N. M. P., Short, S. W., Rana, P., & Evans, S. (2014). A literature and practice review to develop sustainable business model archetypes. *Journal of Cleaner Production, 65*, 42–56.

Bollen, N. P. (2007). Mutual fund attributes and investor behavior. *Journal of Financial and Quantitative Analysis, 42*(3), 683–708.

Boons, F., & Lüdeke-Freund, F. (2013). Business models for sustainable innovation: State-of-the-art and steps towards a research agenda. *Journal of Cleaner Production, 45*, 9–19.

Botsman, R., & Rogers, R. (2010). *What's mine is yours. The rise of collaborative consumption*. New York, NY: HarperCollins.

Bowen, H. R. (1953). *Social responsibilities of the businessman*. New York, NY: Harper & Row.

Brandenburger, A. M., & Nalebuff, B. J. (2011). *Co-opetition*. New York, NY: Crown Business.

Brandt, R. L. (2011). *One click: Jeff Bezos and the rise of Amazon.com*. London: Penguin.

Brown, T. J., & Dacin, P. A. (1997). The company and the product: Corporate associations and consumer product responses. *Journal of Marketing, 61*(1), 68–84.

Brundtland, G. H. (Ed.). (1987). *Report of the World Commission on environment and development: Our common future*. New York, NY: United Nations.

Brynjolfsson, E., & McAfee, A. (2014). *The second machine age: Work, progress, and prosperity in a time of brilliant technologies*. New York, NY: WW Norton & Company.

Carroll, A. B. (1999). Corporate social responsibility: Evolution of a definitional construct. *Business & Society, 38*(3), 268–295.

Carroll, A. B. (2008). A history of corporate social responsibility: Concepts and practices. In A. Crane et al. (Eds.), *The Oxford handbook of corporate social responsibility* (pp. 19–46). Oxford: Oxford University Press.

Carroll, A. B., & Shabana, K. M. (2010). The business case for corporate social responsibility: A review of concepts, research and practice. *International Journal of Management Reviews, 12*(1), 85–105.

Chatterji, A. K., Findley, M., Jensen, N. M., Meier, S., & Nielson, D. (2016). Field experiments in strategy research. *Strategic Management Journal, 37*(1), 116–132.

Chatterji, A. K., & Toffel, M. W. (2010). How firms respond to being rated. *Strategic Management Journal, 31*(9), 917–945.

Cheng, B., Ioannou, I., & Serafeim, G. (2014). Corporate social responsibility and access to finance. *Strategic Management Journal, 35*(1), 1–23.

Chesbrough, H. W. (2006). *Open innovation: The new imperative for creating and profiting from technology*. Cambridge, MA: Harvard Business Press.

Chesbrough, H. (2007). Business model innovation: It's not just about technology anymore. *Strategy & Leadership, 35*(6), 12–17.

Chesbrough, H. (2010). Business model innovation: Opportunities and barriers. *Long Range Planning, 43*(2), 354–363.

Chesbrough, H., & Rosenbloom, R. S. (2002). The role of the business model in capturing value from innovation: Evidence from Xerox Corporation's technology spin-off companies. *Industrial and Corporate Change, 11*(3), 529–555.

Choudary, S. P., Van Alstyne, M. W., & Parker, G. G. (2016). *Platform revolution: How networked markets are transforming the economy—And how to make them work for you*. New York, NY: WW Norton & Company.

Christensen, C. M., Anthony, S. D., Berstell, G., & Nitterhouse, D. (2007). Finding the right job for your product. *MIT Sloan Management Review, 48*(3), 38.

Christensen, C. (2012). *The innovator's dilemma: When new technologies cause great firms to fail.* Cambridge, MA: Harvard Business Review Press.

Christensen, C. (2013). *The innovator's dilemma: When new technologies cause great firms to fail.* Cambridge, MA: Harvard Business Review Press.

Collins, A., & Fairchild, R. (2007). Sustainable food consumption at a subnational level: An ecological footprint, nutritional and economic analysis. *Journal of Environmental Policy & Planning, 9*(1), 5–30.

Cornes, R., & Sandler, T. (1996). *The theory of externalities, public goods, and club goods.* Cambridge: Cambridge University Press.

Crane, A., Henriques, I., & Husted, B. W. (2018). Quants and poets: Advancing methods and methodologies in business and society research. *Business & Society, 57*(1), 3–25.

Crespo, A. H., & del Bosque, I. R. (2005). Influence of corporate social responsibility on loyalty and valuation of services. *Journal of Business Ethics, 61*(4), 369–385.

Das, T. K., & Teng, B. S. (2001). Trust, control, and risk in strategic alliances: An integrated framework. *Organization Studies, 22*(2), 251–283.

Davenport, T. H. (2009). How to design smart business experiments. *Harvard Business Review, 87*(2), 68–76.

Davis, K. (1960). Can business afford to ignore social responsibilities? *California Management Review, 2*(3), 70–76.

Deci, E. L., & Ryan, R. M. (2000). The "what" and "why" of goal pursuits: Human needs and the self-determination of behavior. *Psychological Inquiry, 11*(4), 227–268.

Delmas, M. A., & Aragon-Correa, J. A. (2016). Field experiments in corporate sustainability research: Testing strategies for behavior change in markets and organizations. *Organization & Environment, 29*(4), 391–400.

Dentchev, N., Baumgartner, R., Dieleman, H., Jóhannsdóttir, L., Jonker, J., Nyberg, T., & van Hoof, B. (2016). Embracing the variety of sustainable business models: Social entrepreneurship, corporate intrapreneurship, creativity, innovation, and other approaches to sustainability challenges. *Journal of Cleaner Production, 113*(1), 1–4.

Dewar, R. D., & Dutton, J. E. (1986). The adoption of radical and incremental innovations: An empirical analysis. *Management Science, 32*(11), 1422–1433.

Dhebar, A. (2016). Razor-and-Blades pricing revisited. *Business Horizons, 59*(3), 303–310.

Dierickx, I., & Cool, K. (1989). Asset stock accumulation and sustainability of competitive advantage. *Management Science, 35*(12), 1504–1511.

Dixon, J. A., & Fallon, L. A. (1989). The concept of sustainability: Origins, extensions, and usefulness for policy. *Society & Natural Resources, 2*(1), 73–84.

Døskeland, T., & Pedersen, L. J. T. (2015). Investing with brain or heart? A field experiment on responsible investment. *Management Science, 62*(6), 1632–1644.

Døskeland, T., & Pedersen, L. J. T. (2017). Does the wealth of investors matter? Evidence from a field experiment on responsible investment. *Working paper*, NHH Norwegian School of Economics.

Drechsler, W., & Natter, M. (2012). Understanding a firm's openness decisions in innovation. *Journal of Business Research, 65*(3), 438–445.

Duraiappah, A. K. (1998). Poverty and environmental degradation: A review and analysis of the nexus. *World Development, 26*(12), 2169–2179.

Du, S., Bhattacharya, C. B., & Sen, S. (2010). Maximizing business returns to corporate social responsibility (CSR): The role of CSR communication. *International Journal of Management Reviews, 12*(1), 8–19.

Dyer, J. H., & Singh, H. (1998). The relational view: Cooperative strategy and sources of interorganizational competitive advantage. *Academy of Management Review, 23*(4), 660–679.

Dyllick, T., & Hockerts, K. (2002). Beyond the business case for corporate sustainability. *Business Strategy and the Environment, 11*(2), 130–141.

Eccles, R. G., Feiner, A., & Verheyden, T. (2016). *Sustainability and financial performance of Scandinavian companies*. Unpublished manuscript, Harvard Business School.

Eccles, R. G., Ioannou, I., & Serafeim, G. (2014). The impact of corporate sustainability on organizational processes and performance. *Management Science, 60*(11), 2835–2857.

Eccles, R. G., Ioannou, I., & Serafeim, G. (2015). The impact of corporate sustainability on organizational processes and performance. *Management Science, 60*(11), 2835–2857.

Eccles, R. G., & Krzus, M. P. (2010). *One report: Integrated reporting for a sustainable strategy*. Hoboken, NJ: John Wiley & Sons.

Eccles, R. G., Krzus, M. P., Rogers, J., & Serafeim, G. (2012). The need for sector-specific materiality and sustainability reporting standards. *Journal of Applied Corporate Finance, 24*(2), 65–71.

Eccles, R. G., & Serafeim, G. (2013). The performance frontier. *Harvard Business Review, 91*(5), 50–60.

Eccles, R. G., Serafeim, G., & Krzus, M. P. (2011). Market interest in nonfinancial information. *Journal of Applied Corporate Finance, 23*(4), 113–127.

Edmans, A. (2012). The link between job satisfaction and firm value, with implications for corporate social responsibility. *The Academy of Management Perspectives, 26*(4), 1–19.

Eells, R. S. F., & Walton, C. C. (1969). *Conceptual foundations of business.* Homewood, IL: R.D. Irwin.

Ehrenfeld, J., & Gertler, N. (1997). Industrial ecology in practice: The evolution of interdependence at Kalundborg. *Journal of Industrial Ecology, 1*(1), 67–79.

Eisenhardt, K. M., Graebner, M. E., & Sonenshein, S. (2016). Grand challenges and inductive methods: Rigor without rigor mortis. *Academy of Management Journal, 59*(4), 1113–1123.

Ekins, P. (2002). *Economic growth and environmental sustainability: The prospects for green growth.* London: Routledge.

Elkington, J. (1997). *Cannibals with forks. The triple bottom line of 21st century.* Oxford: Capstone.

Elkington, J., & Zeitz, J. (2014). *The breakthrough challenge: 10 ways to connect today's profits with tomorrow's bottom line.* London: John Wiley & Sons.

Ellen MacArthur Foundation. (2015). *Growth within: A circular economy vision for a competitive Europe.* Cowes, UK: Ellen MacArthur Foundation.

Ellen MacArthur Foundation. (2017). *Beyond plastic waste.* Cowes, UK: Ellen MacArthur Foundation.

Epstein, M. J., & Buhovac, A. R. (2014). *Making sustainability work: Best practices in managing and measuring corporate social, environmental, and economic impacts.* San Francisco, CA: Berrett-Koehler Publishers.

Epstein, M. J., & Roy, M. J. (2001). Sustainability in action: Identifying and measuring the key performance drivers. *Long Range Planning, 34*(5), 585–604.

Esty, D., & Winston, A. (2009). *Green to gold: How smart companies use environmental strategy to innovate, create value, and build competitive advantage.* London: John Wiley & Sons.

Ettlie, J. E., Bridges, W. P., & O'Keefe, R. D. (1984). Organization strategy and structural differences for radical versus incremental innovation. *Management Science, 30*(6), 682–695.

Etzion, D., & Ferraro, F. (2010). The role of analogy in the institutionalization of sustainability reporting. *Organization Science, 21*(5), 1092–1107.

Eurosif. (2014). *European SRI study 2014.* Paris: Eurosif.

Evans, A. (2011). *Resource scarcity, climate change and the risk of violent conflict.* Washington, DC: The World Bank.

Fernandez-Feijoo, B., Romero, S., & Ruiz, S. (2014). Effect of stakeholders' pressure on transparency of sustainability reports within the GRI framework. *Journal of Business Ethics, 122*(1), 53–63.

Figge, F., Hahn, T., Schaltegger, S., & Wagner, M. (2002). The sustainability balanced scorecard–linking sustainability management to business strategy. *Business Strategy and the Environment, 11*(5), 269–284.

Flammer, C. (2015). Does corporate social responsibility lead to superior financial performance? A regression discontinuity approach. *Management Science, 61*(11), 2549–2568.

Flammer, C., & Kacperczyk, A. (2015). The impact of stakeholder orientation on innovation: Evidence from a natural experiment. *Management Science, 62*(7), 1982–2001.

Foss, N. J., Pedersen, T., Pyndt, J., & Schultz, M. (2012). *Innovating organization and management: New sources of competitive advantage*. Cambridge: Cambridge University Press.

Foss, N. J., & Saebi, T. (2017). Fifteen years of research on business model innovation: How far have we come, and where should we go? *Journal of Management, 43*(1), 200–227.

Frank, R. H. (2004). *What price the moral high ground? How to succeed without selling your soul*. Princeton, NJ: Princeton University Press.

Frederick, W. C. (1960). The growing concern over business responsibility. *California Management Review, 2*, 54–61.

Freeman, R. E. (1984). *Strategic management: A stakeholder approach*. Boston, MA: Pitman.

Freeman, R. E. (2010). *Strategic management: A stakeholder approach*. Cambridge: Cambridge University Press.

Frey, B. S., & Oberholzer-Gee, F. (1997). The cost of price incentives: An empirical analysis of motivation crowding-out. *American Economic Review, 87*(4), 746–755.

Friedman, M. (1970, September 13). The social responsibility of business is to increase its profits. *New York Times Magazine*.

Friends of the Earth. (2012). *Cruise ship report card*. Washington, DC: Friends of the Earth.

Gansky, L. (2010). *The mesh: Why the future of business is sharing*. London: Penguin.

Gassmann, O., Frankenberger, K., & Csik, M. (2014). *The business model navigator: 55 models that will revolutionise your business*. Harlow, UK: Pearson UK.

Global Footprint Network. (2011). What happens when infinite-growth economy runs into a finite planet. *Global Footprint Network 2011 Annual Report*. Oakland, CA: Global Footprint Network.

Gond, J. P., Grubnic, S., Herzig, C., & Moon, J. (2012). Configuring management control systems: Theorizing the integration of strategy and sustainability. *Management Accounting Research, 23*(3), 205–223.

Grayson, D., & Hodges, A. (2017). *Corporate social opportunity! Seven steps to make corporate social responsibility work for your business.* Sheffield, UK: Greenleaf.

Guajardo, J. A. (2016). Pay-as-you-go business models in developing economies: Consumer behavior and repayment performance. Available at SSRN.

Gulbrandsen, E. A., Jørgensen, S., Kaarbøe, K., & Pedersen, L. J. T. (2015). Developing management control systems for sustainable business models. *Beta: Scandinavian Journal of Business Research, 29*(1), 10–25.

Gulbrandsen, E. A., Jørgensen, S., & Pedersen, L. J. T. (2017). Sustainability practices and performance in Norwegian knowledge-intensive service companies. *Working paper*, NHH Norwegian School of Economics.

Harman, J. (2013). *The Shark's paintbrush: Biomimicry and how nature is inspiring innovation.* London: Nicholas Brealey Publishing.

Harrison, G. W., & List, J. A. (2004). Field experiments. *Journal of Economic Literature, 42*(4), 1009–1055.

Harrison, H., Kubik, J. D., & Scheinkman, J. A. (2012). Financial constraints on corporate goodness. *NBER Working Paper Series, 18476.*

Harter, J. K., Schmidt, F. L., & Hayes, T. L. (2002). Business-unit-level relationship between employee satisfaction, employee engagement, and business outcomes: A meta-analysis. *Journal of Applied Psychology, 87*(2), 268.

Hawken, P. (1993). *The ecology of commerce: How business can save the planet.* London: Weidenfeld & Nicolson.

Hofmann, H., Busse, C., Bode, C., & Henke, M. (2014). Sustainability-related supply chain risks: Conceptualization and management. *Business Strategy and the Environment, 23*(3), 160–172.

Holmes, B. (2006). Earth without humans. *New Scientist, 192*(2573), 36–41.

Hong, H., & Kacperczyk, M. (2009). The price of sin: The effects of social norms on markets. *Journal of Financial Economics, 93*(1), 15–36.

Horbach, J., Rammer, C., & Rennings, K. (2012). Determinants of eco-innovations by type of environmental impact—The role of regulatory push/pull, technology push and market pull. *Ecological Economics, 78*, 112–122.

Hufford, A. (2017, June 15). Spotify's paid users surged last year but loss doubled. *The Wall Street Journal*. Retrieved January 12, 2018, from https://www.wsj.com/articles/spotify-paid-users-surged-last-year-but-loss-doubled-1497539725.

Hutchins, M. J., & Sutherland, J. W. (2008). An exploration of measures of social sustainability and their application to supply chain decisions. *Journal of Cleaner Production, 16*(15), 1688–1698.

Inagaki, K., & Osawa, J. (2012, January 20). Fujifilm thrived by changing focus. *The Wall Street Journal*. Retrieved January 12, 2018, from https://www.wsj.com/articles/SB10001424052970203750404577170481473958516.

Ingebrigtsen, S., & Jakobsen, O. D. (2007). *Circulation economics: Theory and practice* (Vol. 3). Oxford: Peter Lang.

Intergovernmental Panel on Climate Change. (2014). *Climate change 2014—Impacts, adaptation and vulnerability: Regional aspects*. Cambridge: Cambridge University Press.

Jacobsen, N. B. (2006). Industrial symbiosis in Kalundborg, Denmark: A quantitative assessment of economic and environmental aspects. *Journal of Industrial Ecology, 10*(1–2), 239–255.

Jenkins, H. (2009). A 'business opportunity' model of corporate social responsibility for small-and medium-sized enterprises. *Business Ethics: A European Review, 18*(1), 21–36.

Jeucken, M. (2010). *Sustainable finance and banking: The financial sector and the future of the planet*. London: Routledge.

Johnson, G., Melin, L., & Whittington, R. (2003). Micro strategy and strategizing: Towards an activity-based view. *Journal of Management Studies, 40*(1), 3–22.

Johnson, M. W., Christensen, C. M., & Kagermann, H. (2008). Reinventing your business model. *Harvard Business Review, 86*(12), 57–68.

Jorde, T. M., & Teece, D. J. (1990). Innovation and cooperation: Implications for competition and antitrust. *Journal of Economic Perspectives, 4*(3), 75–96.

Jørgensen, S., & Pedersen, L. J. T. (2011). Organizing for responsibility. In O. Jakobsen & L. J. T. Pedersen (Eds.), *Responsibility, deep ecology & the self: Festschrift in honor of Knut J. Ims*. Oslo: Forlag1.

Jørgensen, S., & Pedersen, L. J. T. (2015). *Responsible and profitable: Strategies for sustainable business models*. Oslo: Cappelen Damm Akademisk.

Jørgensen, S., & Pedersen, L. J. T. (2017a). Designing sustainable business models. In T. W. Andreassen, S. Clatworthy, M. Lüders, & T. Hillestad (Eds.), *Innovating for trust*. Cheltenham, UK: Edward Elgar Publishing.

Jørgensen, S., & Pedersen, L. J. T. (2017b). Towards smarter and more sustainable business models in retail. *Working paper*, NHH Norwegian School of Economics.

Jørgensen, S. & Pedersen, L.J.T. (2018). Towards smart and sustainable business models in retail. In N. Bocken, P. Ritala, L. Albareda, & R. Verburg (Eds.),

Innovation for sustainability: Business transformations towards a better world. London: Palgrave (In press).

Jørgensen, S., Pedersen, L. J. T., & Skard, S. (2018). Does going green build trust? The relationship between sustainability efforts, perceived innovativeness and trust. *Working paper*, NHH Norwegian School of Economics.

Kang, C., Germann, F., & Grewal, R. (2016). Washing away your sins? Corporate social responsibility, corporate social irresponsibility, and firm performance. *Journal of Marketing, 80*(2), 59–79.

Kaplan, S. (2012). *The business model innovation factory: How to stay relevant when the world is changing*. London: John Wiley & Sons.

Karamchandani, A., Kubzansky, M., & Lalwani, N. (2011). Is the bottom of the pyramid really for you. *Harvard Business Review, 89*(3), 107–111.

Karnani, A. (2007). The mirage of marketing to the bottom of the pyramid: How the private sector can help alleviate poverty. *California Management Review, 49*(4), 90–111.

Kastalli, I. V., & Van Looy, B. (2013). Servitization: Disentangling the impact of service business model innovation on manufacturing firm performance. *Journal of Operations Management, 31*(4), 169–180.

Katz, W. G. (1960). Responsibility and the modern corporation. *Journal of Law and Economics, 3*, 75–85.

Keeble, J. J., Topiol, S., & Berkeley, S. (2003). Using indicators to measure sustainability performance at a corporate and project level. *Journal of Business Ethics, 44*(2), 149–158.

Kelly, K. (2016). *The inevitable: Understanding the 12 technological forces that will shape our future*. Penguin.

Khan, M., Serafeim, G., & Yoon, A. (2015). Corporate sustainability: First evidence on materiality. *Accounting Review, 91*(6), 1697–1724.

Khan, M., Serafeim, G., & Yoon, A. (2016). Corporate sustainability: First evidence on materiality. *Accounting Review, 91*(6), 1697–1724.

Kiron, D., Kruschwitz, N., Haanaes, K., Reeves, M., Fuisz-Kehrbach, S. K., & Kell, G. (2015). Joining forces: Collaboration and leadership for sustainability. *MIT Sloan Management Review, 56*(3), 1–31.

Kiron, D., Kruschwitz, N., Haanaes, K., & von Streng Velken, I. (2012). Sustainability nears a tipping point. *MIT Sloan Management Review, 53*(2), 69–74.

Koys, D. J. (2001). The effects of employee satisfaction, organizational citizenship behavior, and turnover on organizational effectiveness: A unit-level, longitudinal study. *Personnel Psychology, 54*(1), 101–114.

Krautkraemer, J. A. (1998). Nonrenewable resource scarcity. *Journal of Economic Literature, 36*(4), 2065–2107.

Lacy, P., & Rutqvist, J. (2015). *Waste to wealth: The circular economy advantage.* London: Palgrave.

Le, K., Bilgir, O., Bianchini, R., Martonosi, M., & Nguyen, T. D. (2010, June). Managing the cost, energy consumption, and carbon footprint of internet services. In *ACM SIGMETRICS performance evaluation review* (Vol. 38, No. 1, pp. 357–358). ACM.

Lehner, M., Mont, O., & Heiskanen, E. (2016). Nudging—A promising tool for sustainable consumption behaviour? *Journal of Cleaner Production, 134*, 166–177.

Levitt, S. D., & List, J. A. (2007). What do laboratory experiments measuring social preferences reveal about the real world? *Journal of Economic Perspectives, 21*(2), 153–174.

Levitt, S. D., & List, J. A. (2009). Field experiments in economics: The past, the present, and the future. *European Economic Review, 53*(1), 1–18.

Levitt, T. (1960). Marketing myopia. *Harvard Business Review, 38*(4), 24–47.

Levitt, T. (1972). Production-line approach to service. *Harvard Business Review, 50*(5), 41–52.

Lewin, K. (1947). Group decision and social change. *Readings in Social Psychology, 3*, 197–211.

Lieder, M., & Rashid, A. (2016). Towards circular economy implementation: A comprehensive review in context of manufacturing industry. *Journal of Cleaner Production, 115*, 36–51.

Linder, M., & Williander, M. (2017). Circular business model innovation: Inherent uncertainties. *Business Strategy and the Environment, 26*(2), 182–196.

List, J., & Gneezy, U. (2014). *The why axis: Hidden motives and the undiscovered economics of everyday life.* New York, NY: Random House.

Lockett, A., Moon, J., & Visser, W. (2006). Corporate social responsibility in management research: Focus, nature, salience and sources of influence. *Journal of Management Studies, 43*(1), 115–136.

Lozano, R. (2008). Envisioning sustainability three-dimensionally. *Journal of Cleaner Production, 16*(17), 1838–1846.

Lusch, R. F., & Vargo, S. L. (2012). *Service-dominant logic.* Cambridge: Cambridge University Press.

Magretta, J. (2002). Why business models matter. *Harvard Business Review, 80*(5), 86–92.

Margolis, J. D., Elfenbein, H. A., & Walsh, J. P. (2007). Does it pay to be good? A meta-analysis and redirection of research on the relationship between corporate social and financial performance. Ann Arbor, 1001, 48109-1234.

Margolis, J. D., & Walsh, J. P. (2003). Misery loves companies: Rethinking social initiatives by business. *Administrative Science Quarterly, 48*(2), 268–305.

McDonough, W., & Braungart, M. (2010). *Cradle to cradle: Remaking the way we make things.* London: Macmillan.

McDonough, W., & Braungart, M. (2013). *The upcycle: Beyond sustainability—Designing for abundance.* London: Macmillan.

McGrath, R. G. (2010). Business models: A discovery driven approach. *Long Range Planning, 43*(2), 247–261.

McWilliams, A., & Siegel, D. (2001). Corporate social responsibility: A theory of the firm perspective. *Academy of Management Review, 26*(1), 117–127.

Miller, K. D. (1992). A framework for integrated risk management in international business. *Journal of International Business Studies, 23*(2), 311–331.

Mitchell, D., & Coles, C. (2003). The ultimate competitive advantage of continuing business model innovation. *Journal of Business Strategy, 24*(5), 15–21.

Mitchell, R. K., Agle, B. R., & Wood, D. J. (1997). Toward a theory of stakeholder identification and salience: Defining the principle of who and what really counts. *Academy of Management Review, 22*(4), 853–886.

Mol, A. P. (2015). Transparency and value chain sustainability. *Journal of Cleaner Production, 107,* 154–161.

Mont, O. K. (2002). Clarifying the concept of product–service system. *Journal of Cleaner Production, 10*(3), 237–245.

Mont, O., & Tukker, A. (2006). Product-service systems: Reviewing achievements and refining the research agenda. *Journal of Cleaner Production, 14*(17), 1451–1454.

Morlet, A., Blériot, J., Opsomer, R., Linder, M., Henggeler, A., Bluhm, A., & Carrera, A. (2016). *Intelligent assets: Unlocking the circular economy potential.* London: Ellen MacArthur Foundation.

Morris, M., Schindehutte, M., & Allen, J. (2005). The entrepreneur's business model: Toward a unified perspective. *Journal of Business Research, 58*(6), 726–735.

Mowery, D. C., Oxley, J. E., & Silverman, B. S. (1996). Strategic alliances and interfirm knowledge transfer. *Strategic Management Journal, 17*(S2), 77–91.

Nalebuff, B. J., & Brandenburger, A. M. (1997). Co-opetition: Competitive and cooperative business strategies for the digital economy. *Strategy & Leadership, 25*(6), 28–33.

Nehrt, C. (1998). Maintainability of first mover advantages when environmental regulations differ between countries. *Academy of Management Review, 23*(1), 77–97.

Ng, I., Parry, G., Smith, L., Maull, R., & Briscoe, G. (2012). Transitioning from a goods-dominant to a service-dominant logic: Visualising the value proposition of Rolls-Royce. *Journal of Service Management, 23*(3), 416–439.

Nidumolu, R., Prahalad, C. K., & Rangaswami, M. R. (2009). Why sustainability is now the key driver of innovation. *Harvard Business Review, 87*(9), 56–64.

O'Higgins, E., & Zsolnai, L. (Eds.). (2017). *Progressive business models: Creating sustainable and pro-social enterprise.* Springer.

O'Higgins, E., & Zsolnai, L. (2018). What is progressive business? In E. O'Higgins & L. Zsolnai (Eds.), *Progressive business models: Creating sustainable and pro-social enterprise* (pp. 3–25). London: Palgrave Macmillan.

Orlitzky, M., Schmidt, F. L., & Rynes, S. L. (2003). Corporate social and financial performance: A meta-analysis. *Organization Studies, 24*(3), 403–441.

Osterwalder, A., & Pigneur, Y. (2010). *Business model generation: A handbook for visionaries, game changers, and challengers.* London: John Wiley & Sons.

Osterwalder, A., Pigneur, Y., Bernarda, G., & Smith, A. (2014). *Value proposition design: How to create products and services customers want.* London: John Wiley & Sons.

Pachauri, R. K., & Meyer, L. (red.) (2014). *Climate change 2014: Synthesis report.* Geneva, Switzerland: IPCC.

Pedersen, L. J. T. (2013). Systems of accountability and personal responsibility. In P. Gooderham, K. Kaarbøe, & H. Nørreklit (Eds.), *Managing in dynamic business environments: Between control and autonomy.* Cheltenham, UK: Edward Elgar.

Peloza, J., & Falkenberg, L. (2009). The role of collaboration in achieving corporate social responsibility objectives. *California Management Review, 51*(3), 95–113.

Peredo, A. M., & McLean, M. (2006). Social entrepreneurship: A critical review of the concept. *Journal of World Business, 41*(1), 56–65.

Perrini, F., & Tencati, A. (2006). Sustainability and stakeholder management: The need for new corporate performance evaluation and reporting systems. *Business Strategy and the Environment, 15*(5), 296–308.

Popp, D. (2012). The role of technological change in green growth (No. w18506). National Bureau of Economic Research.

Prahalad, C. K. (2012). Bottom of the pyramid as a source of breakthrough innovations. *Journal of Product Innovation Management, 29*(1), 6–12.

Richardson, K., Steffen, W., Schellnhuber, H. J., Alcamo, J., Barker, T., Kammen, D. M., & Stern, N. (2009). *Climate change-global risks, challenges & decisions: Synthesis report*. Copenhagen: Museum Tusculanum.

Ries, E. (2011). *The lean startup: How today's entrepreneurs use continuous innovation to create radically successful businesses*. New York, NY: Crown Books.

Rockström, J., Steffen, W., Noone, K., Persson, Å., Chapin, F. S., Lambin, E. F., & Nykvist, B. (2009). A safe operating space for humanity. *Nature, 461*(7263), 472–475.

Rosseland, J. H. (2011). Does it pay to be a responsible company? An examination of the equator principles. *Beta: Scandinavian Journal of Business Research, 25*(1), 49–62.

Salaber, J. M. (2007). The determinants of sin stock returns: Evidence on the European market. *Working paper*, Université Paris-Dauphine.

Schaltegger, S. (2011). Sustainability as a driver for corporate economic success: Consequences for the development of sustainability management control. *Society and Economy, 33*(1), 15–28.

Scholl, G. (2006). Product service systems. In A. Tukker, M. Charter, C. Vezzoli, E. Sto, & M. Munch Andersen (Eds.), *System innovation for sustainability. Perspectives on radical change to sustainable consumption and production* (pp. 25–43). Sheffield, UK: Greenleaf Publishing Ltd.

Schumpeter, J. (1911). *The theory of economic development (1934 translation)*. Piscataway, NJ: Transaction Books.

Schwab, K. (2016). *The fourth industrial revolution*. Geneva: World Economic Forum.

Selsky, J. W., & Parker, B. (2005). Cross-sector partnerships to address social issues: Challenges to theory and practice. *Journal of Management, 31*(6), 849–873.

Sen, S., & Bhattacharya, C. B. (2001). Does doing good always lead to doing better? Consumer reactions to corporate social responsibility. *Journal of Marketing Research, 38*(2), 225–243.

Sen, S., Du, S., & Bhattacharya, C. B. (2016). Corporate social responsibility: A consumer psychology perspective. *Current Opinion in Psychology, 10*, 70–75.

Serafeim, G. (2015). Integrated reporting and investor clientele. *Journal of Applied Corporate Finance, 27*(2), 34–51.

Seuring, S., & Gold, S. (2013). Sustainability management beyond corporate boundaries: From stakeholders to performance. *Journal of Cleaner Production, 56*, 1–6.

Serafeim, G., & Gombos, S. (2015). Turnaround at Norsk Gjenvinning. Harvard Business School Case, 1.

Shamir, B., House, R. J., & Arthur, M. B. (1993). The motivational effects of charismatic leadership: A self-concept based theory. *Organization Science, 4*(4), 577–594.

Short, J. C., Moss, T. W., & Lumpkin, G. T. (2009). Research in social entrepreneurship: Past contributions and future opportunities. *Strategic Entrepreneurship Journal, 3*(2), 161–194.

Simas, M. S., Golsteijn, L., Huijbregts, M. A., Wood, R., & Hertwich, E. G. (2014). The "Bad Labor" footprint: Quantifying the social impacts of globalization. *Sustainability, 6*(11), 7514–7540.

Simester, D. (2017). Field experiments in marketing. *Handbook of Economic Field Experiments, 1*, 465–497.

Skarmeas, D., & Leonidou, C. N. (2013). When consumers doubt, watch out! The role of CSR skepticism. *Journal of Business Research, 66*(10), 1831–1838.

Smith, W. K., Gonin, M., & Besharov, M. L. (2013). Managing social-business tensions: A review and research agenda for social enterprise. *Business Ethics Quarterly, 23*(3), 407–442.

Solomon, R. C. (1992). Corporate roles, personal virtues: An Aristotelean approach to business ethics. *Business Ethics Quarterly, 2*(3), 317–339.

Søreide, T. (2016). *Corruption and criminal justice: Bridging economic and legal perspectives*. Edward Elgar Publishing.

Stahel, W. R. (2016). The circular economy. *Nature, 531*(7595), 435.

Stampfl, G., Prügl, R., & Osterloh, V. (2013). An explorative model of business model scalability. *International Journal of Product Development, 18*(3–4), 226–248.

Steffen, W., Richardson, K., Rockström, J., Cornell, S. E., Fetzer, I., Bennett, E. M., & Folke, C. (2015). Planetary boundaries: Guiding human development on a changing planet. *Science, 347*(6223), 1259855.

Stenmarck, A., Jensen, C., Quested, T., Moates, G., Buksti, M., Cseh, B., & Scherhaufer, S. (2016). *Estimates of European food waste levels*. IVL Swedish Environmental Research Institute.

Stephany, A. (2015). *The business of sharing: Making it in the new sharing economy*. London: Palgrave Macmillan.

Stoknes, P. E. (2015). *What we think about when we try not to think about global warming: Toward a new psychology of climate action*. Chelsea Green Publishing.

Strand, R. (2013). The chief officer of corporate social responsibility: A study of its presence in top management teams. *Journal of Business Ethics, 112*(4), 721–734.

Strand, R. (2014). Strategic leadership of corporate sustainability. *Journal of Business Ethics, 123*(4), 687–706.

Strand, R. (2017). *Strategic management in the era of cooperation: Toward a theory of scandinavian cooperative advantage*. Unpublished manuscript, University of California-Berkeley.

Sullivan, J., & Zutavern, A. (2017). *The mathematical corporation: Where machine intelligence and human ingenuity achieve the impossible*. New York, NY: PublicAffairs.

Sundararajan, A. (2013). From Zipcar to the sharing economy. *Harvard Business Review*, 1.

Sundararajan, A. (2016). *The sharing economy: The end of employment and the rise of crowd-based capitalism*. Cambridge, MA: MIT Press.

Teece, D. J. (2010). Business models, business strategy and innovation. *Long Range Planning, 43*(2), 172–194.

Tencati, A., & Zsolnai, L. (2009). The collaborative enterprise. *Journal of Business Ethics, 85*(3), 367–376.

Thomke, S. (2001). Enlightened experimentation: The new imperative for innovation. *Harvard Business Review, 79*(2), 66–75.

Thompson, J. D., & Macmillan, I. C. (2010). Business models: Creating new markets and societal wealth. *Long Range Planning, 43*(2), 291–307.

Toffler, A. (1981). *The third wave*. New York, NY: Bantam Books.

Tukker, A. (2004). Eight types of product–service system: Eight ways to sustainability? Experiences from SusProNet. *Business Strategy and the Environment, 13*(4), 246–260.

Tukker, A., & Tischner, U. (2006). Product-services as a research field: Past, present and future. Reflections from a decade of research. *Journal of Cleaner Production, 14*(17), 1552–1556.

Turban, D. B., & Greening, D. W. (1997). Corporate social performance and organizational attractiveness to prospective employees. *Academy of Management Journal, 40*(3), 658–672.

Unruh, G., Kiron, D., Kruschwitz, N., Reeves, M., Rubel, H., & Zum Felde, A. M. (2016). Investing for a sustainable future: Investors care more about sustainability than many executives believe. *MIT Sloan Management Review, 57*(4), 3–25.

Varadarajan, P. R., & Cunningham, M. H. (1995). Strategic alliances: A synthesis of conceptual foundations. *Journal of the Academy of Marketing Science, 23*(4), 282.

Visser, W. (2011). *The age of responsibility: CSR 2.0 and the new DNA of business*. Hoboken, NJ: John Wiley & Sons.

Waddock, S. A., & Graves, S. B. (1997). The corporate social performance-financial performance link. *Strategic Management Journal, 18*(4), 303–319.

Walter, E. (2017). *Trust in the sharing economy. Can trust make or break a sharing enterprise?* Anchor Academic Publishing.

Wang, T., & Bansal, P. (2012). Social responsibility in new ventures: Profiting from a long-term orientation. *Strategic Management Journal, 33*(10), 1135–1153.

Weber, O., Scholz, R. W., & Michalik, G. (2010). Incorporating sustainability criteria into credit risk management. *Business Strategy and the Environment, 19*(1), 39–50.

Webster, K. (2015). *The circular economy: A wealth of flows*. Coew, UK: Ellen MacArthur Foundation Publishing.

Wells, P. E. (2013). *Business models for sustainability*. Cheltenham, UK: Edward Elgar Publishing.

World Bank. (2015). Services, etc., value added (% of GDP). Retrieved May 11, 2015, from http://data.worldbank.org/indicator/NV.SRV.TETC.ZS.

Yoon, Y., Gürhan-Canli, Z., & Schwarz, N. (2006). The effect of corporate social responsibility (CSR) activities on companies with bad reputations. *Journal of Consumer Psychology, 16*(4), 377–390.

Zeitz, J. (2011). Puma completes first environmental profit and loss account. *The Guardian*, November 16.

Zott, C., & Amit, R. (2007). Business model design and the performance of entrepreneurial firms. *Organization Science, 18*(2), 181–199.

Zott, C., Amit, R., & Massa, L. (2011). The business model: Recent developments and future research. *Journal of Management, 37*(4), 1019–1042.

Zsolnai, L. (2004). Honesty and trust in economic relationships. *Management Research News, 27*(7), 57–62.

Index

A

Access, 50, 57
Accountability, 160, 161
Accounting, 203
Activities, 28, 59, 62, 130
Adoption, 201
Alliances, 4, 9, 18, 50

B

Behavior, 82
Big data, 99
Biodegradable, 23, 109
Biological, 105
Biomimicry, 114
Bottom of the pyramid, 9
Boundaries, 42, 199
Boundary spanner, 162
Brand, 38

Business case, 194
Business models, xi

C

Capabilities, 157, 193
Capital, 130, 146
Carbon footprint, 159
Channels, 201
Circular, 17
Climate change, ix, xii
Closed-loop, 112
CO_2, 23
Collaborates, 62, 118, 122, 191
Collaboration, 13, 18, 50, 123, 156
Collaborative, 62, 123, 201
Commitment, 155
Companies, 18
Competition, 124

Competitive, 146
Competitors, 123, 129
Compliance, 30
Consumer, 171
Consumer preferences, 1
Cooperate, 171
Cooperation, 157
Corporate responsibility, 4
Corporate social responsibility (CSR), 4, 137
Corporate sustainability, 4
Corruption, x
Costs, 39, 58, 59, 171
Cost structure, 63
Customers, 50, 56, 57, 71, 83, 129
Customization, 99

D

Decision, 67
Decision rights, 161
Deliver, 84
Design, 77, 113
Digital, 14, 56
Digitalization, xiii, 66
Disassembled, 104, 106, 107
Disruptive, 68
Distribution, 201
Distribution channel, 202
Diversity, 41
Downcycling, 106
Drivers, 27–28

E

Economics, 50
Ecosystems, ix, 115, 123, 222–224
Efficiency, 50, 112
Efficient, 50, 93

Emissions, 13
Empirical, 194
Employees, 129, 146
Entrepreneurs, 72
Entrepreneurship, 71
Environment, ix, 14, 24, 106
Equality, x, 41
Ethical, 82
Experimental, 50, 197
Experiments, 72, 79, 96, 184, 199
Externalities, 28

F

Field experiments, 8
Finance, 82
Financial, 29
Footprint, xii
Fourth industrial revolution, xiii
Functionality, 18, 50

G

Goal attainment, 165
Goods, 115
Governance, 8
Governments, 123, 130
Green, 30
Green growth, xi
Greener, 24
Growth, 58, 67, 125

H

Harmful, 115
Human, 115
Human rights, x
Hypothesis, 57, 64–66

I

Impact, 31, 141
Implementation, 29, 122, 161, 201
Incentives, 38, 160, 165, 202
Incremental, 68
Industrial, 105
Industry, 56
Inequality, 41
Infrastructure, 201
Innovations, xiii, 7, 68, 183
Innovativeness, 4, 7, 68, 195
Innovators, 6
Input factors, 26, 139
Institutions, 36
Interests, 140
Internet of Things (IoT), 98
Intrapreneurs, 72
Intrapreneurship, 72
Investments, 82, 123, 148
Investors, 82, 129

J

Job-to-be-done, 59
Joint ventures, 122
Justice, 41

K

Key performance indicators (KPIs), 163, 164
Knowledge, 29, 84

L

Labor, 41
Laws, 130
Leadership, 155
Leasing, 64
Linear, 18, 104
Logistics, 19

M

Management, 30, 156, 183
Management control, 8, 155
Manufacturing, 19
Market, 85
Market share, 155
Marketplace, 93
Materiality, 141
Materials, 90, 104, 144, 159
Measurement, 40, 165
Mechanisms, 195
Money, 61

N

Natural, 105, 109, 180
Natural resources, xii
Non-governmental organizations (NGOs), 130

O

Objectives, 166
Offering, 17, 63
Online, 85
Operations, 31, 180
Opportunity, 27–28, 61, 140
Organizational, 62, 165
Organizational design, 51, 155
Organizations, 51
Organize, 131
Ownership, 18, 50, 92

P

Packaging, 19, 223
Partners, 59, 62, 129
Partnership, 24, 159, 201
Pay-as-you-go, 85
Payment, 57
Payment model, 63
Performance, 26, 137
Performance management, 163
Philanthropy, 137
Physical, 96
Plastic, ix
Platforms, 17, 57
Pollution, ix, 107
Poverty, xii
Price, 61, 78, 114
Prioritization, 51, 164, 195, 202
Processes, 77, 78
Process model, 183
Product-as-service, 64
Product design, 223
Production, 81, 105, 136
Product-logic, 50
Products, 18, 50, 58, 131
Product-service system, 24
Profitability, 19, 25, 63, 90
Profits, 42, 105
Prototypes, 84

Q

Qualitative research, 196
Quantitative research, 196

R

Radical, 68
Recognize, 187
Recycle, 29, 31, 90, 104, 122
Redesign and experimentation (RE), 18
Redesigning, 104
Refurbish/refurbishing, 90, 91, 107
Regeneration, 106
Regulation, 19, 37
Regulatory, 130, 147
Reinvent, 7, 187
Renewable, 106
Renewable energy, 81
Reorganize, 187
Repair, 107
Reporting, 165, 203
Reputation, 38, 78
Research, 85
Resource-efficient, 50
Resources, x, 26, 59, 62, 106
Responsibility, 27–28, 83
RESTART, xiii
Restorative, 115
Results, 38, 51
Results and three-dimensionality (RT), 18
Rethink, 7, 185
Reuse, 90, 91, 105, 107
Revenue model, 63
Revenues, 57–59, 92, 201
Revenue streams, 68
Rights, 37
Risks, 6, 26, 139

S

Scale, 118
Scarce, 50, 111
Segments, 70
Service-logic, the circular economy and alliances (STA), 18
Services, 14, 18, 50, 58

Servitization, 64
Sharing, 17
Sharing economy, 93
Social, 14
Social entrepreneur, 117
Social entrepreneurship, 116
Societal, 36, 188
Society, 24
Stakeholder engagement, 146
Stakeholders, 26, 38, 69, 124, 146
Standards, 37
Stock, 78
Strategy, 38, 62, 124, 129
Structural waste, 93
Subscription, 57, 71
Substitutes, 61
Suppliers, 63, 122
Supply chain, 104, 125
Sustainability, x
    development, 39
    efforts, 155
    report, 34, 37
Sustainable Development Goals (SDGs), x

T

Technical, 105
Technological, xiii
Technologies, 14, 29

Three-dimensional, 160
Three-dimensional (3D) printing, 13, 17
Transaction, 63, 125
Transformation, 17
Transition, 50, 79
Transparency, 26, 226
Triple bottom line, 155
Trust, 8, 93

U

UN Global Compact (UNGC), 189
Upcycling, 105

V

Values, 30, 158
    capture, 59
    chain, 4, 23, 122, 225
    creation, 14, 59
    delivery, 59
    propositions, 59, 61
Venture, 118
Virtual reality (VR), 218

W

Waste, x, 104

The manufacturer's authorised representative in the EU is Springer Nature Customer Service Centre GmbH, Europaplatz 3, 69115 Heidelberg, Germany. If you have any concerns regarding our products, please contact ProductSafety@springernature.com

Printed and bound by CPI Group (UK) Ltd, Croydon, CR0 4YY
24/03/2026
02077755-0001